U.S. Fish & Wildlife Service

2001
National Survey of
Fishing, Hunting, and
Wildlife-Associated
Recreation

2001 National Survey of Fishing, Hunting, and Wildlife-Associated Recreation

Issued October 2002

U.S. Department of the Interior
Gale A. Norton,
Secretary

FISH AND WILDLIFE SERVICE
Steve Williams,
Director

U.S. Department of Commerce
Donald L. Evans,
Secretary
Samuel W. Bodman,
Deputy Secretary

Economics and Statistics Administration
Kathleen B. Cooper,
Under Secretary for Economic Affairs

U.S. CENSUS BUREAU
Charles Louis Kincannon,
Director

ECONOMICS
AND STATISTICS
ADMINISTRATION

Economics and Statistics
Administration

Kathleen B. Cooper,
Under Secretary for Economic Affairs

Department of Interior
Gale A. Norton, Secretary

FISH AND WILDLIFE SERVICE
Steve Williams, Director

U.S. CENSUS BUREAU

Charles Louis Kincannon,
Director

Division of Federal Aid
Kris E. LaMontagne, Chief

As the Nation's principal conservation agency, the Department of the Interior has responsibility for most of our nationally owned public lands and natural resources. This includes fostering the wisest use of our land and water resources, protecting our fish and wildlife, preserving the environmental and cultural values of our national parks and historical places, and providing for the enjoyment of life through outdoor recreation. The Department assesses our energy and mineral resources and works to assure their development in the best interests of all our people. The Department also has a major responsibility for American Indian reservation communities and for people who live in island territories under U.S. administration.

The mission of the Department's Fish and Wildlife Service is to conserve, protect, and enhance fish and wildlife and their habitats for the continuing benefit of the American people. The Service is responsible for national programs of vital importance to our natural resources, including administration of the Federal Aid in Sport Fish Restoration and the Federal Aid of Wildlife Restoration Programs. These two grant programs provide financial assistance to the States for projects to enhance and protect fish and wildlife resources and to assure their availability to the public for recreational purposes. Multistate grants from these programs pay for the National Survey of Fishing, Hunting, and Wildlife-Associated Recreation.

Suggested Citation

U.S. Department of the Interior, Fish and Wildlife Service and U.S. Department of Commerce, U.S. Census Bureau. *2001 National Survey of Fishing, Hunting, and Wildlife-Associated Recreation.*

Contents

List of Tables

State Wildlife-Related Recreation: 2001

Foreword

Fish and wildlife resources are part of our American culture. Whether we are fishing, hunting, watching wildlife or feeding backyard birds, Americans derive many hours of enjoyment from wildlife-related recreation. Wildlife recreation is the cornerstone of our Nation's great conservation ethic.

The 2001 National Survey of Fishing, Hunting, and Wildlife-Associated Recreation is a partnership effort with the States and national conservation organizations, and has become one of the most important sources of information on fish and wildlife recreation in the United States. It is a useful tool that quantifies the economic impact of wildlife-based recreation. Federal, State, and private organizations use this detailed information to manage wildlife, market products, and look for trends. The 2001 Survey is the tenth in a series that began in 1955.

More than 82 million U.S. residents fished, hunted, and watched wildlife in 2001. They spent over $108 billion pursuing their recreational activities, contributing to millions of jobs in industries and businesses that support wildlife-related recreation. Furthermore, funds generated by licenses and taxes on hunting and fishing equipment pay for many of the conservation efforts in this country.

Wildlife recreationists are among the Nation's most ardent conservationists. They not only contribute financially to conservation efforts, but also spend time and effort to introduce children and other newcomers to the enjoyment of the outdoors and wildlife.

I appreciate the assistance of those who took time to participate in this valuable survey. We all can be grateful that America's great tradition of wildlife-related recreation remains strong.

Steve Williams

Steve Williams
Director, U.S. Fish and Wildlife Service
U.S. Department of the Interior

Survey Background and Method

The National Survey of Fishing, Hunting, and Wildlife-Associated Recreation (Survey) has been conducted since 1955 and is one of the oldest and most comprehensive continuing recreation surveys. The purpose of the Survey is to gather information on the number of anglers, hunters, and wildlife-watching participants (formerly known as nonconsumptive wildlife-related participants) in the United States. Information also is collected on how often these recreationists participate and how much they spend on their activities.

Preparations for the 2001 Survey began in 1999 when the International Association of Fish and Wildlife Agencies (IAFWA) asked us, the Fish and Wildlife Service, to conduct the tenth national survey of wildlife-related recreation. Funding came from the Multistate Conservation Grant Programs, authorized by Sport Fish and Wildlife Restoration Acts, as amended.

We consulted with State and Federal agencies and nongovernmental organizations such as the Wildlife Management Institute and American Sportfishing Association to determine survey content. Other sportspersons' organizations and conservation groups, industry representatives, and researchers also provided valuable advice.

Four regional technical committees were set up under the auspices of the IAFWA to ensure that State fish and wildlife agencies had an opportunity to participate in all phases of survey planning and design. The committees were made up of agency representatives.

Data collection for the Survey was carried out in two phases by the U.S. Census Bureau. The first phase was the screen which began in April 2001. During the screening phase, the Census Bureau interviewed a sample of 80,000 households nationwide to determine who in the household had fished, hunted, or engaged in wildlife-watching activities in 2000, and who had engaged or planned to engage in those activities in 2001. In most cases, one adult household member provided information for all household members. The screen primarily covered 2000 activities while the next, more in-depth phase covered 2001 activities. For more information on the 2000 data, refer to Appendix C.

The second phase of the data collection consisted of three detailed interview waves. The first wave began in April 2001, the second in September 2001, and the last in January 2002. Interviews were conducted with samples of likely anglers, hunters, and wildlife watchers who were identified in the initial screening phase. These interviews were conducted primarily by telephone, with in-person interviews for those respondents who could not be reached by telephone. Respondents in the second survey phase were limited to those at least 16 years old. Each respondent provided information pertaining only to his or her activities and

expenditures. Sample sizes were designed to provide statistically reliable results at the State level. Altogether, interviews were completed for 25,070 respondents from the sportspersons sample and 15,303 from the wildlife watchers sample. More detailed information on sampling procedures and response rates is found in Appendix D.

Comparability With Previous Surveys

The 2001 Survey's questions and methodology were similar to those used in the 1996 and 1991 Surveys. Therefore, the estimates of all three surveys are comparable.

The methodology of the 2001, 1996, and 1991 Surveys did differ significantly from the 1985 and 1980 Surveys, so their estimates are not directly comparable to those earlier surveys. The changes in methodology included reducing the recall period over which respondents had to report their activities and expenditures. Previous Surveys used a 12-month recall period which resulted in greater reporting bias. Research found that the amount of activity and expenditures reported in 12-month recall surveys was overestimated in comparison with that reported using shorter recall periods.

The trend information presented in this report takes into account the differences of the earlier surveys in comparing their estimates with those of the 1991, 1996, and 2001 Surveys. See the Summary Section and Appendix B.

Highlights

Introduction

The National Survey of Fishing, Hunting, and Wildlife-Associated Recreation reports results from interviews with U.S. residents about their fishing, hunting, and other wildlife-related recreation. This report focuses on 2001 participation and expenditures of U.S. residents 16 years of age and older.

In addition to the 2001 numbers, we also provide 11-year trend data. The 2001 numbers reported can be compared with those in the 1991 and 1996 Survey reports because these three surveys used similar methodologies. However, the 2001 estimates should not be directly compared with the results from Surveys earlier than 1991 because of changes in methodology. These changes were made to improve accuracy in the information provided. Trend information from 1955 to 1985 is presented in Appendix B.

The report also provides information on participation in wildlife-related recreation in 2000, particularly of persons 6 to 15 years of age. The 2000 information is provided in Appendix C. Additional information about the scope and coverage of the Survey can be found in the Survey Background and Method section of this report. The remainder of this section defines important terms used in the Survey.

Sportspersons

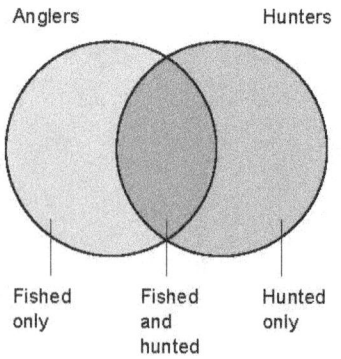

Anglers   Hunters

Fished only   Fished and hunted   Hunted only

Wildlife-Associated Recreation

Wildlife-associated recreation includes fishing, hunting, and wildlife-watching activities. These categories are not mutually exclusive because many individuals enjoyed fish and wildlife in several ways in 2001. Wildlife-associated recreation is reported in two major categories: (1) fishing and hunting and (2) wildlife watching (formerly nonconsumptive wildlife-related recreation). Wildlife watching includes observing, photographing, and feeding fish and wildlife.

Fishing and Hunting

This Survey reports information about residents of the United States who fished or hunted in 2001, regardless of whether they were licensed. The fishing and hunting sections of this report are organized to report three groups: (1) sportspersons, (2) anglers, and (3) hunters.

Sportspersons

Sportspersons are those who fished or hunted. Individuals who fished or hunted commercially in 2001 are reported as sportspersons only if they also fished or hunted for recreation. The sportspersons group is composed of the three subgroups in the diagram below: (1) those who fished and hunted, (2) those who only fished, and (3) those who only hunted. The total number of sportspersons is equal to the sum of people who only fished, only hunted, and both hunted and fished. It is not the sum of all anglers and all hunters, because those people who both fished and hunted are included in both the angler and hunter population and would be incorrectly counted twice.

Anglers

Anglers are sportspersons who only fished plus those who fished and hunted. Anglers include not only licensed hook-and-line anglers, but also those who have no license and those who use special methods such as fishing with spears. Three types of fishing are reported: (1) freshwater, excluding the Great Lakes, (2) Great Lakes, and (3) saltwater. Since many anglers participated in more than one type of fishing, the total number of anglers is less than the sum of the three types of fishing.

Hunters

Hunters are sportspersons who only hunted plus those who hunted and fished. Hunters include not only licensed hunters using common hunting practices, but also those who have no license and those who engaged in hunting with a bow and arrow, muzzleloader, other primitive firearms, or a pistol or handgun. Four types of hunting are reported: (1) big game, (2) small game, (3) migratory bird, and (4) other animals. Since many hunters participated in more than one type of hunting, the sum of hunters for big game, small game, migratory bird, and other animals exceeds the total number of hunters.

Wildlife-Watching Activities
(formerly Nonconsumptive Wildlife-Related Recreation)

Since 1980, the National Survey of Fishing, Hunting, and Wildlife-Associated Recreation has included information on wildlife-watching activities in addition to fishing and hunting. However, the 1991, 1996, and 2001 Surveys, unlike the 1980 and 1985 Surveys, collected data only for those activities where the primary purpose was wildlife watching (observing, photographing, or feeding wildlife). The Survey uses a strict definition of wildlife watching. Participants must either take a "special interest" in wildlife around their homes or take a trip for the "primary purpose" of wildlife watching. Secondary wildlife-watching activities such as incidentally observing wildlife while pleasure driving were included in the 1980 and 1985 Surveys but not in the succeeding ones.

Two types of wildlife-watching activity are reported: (1) nonresidential and (2) residential. Because some people participate in more than one type of wildlife-watching activity, the sum of participants in each type will be greater than the total number of wildlife watchers. The two types of wildlife-watching activities are defined below.

Nonresidential (away from the home)

This group included persons who took trips or outings of at least 1 mile for the primary purpose of observing, feeding, or photographing fish and wildlife. Trips to fish, hunt, or scout and trips to zoos, circuses, aquariums, or museums were not considered wildlife-watching activities.

Residential (around the home)

This group included those whose activities are within 1 mile of home and involve one or more of the following: (1) closely observing or trying to identify birds or other wildlife; (2) photographing wildlife; (3) feeding birds or other wildlife on a regular basis; (4) maintaining natural areas of at least one-quarter acre where benefit to wildlife is the primary concern; (5) maintaining plantings (shrubs, agricultural crops, etc.) where benefit to wildlife is the primary concern; or (6) visiting public parks within 1 mile of home for the primary purpose of observing, feeding, or photographing wildlife.

Summary

The 2001 Survey revealed that 82 million U.S. residents 16 years old and older participated in wildlife-related recreation. During that year, 34.1 million people fished, 13.0 million hunted, and 66.1 million participated in at least one type of wildlife-watching activity including observing, feeding, or photographing fish and other wildlife in the United States.

The information for participation and expenditures of persons 16 years old and older is based on estimates from the detailed phase of the 2001 Survey. This information is comparable with estimates from the 1991 and 1996 Surveys, but not with earlier ones because of changes in methodology. A complete explanation is provided in Appendix B.

Although the focus of this report is based on the detailed phase of the Survey of persons 16 years old and older, we do include information on individuals 6 to 15 years old. An estimate of their participation was calculated using data from the 2001 screening Survey. Based on this data, there were 1.6 million hunters, 10.2 million anglers, and 12.6 million wildlife-watching participants 6 to 15 years old in 2001. More information on 6- to 15-year-olds is provided in Appendix C. For the rest of this report all information pertains to participants 16 years old and older, unless otherwise indicated.

Among anglers, hunters, and wildlife watchers, there was a considerable overlap in activities. In 2001, 71 percent of hunters also fished, and 27 percent of anglers hunted. In addition, 58 percent of anglers and 62 percent of hunters participated in wildlife-watching activities, while 33 percent of all wildlife watchers reported hunting and/or fishing during the year.

Wildlife recreationists' avidity also was reflected in their spending which totaled $108 billion in 2001. This amounted to 1.1 percent of the GDP. Of the total amount spent, $28.1 billion was trip-related, $64.5 billion was spent on equipment, and $15.8 billion was spent on other items.

Sportspersons spent a total of $70 billion in 2001—$35.6 billion on fishing, $20.6 billion on hunting, and $13.8 million on items used for both hunting and fishing. Wildlife watchers spent $38.4 billion on their activities around the home and on trips away from home.

Total Wildlife-Related Recreation

Participants	82 million
Expenditures	$108 billion

Sportspersons

Total participants	37.8 million
Anglers	34.1 million
Hunters	13.0 million
Total days	786 million
Anglers	557 million
Hunters	228 million
Total expenditures	$70.0 billion
Fishing	$35.6 billion
Hunting	$20.6 billion
Unspecified	$13.8 billion

Wildlife Watchers

Total participants	66.1 million
Residential	62.9 million
Nonresidential	21.8 million
Total expenditures	$38.4 billion

Expenditures for Wildlife-Related Recreation
(Total expenditures: $108 billion)

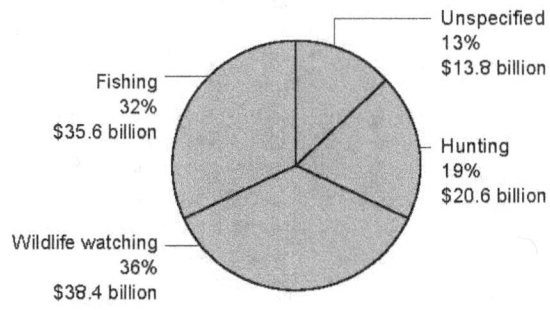

Unspecified
13%
$13.8 billion

Fishing
32%
$35.6 billion

Hunting
19%
$20.6 billion

Wildlife watching
36%
$38.4 billion

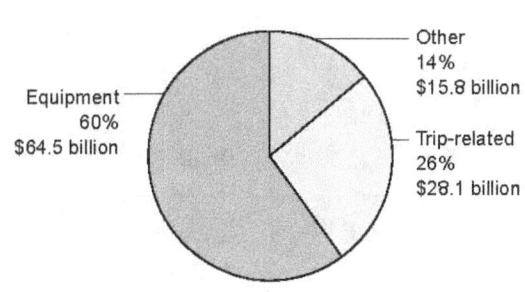

Other
14%
$15.8 billion

Equipment
60%
$64.5 billion

Trip-related
26%
$28.1 billion

Expenditures by Sportspersons
(Total expenditures: $70.0 billion)

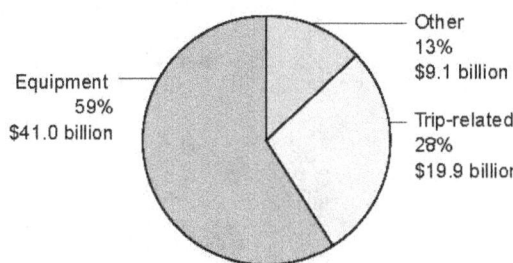

Other
13%
$9.1 billion

Equipment
59%
$41.0 billion

Trip-related
28%
$19.9 billion

Expenditures by Wildlife-Watching Participants
(Total expenditures: $38.4 billion)

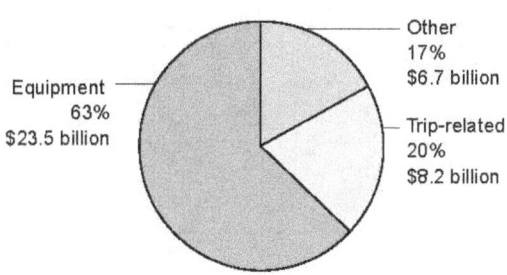

Other
17%
$6.7 billion

Equipment
63%
$23.5 billion

Trip-related
20%
$8.2 billion

Fishing and Hunting

In 2001, 38 million U.S. residents 16 years old and older went fishing and/or hunting. This includes 34.1 million who fished and 13 million who hunted. The overage is accounted for by those who both fished and hunted, 9.3 million.

In 2001, expenditures by sportspersons totaled $70.0 billion. Trip-related expenditures, including those for food, lodging, and transportation, were almost $20.0 billion—28 percent of all fishing and hunting expenditures. Total equipment expenditures amounted to nearly $41.0 billion, 59 percent of the total. Other expenditures—magazines, membership dues, contributions, land leasing and ownership, and licenses, stamps, tags, and permits—accounted for $9.1 billion or 13 percent of all sportspersons' expenditures.

Wildlife-Watching Recreation

Observing, feeding, or photographing wildlife was enjoyed by 66.1 million people 16 years old and older in 2001. Among this group, 21.8 million people took trips away from home (nonresidential) for the purpose of enjoying wildlife, while 62.9 million stayed within a mile of their homes (residential) participating in wildlife-watching activities.

In 2001, wildlife-watching participants spent $38.4 billion. Trip-related expenses, including food, lodging, and transportation, totaled $8.2 billion, 20 percent of all expenditures. A total of $23.5 billion was spent on equipment, 63 percent of all wildlife-watching expenses. The remaining $6.7 billion, 17 percent of the total, was spent on magazines, membership dues, and contributions made to conservation or wildlife-related organizations.

1991, 1996, and 2001 Comparison

A comparison of estimates from the 1991, 1996, and 2001 Surveys reveals that millions of Americans continue to enjoy wildlife-related recreation. While the number of sportspersons fell from 40 million in 1991 to 37.8 million in 2001, expenditures by sportspersons increased from $53 billion (in 2001 dollars) in 1991 to $70 billion in 2001. In 1991, there were 35.6 million anglers and 14.1 million hunters. In 1996, 35.2 million fished and 14.0 million hunted. And in 2001, there were 34.1 million anglers and 13.0 million hunters. In 2001, hunters spent 29 percent more than they did in 1991 for their trips and equipment, while anglers' expenditures showed a 14 percent increase that was not a statistically significant difference[1].

Participation in wildlife watching (observing, feeding, and photographing wildlife) decreased from 76.1 million in 1991 to 62.9 million in 1996, but it increased to 66.1 million from 1996 to 2001. Expenditures for trips and equipment increased by 21 percent from 1991 to 1996 and 10 percent from 1996 to 2001.

_____

[1]At a 5 percent level of significance.

Anglers and Hunters: 1955-2001

(Indices are used to simplify comparisons between the wildlife-related recreation activities.)

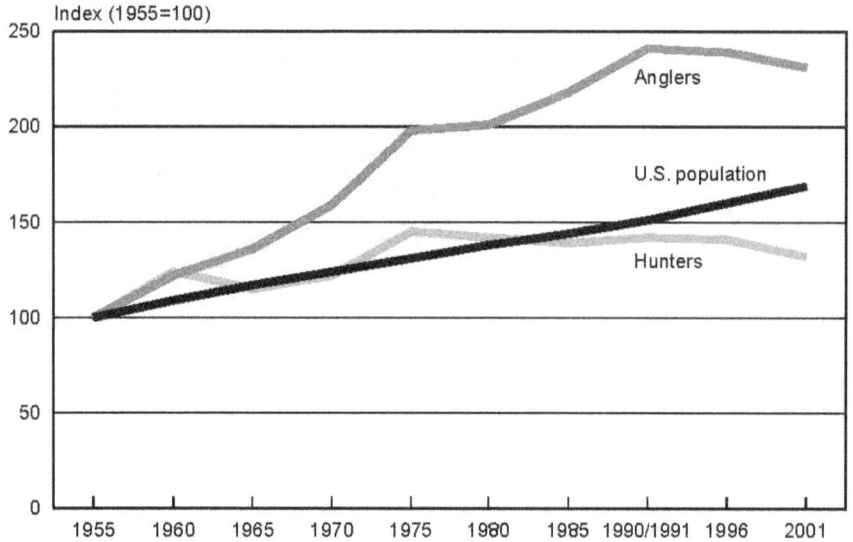

Index (1955=100)

Wildlife-Watching Participants: 1980-2001

(Indices are used to simplify comparisons between the wildlife-related recreation activities.)

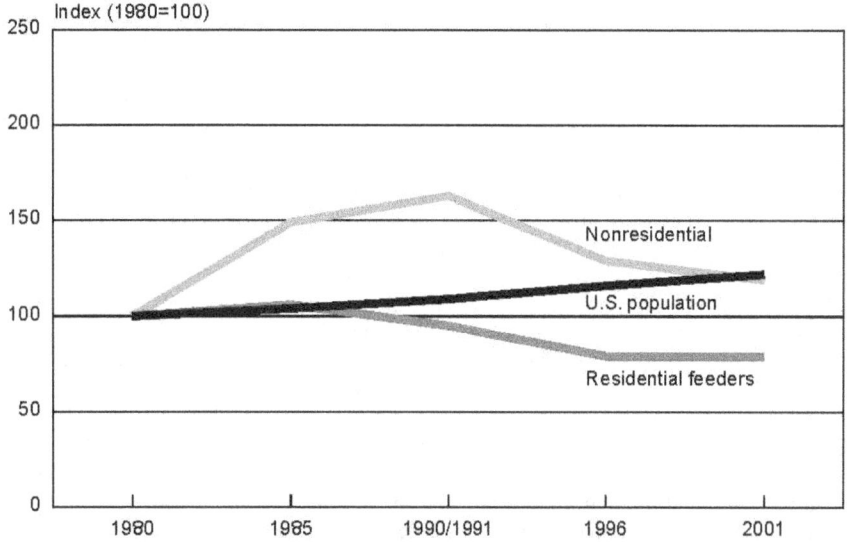

Index (1980=100)

1955 to 2001 Findings

The U.S. Fish and Wildlife Service has conducted these National Surveys at approximate 5-year intervals since 1955 (see Appendix B). A 46-year trend can be traced for the number of anglers and hunters that participated in a given year. The number of wildlife-watching participants can be traced over 21 years because wildlife watching has been part of the Survey only since 1980.

Trends show that the number of anglers increased at nearly twice the rate of the U.S. population growth from 1955 to 2001. The U.S. population increased by 71 percent while the fishing population increased by 130 percent during that period.

The number of hunters also increased over the 46-year period, but not at a rate equal to the overall 71 percent population growth. The number of hunters increased 31 percent from 1955 to 2001.

The number of wildlife-watching participants who took trips away from home to observe, feed, or photograph wildlife decreased 19 percent from 1980 to 2001. The number of people who fed wildlife around their home decreased by 18 percent.

This trend information is based on published findings from the 1955 to the 2001 Survey reports and unpublished screening data from the 1985 to 1990 Surveys. As explained in Appendix B, the estimates from the published reports of the 1985 and 1991 Surveys are not directly comparable because of methodological changes.

Fishing

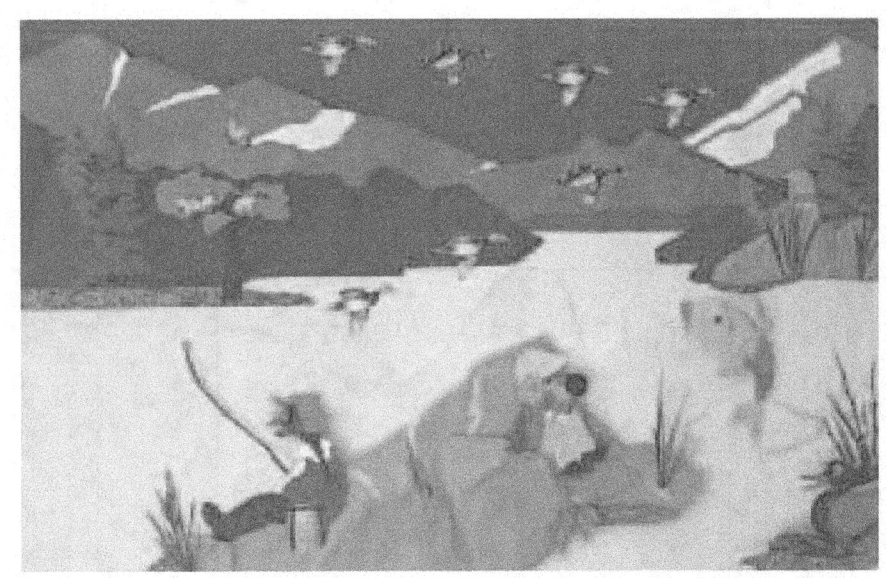

Fishing Highlights

In 2001, 34.1 million U.S. residents 16 years old and older enjoyed a variety of fishing opportunities throughout the United States. Anglers fished 557 million days and took 437 million fishing trips. They spent over $35.6 billion on fishing-related expenses during the year. Freshwater anglers numbered 28.4 million and spent 467 million days fishing on 365 million trips in 2001. Freshwater anglers spent more than $21.3 billion on freshwater fishing trips and equipment. Saltwater fishing attracted 9.1 million anglers who enjoyed nearly 72 million trips on 91 million days. They spent $8.4 billion on their trips and equipment.

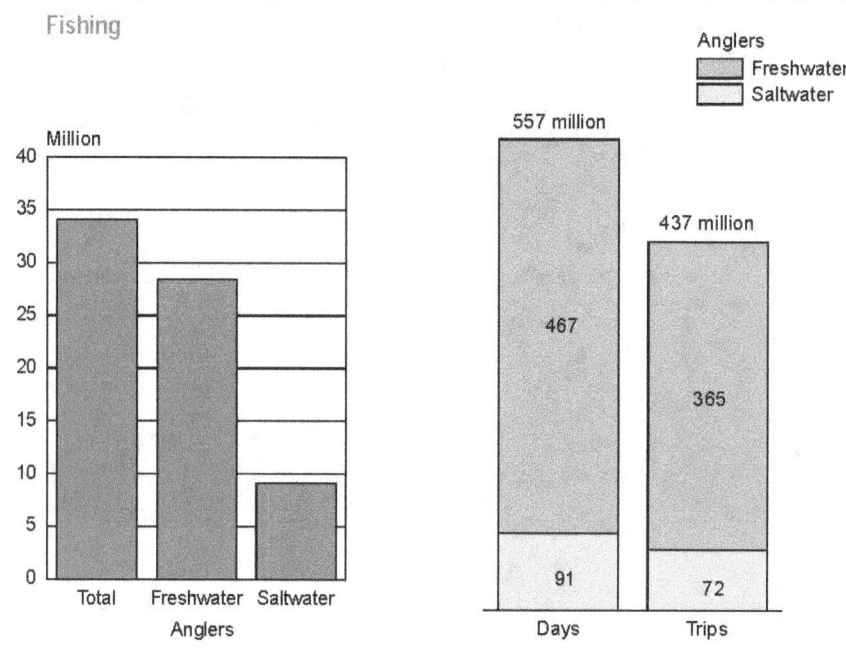

Detail does not add to total because of multiple responses and nonresponse.

Total Fishing		
Anglers	**34.1 million**	
Freshwater	28.4 million	
Saltwater	9.1 million	
Days	**557 million**	
Freshwater	467 million	
Saltwater	91 million	
Trips	**437 million**	
Freshwater	365 million	
Saltwater	72 million	
Expenditures	**$35.6 billion**	
Freshwater	21.3 billion	
Saltwater	8.4 billion	
Unspecified	5.9 billion	

Detail does not add to total because of multiple responses and nonresponse.
Source: Tables 1, 13, 14, and 17.

Fishing Expenditures

Anglers spent $35.6 billion in 2001 including $14.7 billion on travel-related costs, 41 percent of all fishing expenditures. Food and lodging resulted in $6 billion, 40 percent of all trip-related costs, and $3.5 billion, 24 percent of trip-related expenditures, was spent on transportation. Other trip expenditures such as land use fees, guide fees, equipment rental, boating expenses, and bait cost anglers nearly $5.3 billion, 36 percent of all trip expenses.

For that same year, fishing equipment expenditures totaled $17 billion, 48 percent of all fishing expenditures. Anglers spent $4.6 billion on fishing equipment such as rods, reels, tackle boxes, depth finders, and artificial lures and flies. This amounted to 27 percent of all equipment expenditures. Auxiliary equipment—camping equipment, binoculars, and special fishing clothing—amounted to $721 million, 4 percent of equipment costs. Special equipment such as boats, vans, and cabins cost anglers $11.6 billion, 69 percent of all equipment costs.

Anglers also spent a considerable amount on land leasing and ownership—nearly $3.2 billion or 9 percent of all expenditures. They spent $860 million on magazines, books, membership dues and contributions, licenses, stamps, tags, and permits.

Total Fishing Expenditures

Total fishing expenditures	**$35.6 billion**
Total trip-related	**$14.7 billion**
Food and lodging	6.0 billion
Transportation	3.5 billion
Other trip costs	5.3 billion
Total equipment expenditures	**$17.0 billion**
Fishing equipment	4.6 billion
Auxiliary equipment	0.7 billion
Special equipment	11.6 billion
Total other fishing expenditures	**$4.0 billion**
Magazines, books	0.1 billion
Membership dues and contribution	0.1 billion
Land leasing and ownership	3.2 billion
Licenses, stamps, tags, and permits	0.6 billion

Source: Table 13.

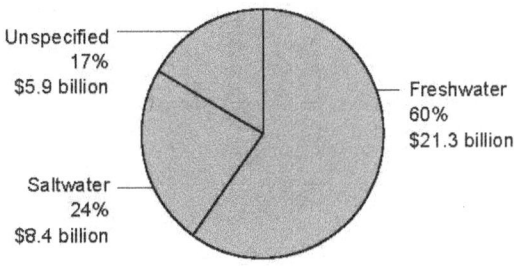

Fishing Expenditures
(Total expenditures: $35.6 billion)

Unspecified 17% $5.9 billion

Freshwater 60% $21.3 billion

Saltwater 24% $8.4 billion

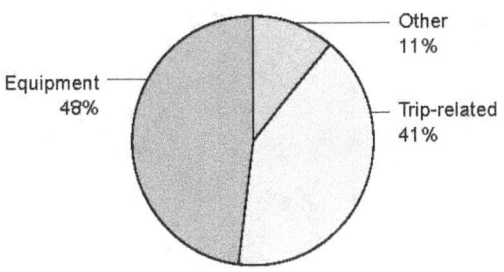

Percent of Total Fishing Expenditures
(Total expenditures: $35.6 billion)

Other 11%

Equipment 48%

Trip-related 41%

Freshwater Fishing

Anglers	**28.4 million**
Freshwater except Great Lakes	28.0 million
Great Lakes	1.8 million
Days	**467 million**
Freshwater except Great Lakes	443 million
Great Lakes	23 million
Trips	**365 million**
Freshwater except Great Lakes	349 million
Great Lakes	16 million
Trip and equipment expenditures	**$21.3 billion**
Freshwater except Great Lakes	20.0 billion
Great Lakes	1.3 billion

Detail does not add to total because of multiple responses and nonresponse.
Source: Tables 1, 14, and 15.

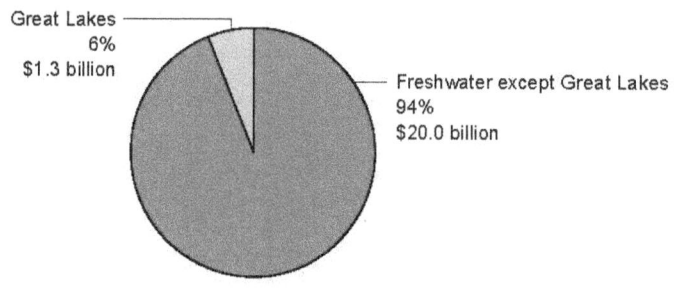

Freshwater Trip and Equipment Expenditures
(Total expenditures: $21.3 billion)

Great Lakes
6%
$1.3 billion

Freshwater except Great Lakes
94%
$20.0 billion

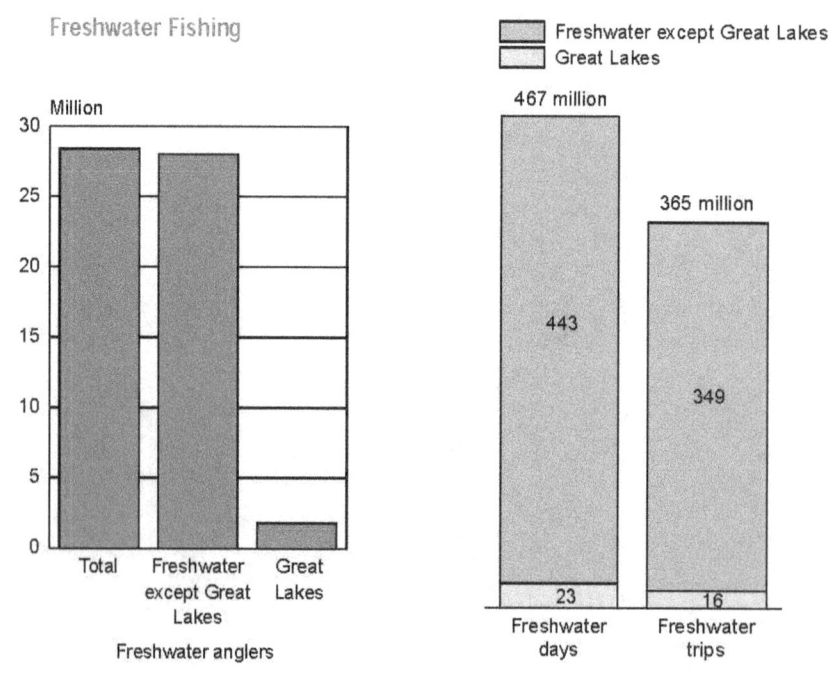

Freshwater Fishing

Freshwater except Great Lakes
Great Lakes

Million

Freshwater anglers: Total, Freshwater except Great Lakes, Great Lakes

467 million — Freshwater days (443, 23)
365 million — Freshwater trips (349, 16)

Detail does not add to total because of multiple responses.

Freshwater Fishing Highlights

Freshwater fishing was the most popular type of fishing. In 2001, 28.4 million Americans fished 467 million days and took 365 million trips. Their expenditures for trips and equipment totaled $21.3 billion for the year. Excluding those who fished the Great Lakes, freshwater anglers numbered 28.0 million, 82 percent of all anglers. Freshwater anglers who did not fish the Great Lakes took 349 million trips on 443 million days and spent $20 billion on trips and equipment for an average of $716 per angler.

The 1.8 million anglers who fished the Great Lakes enjoyed 23 million days and 16 million trips fishing. Their trip and equipment expenditures, $1.3 billion, were 6 percent of the total freshwater trip and equipment expenditures. Great Lakes anglers averaged $690 for the year.

Freshwater Fishing Expenditures

Trip and equipment expenditures for freshwater fishing (excluding the Great Lakes) totaled $20 billion in 2001. Total trip-related expenditures came to $9.4 billion. Food and lodging amounted to $4.0 billion, 43 percent of all trip costs. Transportation costs slightly exceeded $2.6 billion, 28 percent of trip costs. Other trip-related expenses amounted to $2.7 billion and included guide fees, equipment rental, and bait.

Nearly $10.6 billion was spent on equipment for freshwater fishing, excluding the Great Lakes. Non-Great Lakes freshwater anglers purchased $3.0 billion of fishing equipment such as rods and reels, tackle boxes, depth finders, and artificial lures and flies. Expenditures for auxiliary equipment, including camping equipment and binoculars, totaled $498 million for the year. Expenditures for special equipment such as boats, vans, and cabins accounted for $7.1 billion.

Great Lakes anglers spent $1.3 billion on trips and equipment in 2001. Trip-related expenses totaled $776 million. Of these expenditures, $310 million was spent on food and lodging, 40 percent of trip costs; $158 million went for transportation, 20 percent of trip costs; and $308 million was spent on other items such as guide fees, equipment rental, and bait, 40 percent of trip costs. Great Lakes anglers spent $498 million on equipment. They bought $175 million worth of fishing equipment (rods, reels, etc.). They spent $33 million on auxiliary equipment (camping equipment, binoculars, etc.) and $290 million on special equipment (boats, vans, etc.).

Saltwater Fishing Highlights

In 2001, almost 9.1 million anglers enjoyed saltwater fishing on 72 million trips totaling 91 million days. Overall, they spent $8.4 billion during the year on trips and equipment. Of their expenditures, trip-related costs garnered the largest portion, $4.5 billion. Food and lodging cost $1.5 billion, 34 percent of trip expenditures; transportation costs totaled $773 million, 16 percent of trip costs; and other trip costs such as equipment rental, bait, and guide fees were $2.2 billion.

Saltwater Fishing

Anglers	9.1 million
Days	91 million
Trips	72 million
Trip and equipment expenditures	$8.4 billion

Source: Tables 1 and 17.

Saltwater anglers spent a total of $3.9 billion on equipment—$987 million on fishing equipment (rods, reels, etc.), $103 million on auxiliary equipment (camping equipment, binoculars, etc.), and $2.8 billion on special equipment (boats, vans, etc.).

Comparative Trip and Equipment Expenditures

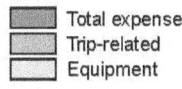
- Total expenses
- Trip-related
- Equipment

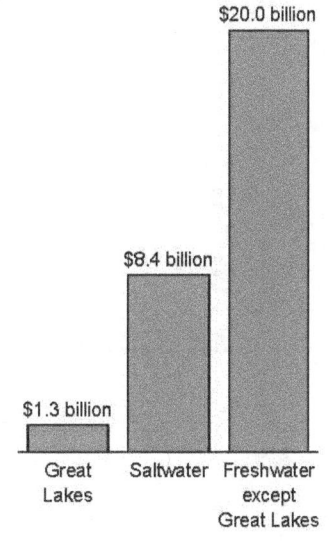

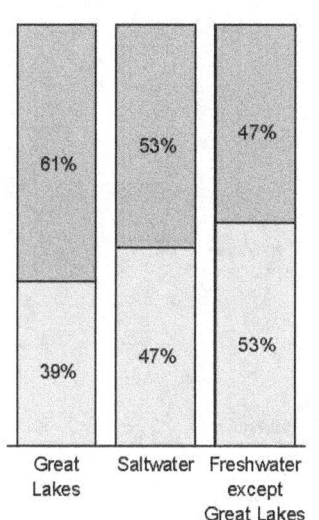

Comparative Fishing by Type of Fishing

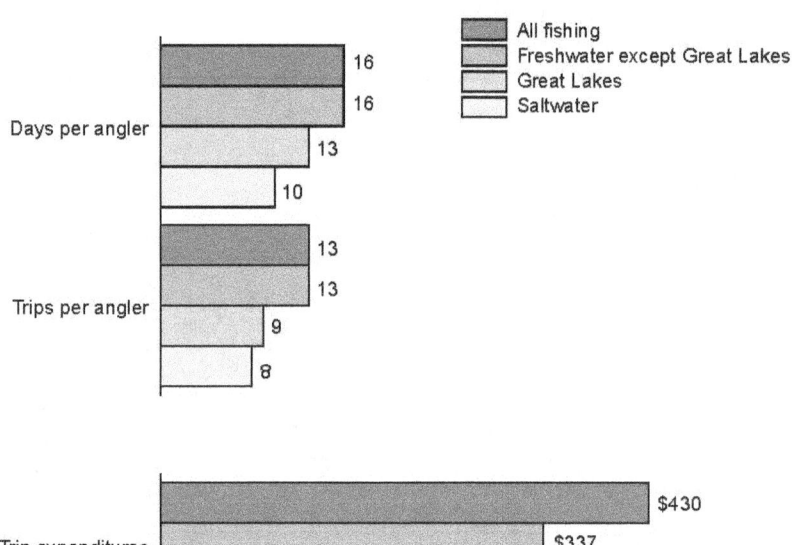

Days per angler
- All fishing: 16
- Freshwater except Great Lakes: 16
- Great Lakes: 13
- Saltwater: 10

Trips per angler
- All fishing: 13
- Freshwater except Great Lakes: 13
- Great Lakes: 9
- Saltwater: 8

Trip expenditures per angler
- All fishing: $430
- Freshwater except Great Lakes: $337
- Great Lakes: $420
- Saltwater: $496

Trip expenditures per day
- All fishing: $26
- Freshwater except Great Lakes: $21
- Great Lakes: $34
- Saltwater: $49

Selected Fish by Type of Fishing
(In millions)

Type of Fishing	Anglers	Days
Freshwater except Great Lakes		
Black bass	10.7	160
Panfish	7.9	103
Trout	7.8	83
Catfish/bullhead	7.5	104
Crappie	6.7	95
White bass, striped bass, and striped bass hybrids	4.9	62
Great Lakes		
Perch	0.7	7
Walleye, sauger	0.6	6
Black bass	0.6	6
Salmon	0.5	4
Lake trout	0.3	4
Steelhead	0.3	4
Saltwater		
Flatfish (flounder, halibut)	2.3	21
Striped bass	1.7	17
Sea trout	1.5	17
Bluefish	1.1	12
Salmon	0.7	5
Mackerel	0.6	6

Comparative Fishing Highlights

In 2001, anglers spent an average of 16 days fishing and took an average of 13 fishing trips. Freshwater, non-Great Lakes anglers averaged 16 days fishing and 13 trips while Great Lakes anglers averaged 13 days fishing and 9 trips. Saltwater anglers fished less frequently—an average of 10 days with an average of 8 trips.

Overall, anglers spent an average of $1,046 on fishing-related expenses in 2001. They averaged $430 per angler on their trips, a daily average of $26. Freshwater anglers, excluding the Great Lakes, averaged $337 per participant for their trips in 2001, equaling $21 per day. Great Lakes anglers spent an average of $420 on trip-related expenses, $34 per day. Saltwater anglers had the highest average expenditure rate at $496—amounting to an average of $49 per day.

Fishing for Selected Fish

Of the 28.0 million anglers who fished freshwater other than the Great Lakes, 10.7 million spent 160 million days fishing for black bass. Panfish were sought by 7.9 million anglers on 103 million days. Catfish and bullheads drew 7.5 million anglers on 104 million days. Nearly 6.7 million anglers fished for crappie on 95 million days. Trout fishing attracted 7.8 million anglers on 83 million days, and 4.9 million anglers fished for white bass and striped bass on 62 million days. Freshwater anglers also commonly fished for walleye, sauger, salmon, and steelhead.

In 2001, 1.8 million anglers fished the Great Lakes. Perch, the most commonly sought fish for these waters, attracted 693 thousand anglers, fishing 7 million days. Next, black bass drew 589 thousand anglers on 6.4 million days, followed by walleye which appealed to 570 thousand anglers who fished more than 5 million days. Salmon drew 516 thousand anglers for almost 4 million days of fishing.

Among the nearly 9.1 million saltwater anglers, 2.3 million fished for flatfish, including flounder and halibut on 21 million days. Bluefish were a favorite of 1.1 million anglers on 12 million days. Sea trout were sought by 1.5 million anglers on 17 million days, and 609 thousand anglers fished for mackerel on 6 million days. Striped bass were sought by 1.7 million anglers on 17 million days. Five million days were spent fishing for salmon by 722 thousand anglers.

Participation by Geographic Division

In 2001, 212 million people 16 years old and older lived in the United State and 1 of every 6 went fishing. While the national participation rate was 16 percent, the regional rates ranged from 11 percent in the Middle Atlantic to 27 percent in the West North Central. The East North Central, East South Central, West South Central, and Mountain Regions all reported participation rates above the national rate. The South Atlantic tied the national rate with 16 percent while the New England (13 percent) and Pacific (12 percent) Regions fell below the national rate.

Fishing in State of Residence and in Other States

A vast majority of the 34.1 million anglers who fished in 2001 did so within their home state. Approximately 31.2 million participants, 92 percent of all anglers, fished in their resident state, while nearly 7.9 million, 23 percent, fished out-of-state. Percentages do not add to 100 because those anglers who fished both in-state and out-of-state were included in both categories.

Of the 28 million non-Great Lakes anglers, 93 percent (25.8 million) fished within their resident state. Nearly 6 million, 20 percent, of these freshwater anglers fished out-of-state.

Eighty-seven percent, 1.6 million, of all Great Lakes anglers enjoyed fishing within their home state in 2001. Nineteen percent, 348 thousand, of all Great Lakes anglers fished out-of-state.

Of all the different types of fishing, saltwater fishing had both the highest percentage of anglers fishing outside their resident state (29 percent) and the lowest percentage fishing within their resident state (76 percent). Nonresident saltwater anglers numbered 2.7 million and resident anglers, 6.9 million.

Fishing in State of Residence and in Other States
(In millions)

	In-State	Out-of-State
Total Anglers	31.2	7.9
Freshwater except		
Great Lakes	25.8	5.6
Great Lakes	1.6	0.3
Saltwater	6.9	2.7

Source: Table 2.

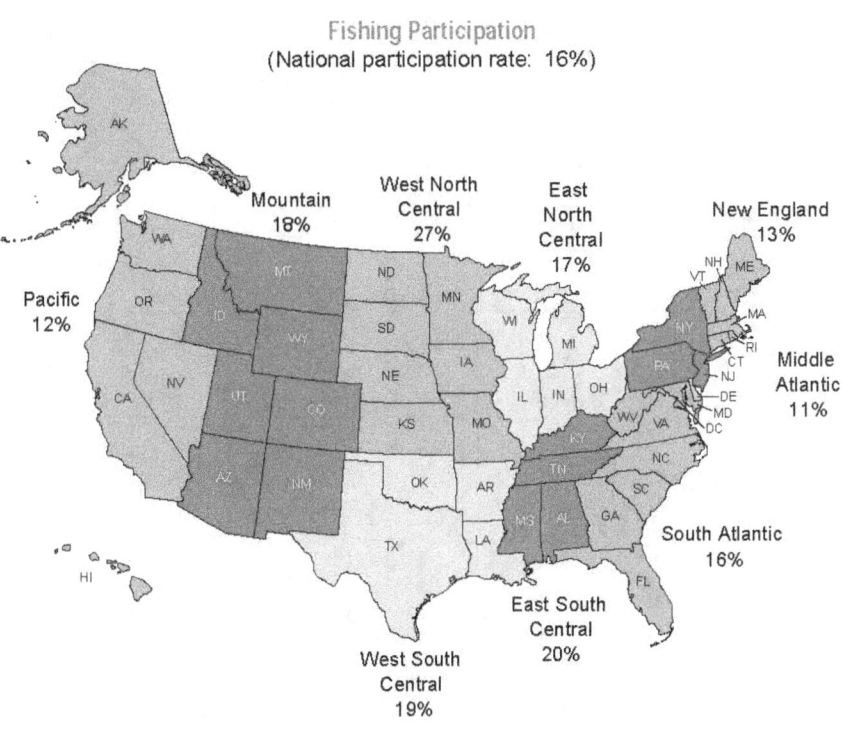

Fishing Participation
(National participation rate: 16%)

Mountain 18%
West North Central 27%
East North Central 17%
New England 13%
Pacific 12%
Middle Atlantic 11%
South Atlantic 16%
East South Central 20%
West South Central 19%

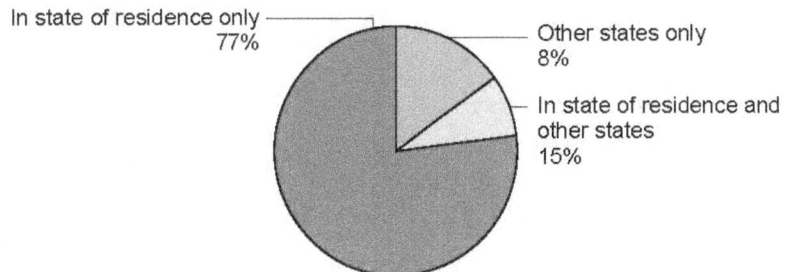

Percent of All Fishing—in State of Residence and Other States
(Total: 34.1 million participants)

In state of residence only 77%
Other states only 8%
In state of residence and other states 15%

Types of Freshwater Fished Excluding Great Lakes
(In millions)

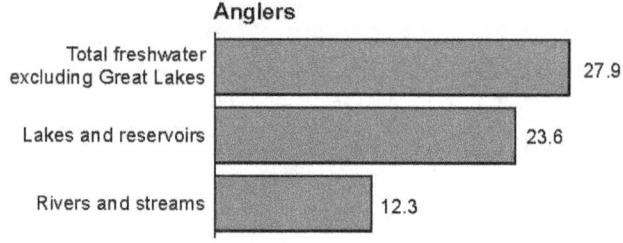

Anglers

Total freshwater excluding Great Lakes	27.9
Lakes and reservoirs	23.6
Rivers and streams	12.3

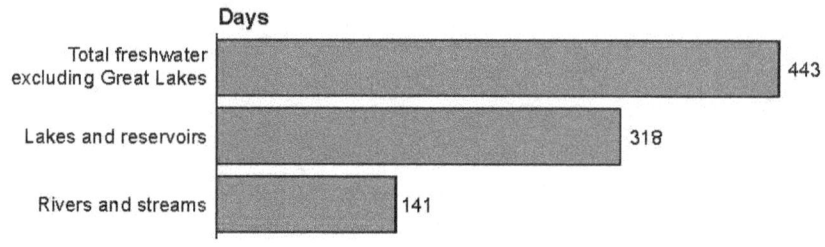

Days

Total freshwater excluding Great Lakes	443
Lakes and reservoirs	318
Rivers and streams	141

Great Lakes Fishing

	Anglers (thousands)	Percentage of all Great Lakes anglers
Total, all Great Lakes	1,847	100
Lake Erie	645	35
Lake Michigan	561	30
Tributaries to the Great Lakes	284	15
Lake Ontario	241	13
Lake Huron	155	8
St. Lawrence River	111	6
Lake St. Clair	96	5
Lake Superior	93	5

Source: Table 27.

Types of Freshwater Fished, Excluding Great Lakes

Freshwater anglers fished in a variety of waters. Most non-Great Lakes freshwater anglers, 23.6 million (85 percent), fished in flatwater including ponds, lakes, or reservoirs on 318 million days. Rivers and streams were utilized by 12.3 million freshwater anglers (44 percent) on 141 million days.

Great Lakes Anglers

Great Lakes fishing includes not only the Great Lakes, but also their tributaries, bodies of water that connect the Great Lakes, and the St. Lawrence River south of the bridge at Cornwall. The most popular of the lakes among anglers was Lake Erie, attracting 35 percent of all the Great Lakes anglers on an average of 12 days during 2001. Lake Michigan ranked second in popularity and hosted 30 percent of the anglers with an average of 9 days per angler. The tributaries to the lakes drew 15 percent of all Great Lakes anglers with an average of 12 days per angler. Lake Ontario attracted 13 percent of the anglers, 241 thousand, averaging 15 fishing day; Lake Huron drew 8 percent, 155 thousand anglers, who averaged 8 days of fishing.

Sex and Age of Anglers

Although more males than females fished in 2001, a substantial number of females fished as well. Approximately 25 percent of all males 16 years and older went fishing, while 8 percent of all females fished. Of the 34.1 million anglers who fished in the United States, 74 percent (25.2 million) were male and 26 percent (8.9 million) were female.

Of the age categories, 9 million anglers, 27 percent of all anglers, were 35 to 44 years old—21 percent of the U.S. population in that age group. They were followed by 6.9 million anglers 45 to 54 years old who comprised 20 percent of all anglers and had a participation rate of 17 percent. Next came the 25- to 34-year-old age group, 6.6 million participants who accounted for 19 percent of all anglers and had a participation rate of 19 percent. The 4.2 million 55- to 64-year-olds who fished comprised 12 percent of all anglers and had a participation rate of 16 percent. Anglers 65 years old and older numbered 3.1 million, 9 percent of total anglers, and recorded an 8 percent participation rate. The 2.9 million anglers 18 to 24 years old also made up 9 percent of the angler population, but they had a participation rate of 13 percent. The 16- and 17-year-olds added 1.3 million individuals to the angler population. They made up 4 percent of the total angler population and had a 17 percent participation rate.

Anglers—by Gender and Age	
Total, both sexes	**34.1 million**
Male	25.2 million
Female	8.9 million
Total, all ages	**34.1 million**
16 and 17	1.3 million
18 to 24	2.9 million
25 to 34	6.6 million
35 to 44	9.0 million
45 to 54	6.9 million
55 to 64	4.2 million
65 and older	3.1 million

Source: Table 9.

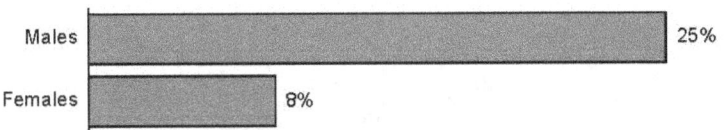

Percent of Males and Females Who Fished in the United States

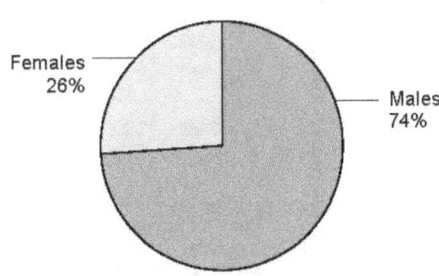

Percent of Anglers—by Gender

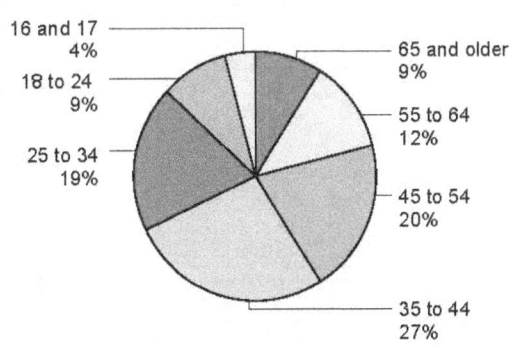

Percent of Anglers—by Age

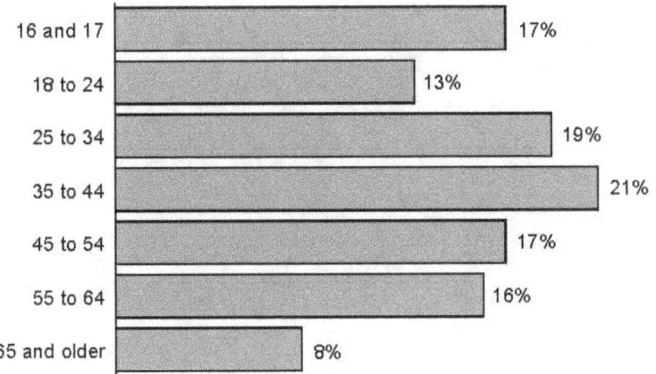

Percent of U.S. Population Who Fished—by Age

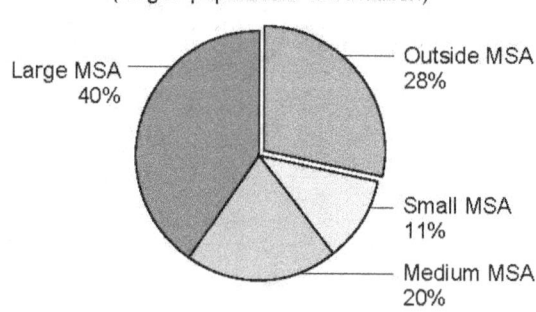

Percent of Anglers—by Residence
(Angler population: 34.1 million)

Large MSA 40%
Outside MSA 28%
Small MSA 11%
Medium MSA 20%

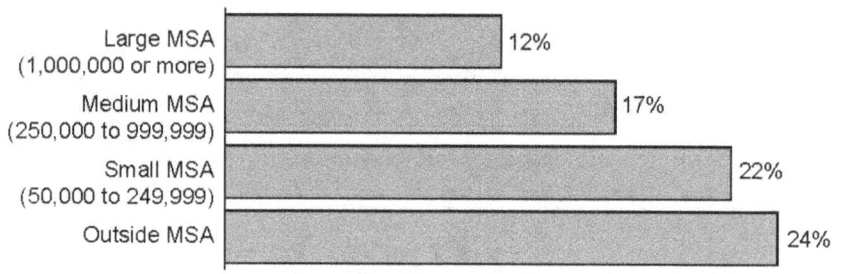

Percent of U.S. Population Who Fished—by Residence
(16% of total U.S. population fished)

Large MSA (1,000,000 or more) — 12%
Medium MSA (250,000 to 999,999) — 17%
Small MSA (50,000 to 249,999) — 22%
Outside MSA — 24%

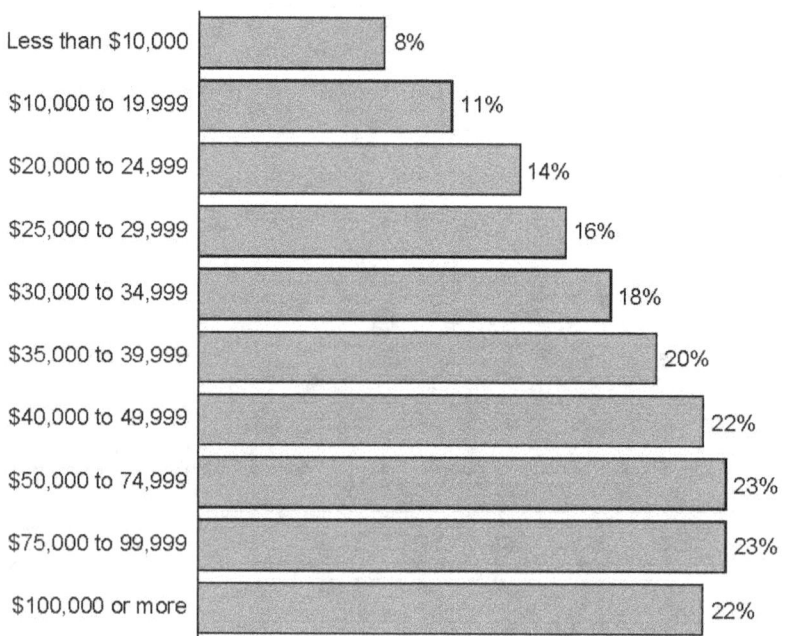

Percent of U.S. Population Who Fished—by Household Income

Less than $10,000 — 8%
$10,000 to 19,999 — 11%
$20,000 to 24,999 — 14%
$25,000 to 29,999 — 16%
$30,000 to 34,999 — 18%
$35,000 to 39,999 — 20%
$40,000 to 49,999 — 22%
$50,000 to 74,999 — 23%
$75,000 to 99,999 — 23%
$100,000 or more — 22%

Metropolitan and Nonmetropolitan Anglers

In 2001, 72 percent of U.S. residents who fished lived in a metropolitan statistical area (MSA) with most anglers coming from large MSAs. People living in MSAs with populations of 1,000,000 or more had a participation rate of 12 percent. Forty percent of all anglers came from these large urban areas. Residents of MSAs with a population of 250,000 to 999,999 had a 17 percent participation rate and represented 20 percent of all anglers. MSAs with populations of 50,000 to 249,999 had a participation rate of 22 percent; they made up 11 percent of all anglers. In areas outside of MSAs, 24 percent of the population fished in 2001. These participants made up 28 percent of all anglers.

Income of Anglers

Anglers at all income levels fished in 2001. Participation rates ranged from 8 percent of all individuals with household incomes of $10,000 or less to 23 percent for those who reported incomes of $50,000 to $99,999. Those living in households with incomes of $10,000 or less comprised 3 percent of all anglers, while those with $50,000 to $74,999 incomes made up 21 percent. Those with $75,000 to $99,999 incomes comprised 12 percent of all anglers. Both household groups with incomes of $40,000 to $49,999 and $100,000 or more garnered participation rates of 22 percent, but only comprised 11 and 12 percent of all anglers, respectively. Next came households earning $35,000 to $39,999 with a participation rate of 20 percent and comprising 6 percent of all anglers. Anglers with household incomes of $30,000 to $34,999 had a participation rate of 18 percent and made up 6 percent of all anglers. A 16 percent participation rate was reported by households with incomes of $25,000 to $29,999—they represented 5 percent of all anglers. Households with $20,000 to $24,999 incomes represented 4 percent of all anglers and had a participation rate of 14 percent. Lastly, 5 percent of all anglers lived in households earning $10,000 to $19,999. These households had a participation rate of 11 percent. Fifteen percent of anglers did not report their income.

Education, Race, and Ethnicity

People from a variety of educational backgrounds fished in 2001. The lowest participation rate, 13 percent, was found among those with 11 years of education or less. They made up 12 percent of all anglers. The highest participation rate, 18 percent, was found among those individuals with 1 to 3 years of college. They made up 27 percent of all anglers. Persons who had 12 years of education, 4 years of college, or 5 years or more of college all had a participation rate of 16 percent. The 12 year education category represented 35 percent of all anglers, while the 4 years of college and the 5 years of more college categories were significantly lower—16 and 10 percent of all anglers.

Fishing was a popular pastime among diverse racial and ethnic populations in the United States. Eighteen percent of the White population fished, compared with 7 percent of the Black population and 5 percent of the Asian population. Among anglers, 93 percent of the total were White, 5 percent Black, 1 percent Asian, and 1 percent other races. Hispanics, a growing percentage of the U.S. population, participated at a rate of 7 percent and represented 5 percent of all anglers.

Anglers—by Education, Race, and Ethnicity (In millions)	
Total anglers	**34.1**
Education	
0-11 years	4.1
12 years	11.8
1 to 3 years of college	9.1
4 years of college	5.5
5 years or more of college .	3.5
Race	
White	31.7
Black	1.6
Asian	0.3
Other	0.4
Ethnicity	
Hispanic	1.6
Non-Hispanic	32.5
Source: Table 9.	

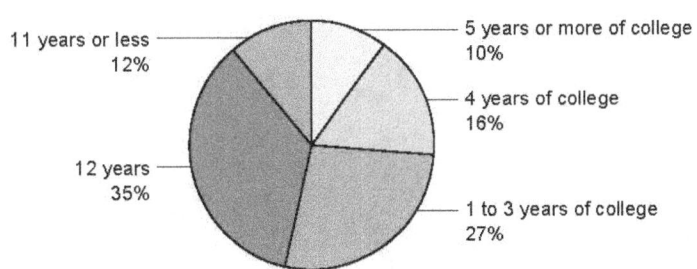

Percent of Anglers—by Education

11 years or less 12%
5 years or more of college 10%
4 years of college 16%
1 to 3 years of college 27%
12 years 35%

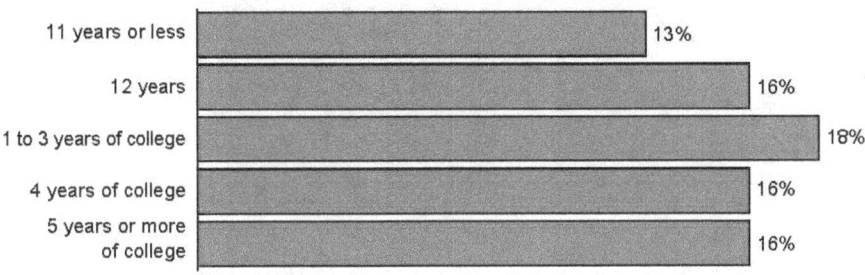

Percent of U.S. Population Who Fished—by Education

11 years or less 13%
12 years 16%
1 to 3 years of college 18%
4 years of college 16%
5 years or more of college 16%

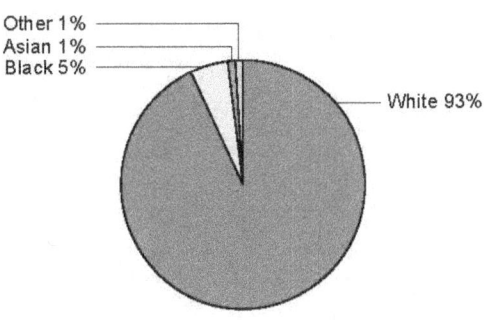

Percent of Anglers—by Race

Other 1%
Asian 1%
Black 5%
White 93%

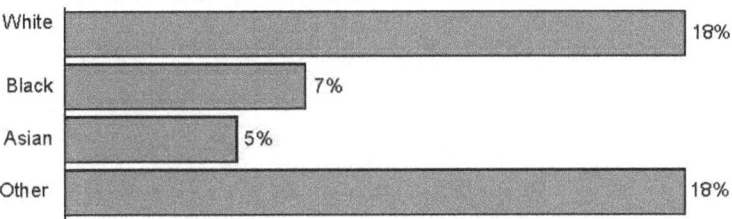

Percent of U.S. Population Who Fished—by Race

White 18%
Black 7%
Asian 5%
Other 18%

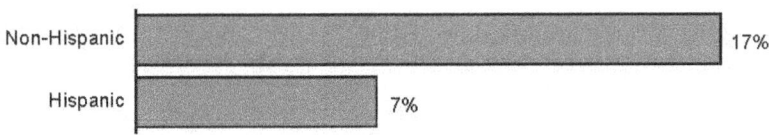

Percent of U.S. Population Who Fished—by Ethnicity

Non-Hispanic 17%
Hispanic 7%

1991-2001 Comparison of Fishing Activity

The number of all anglers in the United States has not changed significantly[1] over the past three Surveys. There was a drop of 1 percent in the number of anglers from 1991 to 1996 and a drop of 3 percent from 1996 to 2001—all well within the survey's margin of error (the 95 percent confidence interval). However, when the angling estimates are examined by type of fishing, there are significant differences. For example, the number of freshwater anglers did change significantly, with an 8 percent drop in the number of non-Great Lakes freshwater

_____

[1]At the 5 percent level of significance.

anglers from 1991 to 2001 and a 28 percent drop in the number of Great Lakes anglers over the same time period. Although saltwater fishing participation shows an increase of 2 percent from 1991 to 2001, it is not statistically significant.

The number of fishing days rose 22 percent from 1991 to 1996 and dropped 11 percent—a statistically insignificant change from 1996 to 2001. This pattern held true for both freshwater fishing and saltwater fishing.

Total fishing expenditures rose 37 percent from 1991 to 1996 and fell 17 percent from 1996 to 2001. Comparing 1991 fishing expenditures with 2001 expenditures finds a 14 percent increase, but this is not a statistically significant

change. Looking at the trip-related expenditure component, there was a similar trend with a 13 percent increase from 1991 to 1996, a 16 percent decrease from 1996 to 2001, and a 5 percent drop (not statistically significant) from 1991 to 2001. Equipment expenditures had a different pattern, with a 78 percent increase from 1991 to 1996, a 22 percent decrease from 1996 to 2001, and a significant 39 percent increase from 1991 to 2001. The purchase of special equipment, such as boats and campers, was primarily responsible for the increase in total equipment purchases. Expenditures for fishing equipment, such as rods and reels, decreased 23 percent from 1996 to 2001 and 5 percent (which is not statistically significant) from 1991 to 2001.

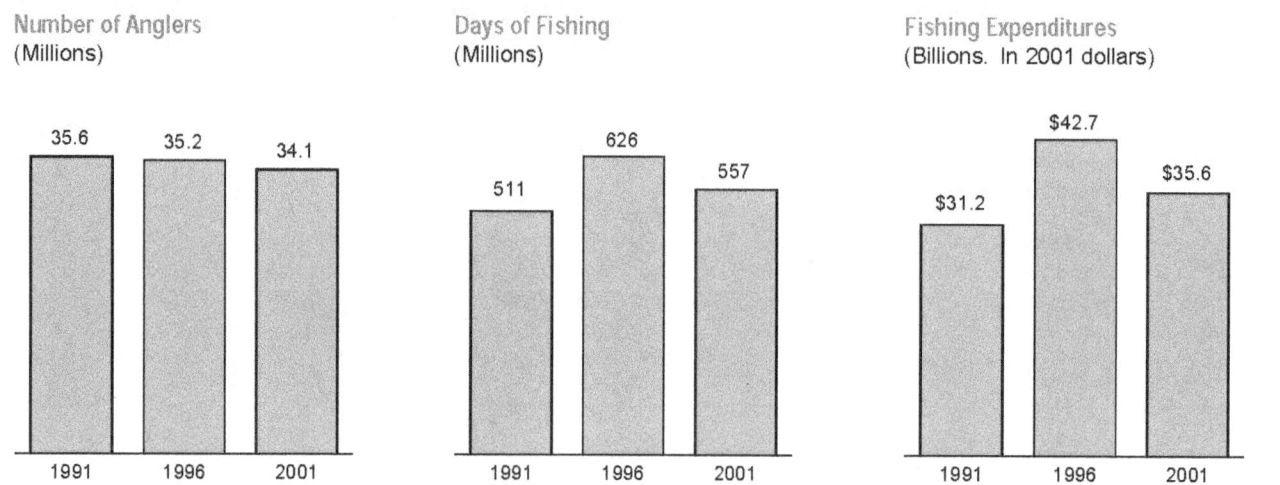

Number of Anglers (Millions): 1991: 35.6, 1996: 35.2, 2001: 34.1

Days of Fishing (Millions): 1991: 511, 1996: 626, 2001: 557

Fishing Expenditures (Billions. In 2001 dollars): 1991: $31.2, 1996: $42.7, 2001: $35.6

1991-2001 Fishing Participants, Days, and Expenditures

(U.S. population 16 years old and older. Numbers in thousands)

	1991		2001		1991-2001 percent change
	Number	Percent	Number	Percent	
Anglers, total..	**35,578**	**100**	**34,067**	**100**	-4*
All freshwater...................................	31,041	87	28,439	83	-8
Freshwater except Great Lakes	30,186	85	27,913	82	-8
Great Lakes....................................	2,552	7	1,847	5	-28
Saltwater......................................	8,885	25	9,051	26	2*
Days, total	**511,329**	**100**	**557,394**	**100**	**9***
All freshwater....................................	439,536	86	466,984	84	6*
Freshwater except Great Lakes	430,922	84	443,247	80	3*
Great Lakes....................................	25,335	5	23,138	4	-9*
Saltwater......................................	74,696	15	90,838	16	22*
Fishing expenditures, total (2001 dollars)	**$31,175,168**	**100**	**$35,632,132**	**100**	**14***
Trips	15,396,151	49	14,656,001	41	-5*
Equipment.....................................	12,170,062	39	16,963,398	48	39
Fishing equipment.............................	4,860,266	16	4,617,488	13	-5*
Auxiliary equipment...........................	804,953	3	721,048	2	-10*
Special equipment.............................	6,504,844	21	11,624,862	33	79
Other..	3,608,953	12	4,012,733	11	11*

* Not different from zero at the 5 percent level.

1996-2001 Fishing Participants, Days, and Expenditures

(U.S. population 16 years old and older. Numbers in thousands)

	1996		2001		1996-2001 percent change
	Number	Percent	Number	Percent	
Anglers, total..	**35,246**	**100**	**34,067**	**100**	-3*
All freshwater....................................	29,734	84	28,439	83	-4*
Freshwater except Great Lakes	28,921	82	27,913	82	-3*
Great Lakes....................................	2,039	6	1,847	5	-9*
Saltwater......................................	9,438	27	9,051	26	-4*
Days, total	**625,893**	**100**	**557,394**	**100**	**-11***
All freshwater....................................	515,115	82	466,984	84	-9*
Freshwater except Great Lakes	485,474	78	443,247	80	-9*
Great Lakes....................................	20,095	3	23,138	4	15*
Saltwater......................................	103,034	17	90,838	16	-12*
Fishing expenditures, total (2001 dollars)	**$42,710,679**	**100**	**$35,632,132**	**100**	**-17**
Trips	17,380,775	41	14,656,001	41	-16
Equipment.....................................	21,666,341	51	16,963,398	48	-22
Fishing equipment.............................	5,998,802	14	4,617,488	13	-23
Auxiliary equipment...........................	1,171,540	3	721,048	2	-38
Special equipment.............................	14,495,999	34	11,624,862	33	-20*
Other..	3,663,563	9	4,012,733	11	10*

* Not different from zero at the 5 percent level.

Hunting

Hunting Highlights

In 2001, 13 million people 16 years old and older enjoyed hunting a variety of animals within the United States. They hunted 228 million days and took 200 million trips. Hunting expenditures totaled $20.6 billion.

Big game hunting was most popular in 2001. Approximately 11.0 million

hunters pursued big game such as deer and elk on 153 million days. They spent $10.1 billion on trips and equipment during the year. A total of 5.4 million people hunted small game including squirrels and rabbits. They hunted small game on 60 million days and spent $1.8 billion on their hunting trips and equipment. Migratory bird hunters

numbered 3.0 million. They spent 29 million days hunting birds such as waterfowl and dove. Their trip and equipment expenditures totaled $1.4 billion. More than 1.0 million hunters sought other animals such as raccoons and groundhogs on 19 million days. They spent $244 million on trips and equipment for the year.

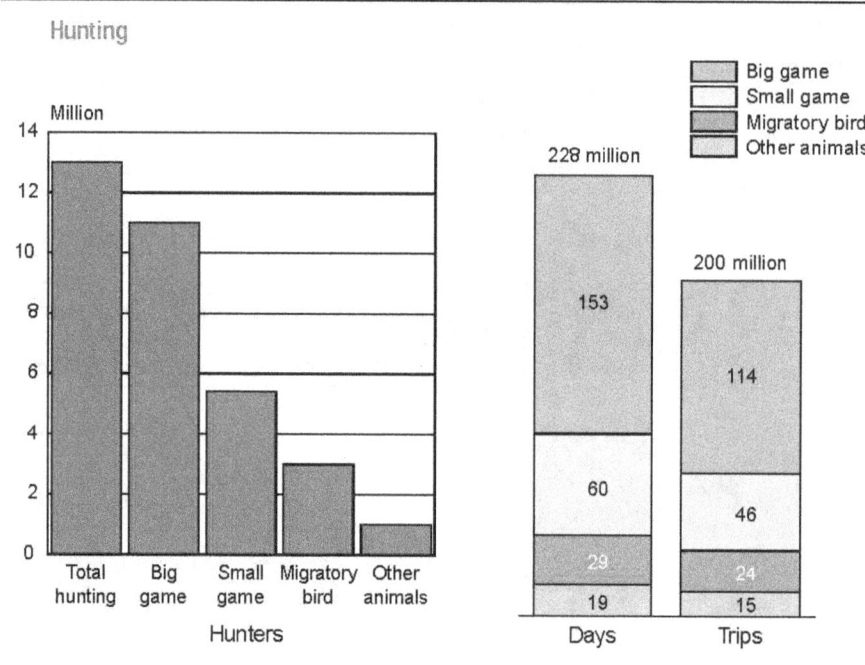

Hunting

Detail does not add to total because of multiple responses and nonresponse.

Total Hunting		
Hunters	**13.0 million**	
Big game	10.9 million	
Small game	5.4 million	
Migratory bird ...	3.0 million	
Other animals	1.0 million	
Days	**228 million**	
Big game	153 million	
Small game	60 million	
Migratory bird ...	29 million	
Other animals	19 million	
Trips	**200 million**	
Big game	114 million	
Small game	46 million	
Migratory bird ...	24 million	
Other animals	15 million	
Expenditures	**$20.6 billion**	
Big game	10.1 billion	
Small game	1.8 billion	
Migratory game ..	1.4 billion	
Other animals	0.2 billion	
Unspecified	7.1 billion	

Detail does not add to total because of multiple responses and nonresponse.
Source: Tables 1 and 18-22.

Hunting Expenditures

Of the $20.6 billion spent by hunters in 2001, 25 percent, $5.3 billion, was spent on trip-related expenses. Food and lodging totaled to $2.4 billion—47 percent of all trip-related expenses. Transportation cost hunters $1.8 billion, 34 percent of their trip expenditures. Other trip expenses such as guide fees, land use fees, and equipment rental were $1.0 billion or 19 percent of all trip-related expenses.

Total hunting equipment expenditures were $10.4 billion in 2001—50 percent of all hunting expenses. Hunting equipment, such as guns and rifles, telescopic sights, and ammunition, cost hunters $4.6 billion, 44 percent of all equipment costs. Expenditures for auxiliary equipment, including camping equipment, binoculars, and special hunting clothing, accounted for $1.2 billion or 12 percent of all equipment expenses. Special equipment, such as campers or trail bikes, amounted to $4.6 billion or 44 percent of all equipment expenditures.

Land leasing and ownership for hunting was a large expenditure category. Hunters spent $4.0 billion on land leasing and ownership—19 percent of their total expenditures in 2001. Expenditures for magazines, books, membership dues, and contributions, and licenses, tags, and permits totaled $1 billion.

Total Hunting Expenditures

Total hunting expenditures	**$20.6 billion**
Total trip-related	**$5.3 billion**
Food and lodging	2.4 billion
Transportation	1.8 billion
Other trip costs	1.0 billion
Total equipment expenditures	**$10.4 billion**
Hunting equipment	$4.6 billion
Auxiliary equipment	1.2 billion
Special equipment	4.6 billion
Total other hunting expenditures	**$5.0 billion**
Magazines, books	0.1 billion
Membership dues and contributions	0.2 billion
Land leasing and ownership	4.0 billion
Licenses, stamps, tags, and permits	0.7 billion

Source: Table 18.

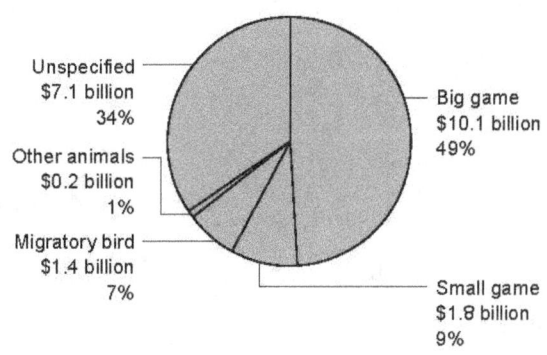

Expenditures
(Total expenditures: $20.6 billion)

Unspecified $7.1 billion 34%
Other animals $0.2 billion 1%
Migratory bird $1.4 billion 7%
Big game $10.1 billion 49%
Small game $1.8 billion 9%

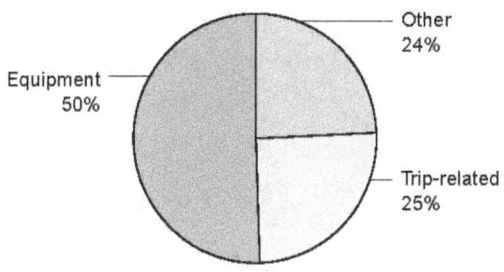

Percent of Total Hunting Expenditures
(Total expenditures: $20.6 billion)

Other 24%
Equipment 50%
Trip-related 25%

Big Game Hunting

In 2001, the majority of hunters, 11.0 million, devoted 153 million days to hunting big game including deer, elk, bear, and wild turkey. They took 114 million trips and spent an average of 14 days hunting big game during the year.

Trip and equipment expenditures for big game hunters amounted to $10.1 billion. Trip-related expenses totaled $3.6 billion. Of that amount, food and lodging totaled $1.7 billion or 47 percent of all trip-related costs. Transportation costs reached $1.1 billion—32 percent of trip costs. Other trip-related expenses amounted to $749 million or 21 percent of trip costs.

Big game hunters spent the majority of their money on equipment—$6.5 billion. Hunting equipment (guns, ammunition, etc.) accounted for $2.2 billion. Purchases of auxiliary equipment (camping equipment, binoculars, etc.) totaled $935 million. And special equipment (vans, trail bikes, etc.) cost big game hunters $3.4 billion.

Small Game Hunting

Also popular with hunters was small game such as rabbits, squirrel, pheasants, quail, and grouse. In 2001, approximately 5.4 million hunters pursued small game on a total of 60 million days. They took 46 million trips. Small game hunters averaged 11 days in the field hunting.

These hunters spent $1.8 billion on trips and equipment. Of their $909 million trip expenditures, $438 million or 48 percent was spent on food and lodging. Transportation costs totaled $348 million or 38 percent of small game trip expenses. Other trip-related expenditures amounted to $124 million or 14 percent of all trip costs.

During 2001, equipment expenditures for small game hunting totaled $907 million. Of that amount, hunting equipment (guns, ammunition, etc.) amounted to $660 million, auxiliary equipment (camping equipment, binoculars, etc.) $63 million, and special equipment (vans, trail bikes, etc.) $183 million.

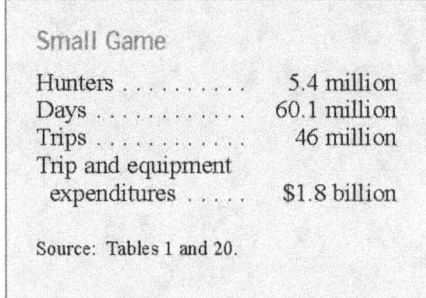

Big Game

Hunters	11.0 million
Days	153 million
Trips	114 million
Trip and equipment expenditures	$10.1 billion

Source: Tables 1 and 19.

Small Game

Hunters	5.4 million
Days	60.1 million
Trips	46 million
Trip and equipment expenditures	$1.8 billion

Source: Tables 1 and 20.

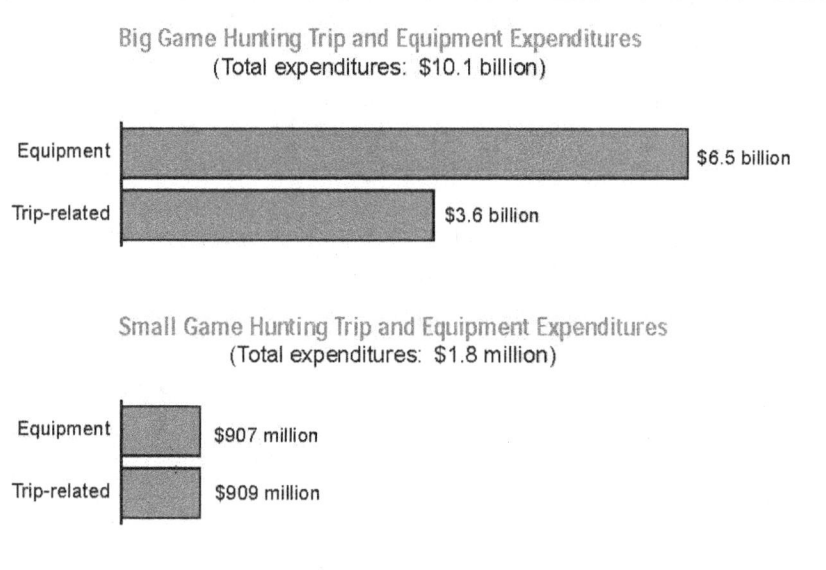

Big Game Hunting Trip and Equipment Expenditures
(Total expenditures: $10.1 billion)

Equipment — $6.5 billion
Trip-related — $3.6 billion

Small Game Hunting Trip and Equipment Expenditures
(Total expenditures: $1.8 million)

Equipment — $907 million
Trip-related — $909 million

Migratory Bird Hunting

In 2001, 3.0 million migratory bird hunters devoted 29 million days on 24 million trips for hunting birds such as doves, ducks, and geese. Migratory bird hunters spent an average of 10 days hunting for the year.

The $1.4 billion spent by migratory bird hunters in 2001 was for hunting trips and equipment. Of the items contributing to this sum, $657 million was spent on hunting trips, including $280 million on food and lodging (43 percent of trip-related expenses), and $247 million on transportation (38 percent of all trip costs). Other trip expenses amounted to $130 million—20 percent of the total trip-related expenditures for migratory bird hunters.

Migratory bird hunters purchased nearly $732 million worth of equipment in 2001. They spent $534 million on hunting equipment (guns, ammunition, etc.). Another $68 million was spent by migratory bird hunters on auxiliary equipment (camping equipment, binoculars, etc.), and $130 million was spent on special equipment (vans, trail bikes, etc.).

Hunting Other Animals

During 2001, more than 1 million hunters reported spending 19 million days on 15 million trips pursuing animals such as groundhogs, raccoons, foxes, and coyotes. They averaged 18 days of hunting for the year.

These hunters spent $244 million in 2001 on trips and equipment. Trip-related costs totaled $121 million. Of that, food and lodging were $44 million or 36 percent of all trip costs; transportation was $67 million, 55 percent of trip expenses; and other trip expenses were $10 million, 9 percent of all trip costs.

Equipment expenditures for hunting other animals totaled $123 million. Hunters pursuing other animals spent $85 million on hunting equipment (guns, ammunition, etc.), and $6 million on auxiliary equipment (camping equipment, binoculars, etc.).

Comparative Hunting Highlights

In 2001, big game hunters averaged 14 days of hunting and 10 trips per hunter. Small game hunters spent an average of 11 days hunting in the field on an average of 9 trips. In comparison, migratory bird

Migratory Birds

Hunters	3.0 million
Days	29 million
Trips	24 million
Trip and equipment expenditures	$1.4 billion

Source: Tables 1 and 21.

Other Animals

Hunters	1.0 million
Days	19 million
Trips	15 million
Trip and equipment expenditures	$244 million

Source: Table 1 and 22.

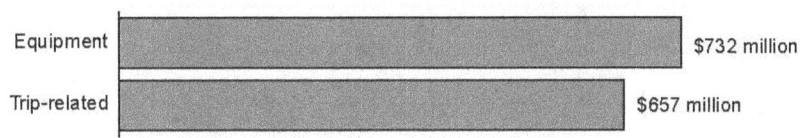

Migratory Bird Hunting Trip and Equipment Expenditures
(Total expenditures: $1.4 million)

Equipment — $732 million
Trip-related — $657 million

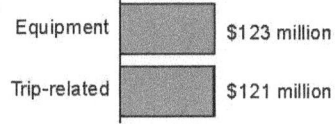

Trip and Equipment Expenditures for Hunting Other Animals
(Total expenditures: $244 million)

Equipment — $123 million
Trip-related — $121 million

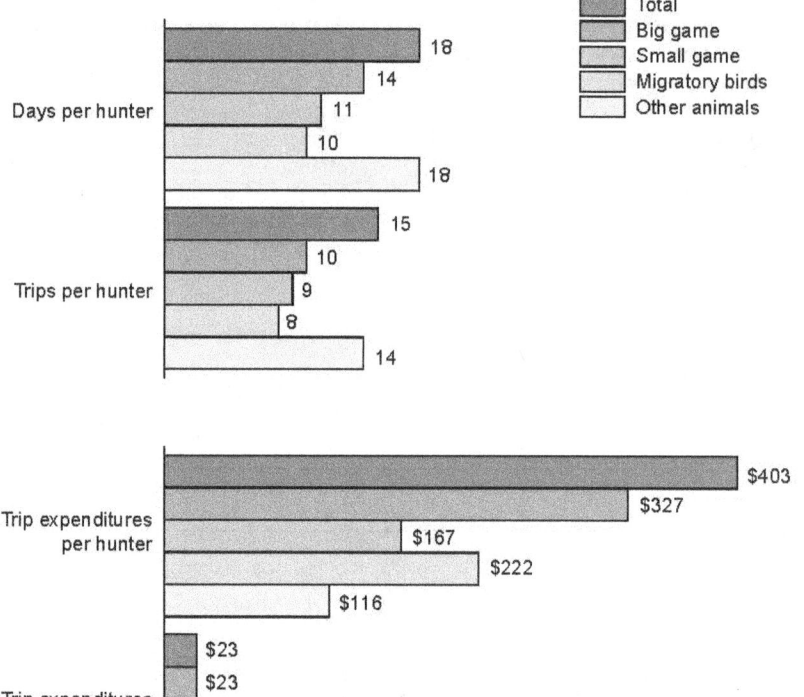

Comparative Hunting by Type of Hunting

Legend: Total, Big game, Small game, Migratory birds, Other animals

Days per hunter: 18, 14, 11, 10, 18

Trips per hunter: 15, 10, 9, 8, 14

Trip expenditures per hunter: $403, $327, $167, $222, $116

Trip expenditures per day: $23, $23, $15, $22, $6

Hunting for Selected Game
(In millions)

Type of Hunting	Hunters	Days
Big game	10.9	153
Deer	10.3	133
Wild turkey	2.5	23
Elk	0.9	6
Bear	0.3	3
Small game	5.4	60
Squirrel	2.1	22
Rabbit and hare	2.1	23
Pheasant	1.7	13
Grouse/prairie chicken	1.0	9
Quail	0.9	8
Migratory birds	3.0	29
Ducks	1.6	18
Doves	1.5	9
Geese	1.0	11
Other animals	1.0	19

Source: Table 7.

hunters spent an average of 10 days and 8 trips hunting. Individuals hunting other animals averaged 18 days and 14 trips pursuing their game.

On average, big game hunters spent more money on trips and equipment than other hunters in 2001. They averaged $925 per hunter for the year. Small game hunters spent an average of $334 per hunter while migratory bird hunters averaged $470. Those hunting other animals spent $233 per hunter for the year.

During 2001, trip expenditures for all hunting averaged $403 per hunter, a daily average of $23. The average for trip expenditures varied by type of hunting. Big game hunting trips averaged $327 per hunter for lodging, food, transportation, and other trip-related expenses ($23 per day). Small game hunters spent $167 on average for trip expenses ($15 per day). Persons taking trips for migratory bird hunting spent an average of $222 ($22 per day) while for hunting other animals averaged $116 per hunter for their trips ($6 per day).

Hunting for Selected Game

For big game hunting, deer was the most popular animal pursued—attracting 10.3 million hunters on 133 million days. Turkey attracted 2.5 million hunters on 23 million days, while elk drew 910 thousand on 6 million days, and bear 360 thousand on 3 million days. In addition, 527 thousand hunters spent 5 million days hunting other big game animals.

In 2001, nearly 2.1 million small game hunters hunted rabbits and hares on 23 million days. Quail was flushed by 991 thousand hunters on 8 million days, while grouse and prairie chicken were favorites of 1 million hunters on 9 million days. Squirrels were hunted by 2.1 million participants on 22 million days, and pheasants attracted 1.7 million hunters on 13 million days. In addition, 505 thousand hunters spent 5.2 million days hunting other small game animals.

Among those hunting migratory birds, 1.6 million enthusiasts hunted duck on 18 million days. Nearly 1.5 million participants hunted dove on 9 million days. On 11 million days, 1 million hunters hunted geese in 2001. Other migratory bird species attracted 210 thousand people who hunted on 1.5 million days.

Participation by Geographic Regions

In 2001, 212 million people 16 years old and older lived in the United States. Six percent of all those people hunted that year.

Regionally, participation rates ranged from 2 percent in the Pacific Region to 12 percent in the West North Central Region. The East North Central, East South Central, West South Central, and Mountain Regions also had participation rates above the national average of 6 percent. Both the East South Central and the West South Central Regions garnered participation rates of 9 percent. While the Mountain Region's rate was 8 percent, the East North Central's was 7 percent. The Middle Atlantic and South Atlantic Regions' participation rate was 5 percent, and New England's was 4 percent.

Hunting in State of Residence and in Other States

An overwhelming majority of participants hunted within their resident state—12.4 million or 95 percent of all hunters. Only 2.1 million, 16 percent, hunted in another state. Percentages do not add to 100 because those sportspersons who hunted both in-state and out-of-state were included in both categories.

In 2001, 10.4 million big game hunters, 95 percent of all big game hunters, hunted within their state of residence, while only 13 percent, 1.5 million people, traveled to another state to hunt big game. Nearly 5.1 million small game hunters, 94 percent of all small game hunters, pursued game in their resident state. Approximately 672 thousand, 12 percent, ventured across state lines to hunt small game. Ninety-four percent of all migratory bird hunters, 2.8 million participants, hunted within their resident state. Fourteen percent or 410 thousand of these sportspersons hunted out-of-state. Among sportspersons who hunted other animals, 96 percent, 1.0 million, hunted in-state and 10 percent, 102 thousand participants, hunted out-of-state.

Hunting in State of Residence and in Other States

(In millions)

	In-State	Out-of-State
All hunters	12.4	2.1
Big game	10.4	1.5
Small game	5.1	0.7
Migratory birds	2.8	0.4
Other animals	1.0	0.1

Source: Table 6.

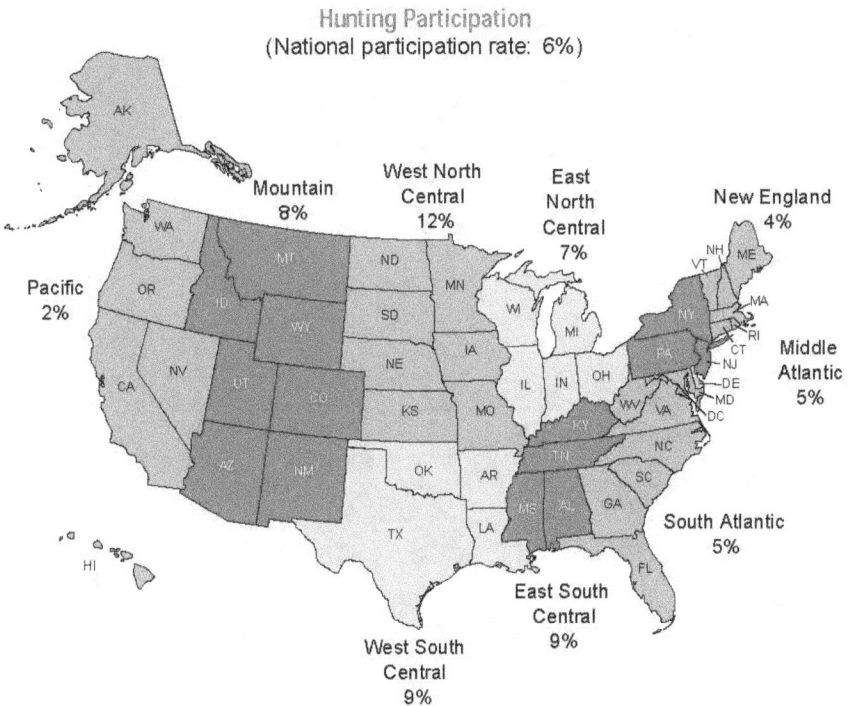

Hunting Participation
(National participation rate: 6%)

Hunting on Public and Private Lands

In 2001, 13 million hunters 16 years old and older hunted on public land, private land, or both. Of this number, 5.2 million or 40 percent hunted on publicly owned lands compared to 10.7 million or 82 percent who hunted on privately owned land. Some hunters, 1.9 million—14 percent of all hunters—used publicly owned lands exclusively while 7.4 million hunted only on private land and represented 57 percent of all hunters. Slightly over 3 million hunters (25 percent) hunted on both public and private lands.

During 2001, 5.2 million hunters used public lands on 60 million days— 26 percent of all hunting days.

Thirty-seven percent of big game hunters spent 36 million days on public lands. Among the 5.4 million small game hunters, 36 percent used public land on 16 million days. Approximately 1.0 million migratory bird hunters, 35 percent of all migratory bird hunters, spent 9.1 million days on public lands. Twenty-seven percent, 287 thousand of other animal hunters pursued their game on public land for 3 million days.

In contrast, 10.7 million hunters spent 170 million days—74 percent of all hunting days—pursuing their sport on private lands in 2001. A vast majority of all hunters (82 percent) pursued their game on private lands as did big game hunters (80 percent), small game hunters (80 percent), migratory bird hunters (76 percent), and other animal hunters (86 percent).

Days spent hunting on private land also varied by type of hunting. In 2001, big game hunters spent 72 percent (110 million days) of their total hunting days on private lands; small game hunters spent 70 percent (42 million days) of their hunting days on private lands, and migratory bird hunters spent 67 percent (20 million days) of their hunting days on private lands. Participants hunting other animals spent 84 percent (16 million days) of their hunting days on private lands.

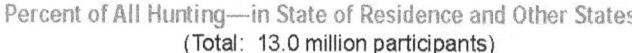

Percent of All Hunting—in State of Residence and Other States
(Total: 13.0 million participants)

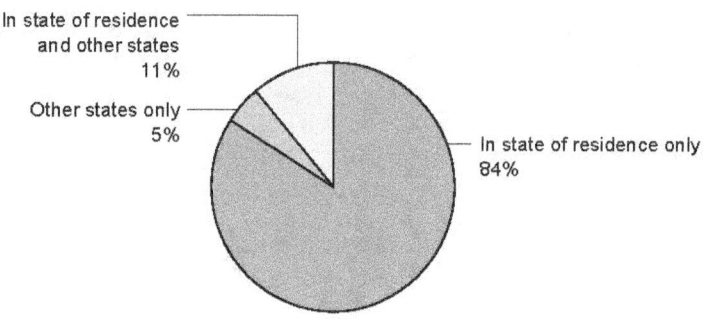

People Hunting on Public and Private Lands

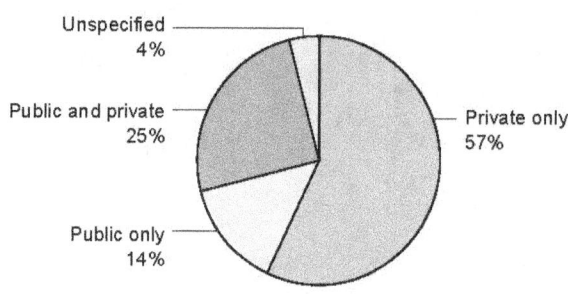

Sex and Age of Hunters

Of the U.S. population 16 years old and older, 12 percent of the males and 1 percent of the females enjoyed hunting in 2001. Of the 13 million participants who hunted, 91 percent (11.8 million) were male and 9 percent (1.2 million) were female.

Hunter participation was seen in all age groups across the country. The proportion of hunters by age group ranged from 4 percent among hunters 16 and 17 years old to 27 percent for those hunters 35 to 44 years old. During 2001, 8 percent of all 16- and 17-year olds hunted. They numbered 584 thousand hunters. The participation rate for 35- to 44-year olds also was 8 percent, but they numbered 3.6 million hunters. The 18- to 24-year olds showed a 6 percent participant rate with nearly 1.3 million participants (10 percent of all hunters). The participation rate for the 25- to 34-year olds was 7 percent, numbering 2.4 million hunters—19 percent of all hunters. Hunters 45 to 54 years old also had a 7 percent participation rate with approximately 2.8 million hunters (22 percent of all hunters). The 55- to 64-year old hunters numbered 1.5 million, capturing 11 percent of all hunters with a participation rate of 6 percent. Finally, 965 thousand people 65 years old and older made up 7 percent of all hunters and garnered a participation rate of 3 percent.

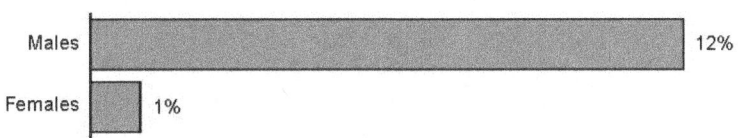

Percent of Males and Females Who Hunted in the United States

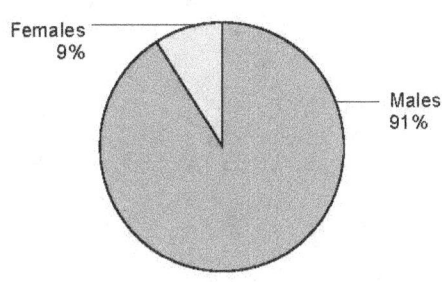

Percent of Hunters—by Gender

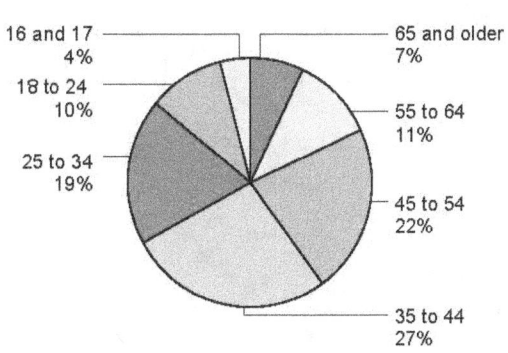

Percent of Hunters—by Age

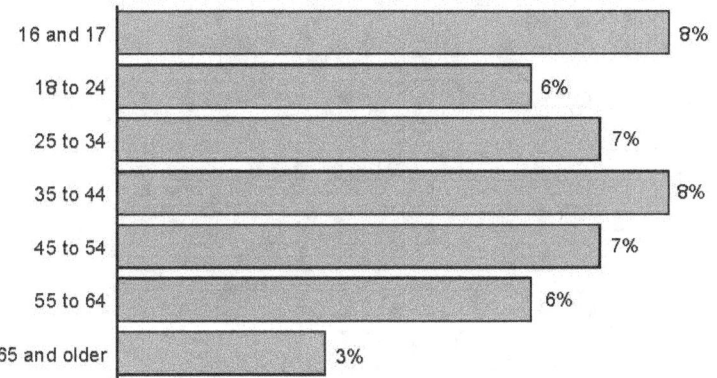

Percent of U.S. Population Who Hunted—by Age

Hunters—by Gender and Age	
Total, both sexes	**13.0 million**
Male	11.8 million
Female	1.2 million
Total, all ages	
16 and 17	0.6 million
18 to 24	1.3 million
25 to 34	2.4 million
35 to 44	3.6 million
45 to 54	2.8 million
55 to 64	1.5 million
65 and older	1.0 million

Source: Table 10.

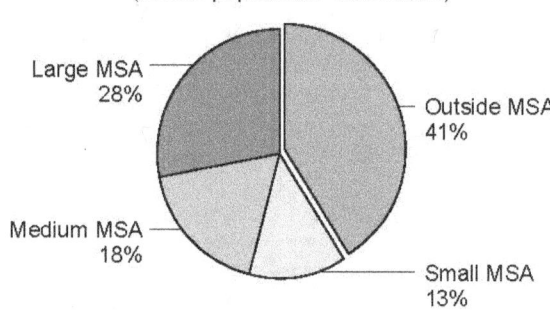

Percent of Hunters—by Residence
(Hunter population: 13.0 million)

- Large MSA 28%
- Outside MSA 41%
- Medium MSA 18%
- Small MSA 13%

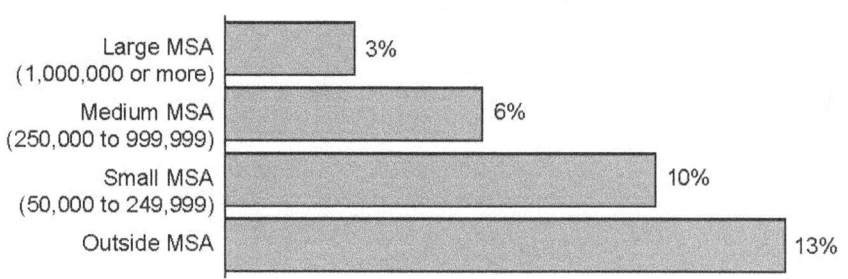

Percent of U.S. Population Who Hunted—by Residence
(6% of total U.S. population hunted)

- Large MSA (1,000,000 or more) — 3%
- Medium MSA (250,000 to 999,999) — 6%
- Small MSA (50,000 to 249,999) — 10%
- Outside MSA — 13%

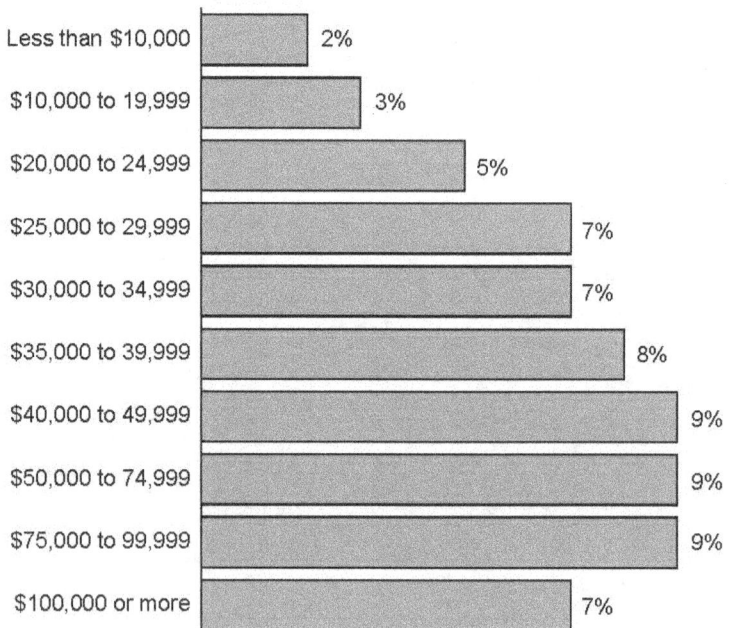

Percent of U.S. Population Who Hunted—by Household Income

- Less than $10,000 — 2%
- $10,000 to 19,999 — 3%
- $20,000 to 24,999 — 5%
- $25,000 to 29,999 — 7%
- $30,000 to 34,999 — 7%
- $35,000 to 39,999 — 8%
- $40,000 to 49,999 — 9%
- $50,000 to 74,999 — 9%
- $75,000 to 99,999 — 9%
- $100,000 or more — 7%

Metropolitan and Nonmetropolitan Hunters

While most hunters in 2001 resided outside the nation's largest metropolitan statistical areas (MSAs), a substantial number of those area residents were hunters. Twenty-eight percent of all hunters were from MSAs with populations of 1,000,000 or more. Three percent of the total residents of these large MSAs hunted. For MSAs with populations of 250,000 to 999,999, 6 percent of their residents hunted and comprised 18 percent of all hunters. Ten percent of all residents of MSAs with populations of 50,000 to 249,999 hunted in 2001. Thirteen percent of all hunters resided in these areas.

Although only 19 percent of the U.S. population 16 years of age and older resided in areas outside of MSAs in 2001, 41 percent of all hunters lived outside MSAs. Thirteen percent of those nonmetropolitan residents hunted in 2001 in contrast with 5 percent of all metropolitan residents who hunted.

Income of Hunters

Participation rates among hunters varied by household income from 2 percent of persons with household incomes of less than $10,000 a year (2 percent of all hunters came from these households) to 9 percent of those reporting incomes of $40,000 to $49,999 (13 percent of all hunters), $50,000 to $74,999 (22 percent of all hunters), and $75,999 to $99,999 (12 percent of all hunters). Households reporting $10,000 to $19,999 incomes had a 3 percent participation rate and comprised 4 percent of all hunters. Five percent of the nation's population with household incomes of $20,000 to $24,999 hunted in 2001 and made up 4 percent of all hunters. Households with incomes of $25,000 to $29,999 had a 7 percent participation rate, representing 6 percent of all hunters. In households reporting incomes of $30,000 to $34,999, 7 percent was the participation rate. Residents of these households represented 6 percent of all hunters. Eight percent of the persons in households reporting incomes of $35,000 to $39,999 totaled 6 percent of all hunters. Finally, 7 percent of persons with household incomes of $100,000 or more hunted and comprised 10 percent of all hunters.

Education and Race of Hunters

During 2001, people from a variety of educational backgrounds went hunting in the United States. Participation rates ranged from 5 percent for individuals with less than 12 years of school or 4 years or more of college to 7 percent for individuals with 12 years of school or 1 to 3 years of college.

Hunters with 12 years of education accounted for 38 percent of the hunting population. Those possessing 1 to 3 years of college represented 26 percent of all hunters. Those with 11 years or less of education represented 14 percent of all hunters. Others with at least 4 years of college comprised 14 percent of all hunters. And individuals with 5 years of more of college totaled 8 percent of all hunters.

While 6 percent of the U.S. population went hunting in 2001, participation among races varied. Seven percent of the nation's White population hunted, 1 percent of the Black population hunted, and 6 percent of the other races hunted. Of the 13 million hunters, 96 percent were White, 2 percent were Black, and 1 percent were of other races.

Hunters—by Education and Race

(In millions)

Total hunters	**13.0**
Education	
0-11 years	1.8
12 years	5.0
1 to 3 years of college	3.4
4 years of college	1.8
5 years or more of college .	1.1
Race	
White	12.6
Black	0.3
Other	0.2

Source: Table 10.

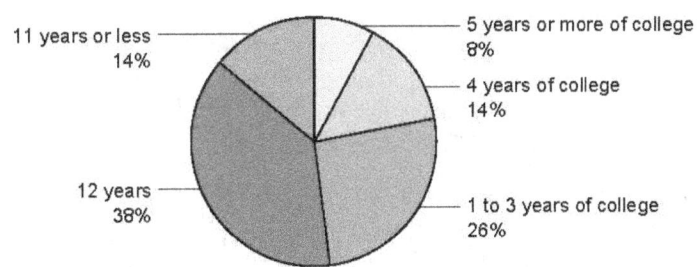

Percent of Hunters—by Education

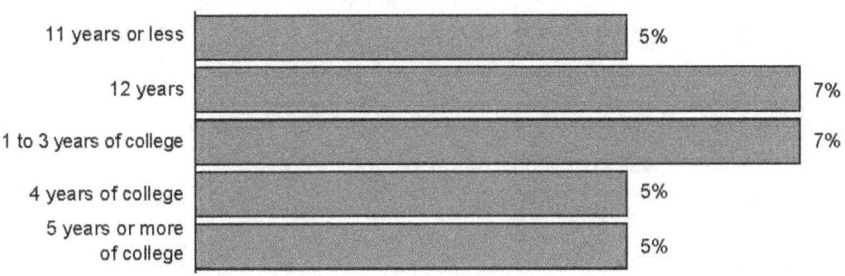

Percent of U.S. Population Who Hunted—by Education

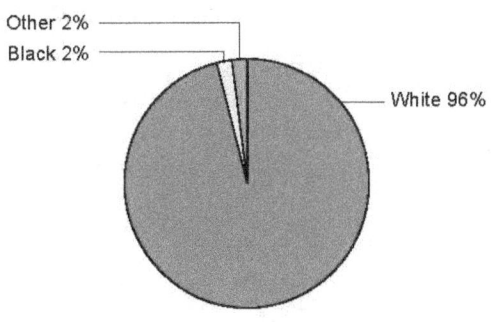

Percent of Hunters—by Race

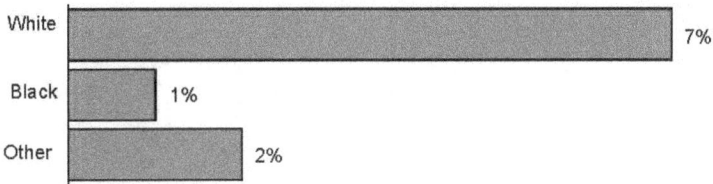

Percent of U.S. Population Who Hunted—by Race

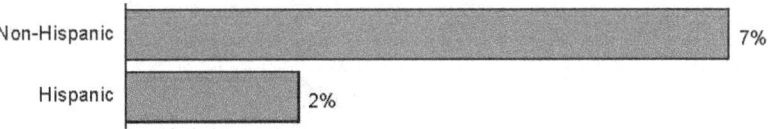

Percent of U.S. Population Who Hunted—by Ethnicity

1991, 1996, 2001 Comparison of Hunting Activity

The overall number of people who hunted in 2001 dropped 7 percent from the 1991/1996 level, and their days afield tended downward as well. However, looking at the various types of hunting, big game and migratory bird hunting did not see this drop in hunting participation—either in the number of hunters or the number of hunting days. The number of big game and migratory bird hunters stayed roughly the same throughout the three surveys, and the number of days hunting these animals increased from 1991 to 2001. The drop in hunting participation can be traced to small game and other animal hunting, which saw significant drops in both hunters and days.

Hunting expenditures increased from 1991 to 1996 for both trip-related and equipment expenditures and then tended downward from 1996 to 2001. The robust 1996 economy, compared to the recessionary years of 1991 and 2001, can at least partly explain this finding. The category that experienced the biggest increase from 1991 to 2001 was special equipment, such as pickups and campers, which nearly tripled. Purchases of hunting equipment, such as firearms and ammunition, increased by 7 percent—not a statistically significant change at the 95 percent confidence level.

1991-2001 Hunting Participants, Days, and Expenditures

(U.S. population 16 years old and older. Numbers in thousands)

	1991		2001		1991-2001
	Number	Percent	Number	Percent	percent change
Hunters, total.....................................	**14,063**	**100**	**13,034**	**100**	-7
Big game..................................	10,745	76	10,911	84	2*
Small game...............................	7,642	54	5,434	42	-29
Migratory bird............................	3,009	21	2,956	23	-2*
Other animal..............................	1,411	10	1,047	8	-26
Days, total......................................	**235,806**	**100**	**228,368**	**100**	-3*
Big game..................................	128,411	54	153,191	67	19
Small game...............................	77,132	33	60,142	26	-22
Migratory bird............................	22,235	9	29,310	13	32
Other animal..............................	19,340	8	19,207	8	-1*
Hunting expenditures, total (2001 dollars)...........	**$16,031,197**	**100**	**$20,611,025**	**100**	29
Trips.....................................	4,471,065	28	5,252,391	25	17*
Equipment.................................	6,716,497	42	10,361,495	50	54
Hunting equipment.........................	4,266,795	27	4,561,708	22	7*
Auxiliary equipment.......................	825,616	5	1,202,845	6	46
Special equipment.........................	1,624,086	10	4,596,942	22	183
Other.....................................	4,843,635	30	4,997,139	24	3*

* Not different from zero at the 5 percent level.

U.S. Fish & Wildlife Service

1996-2001 Hunting Participants, Days, and Expenditures

(U.S. population 16 years old and older. Numbers in thousands)

	1996		2001		1996-2001 percent change
	Number	Percent	Number	Percent	
Hunters, total.....................................	**13,975**	**100**	**13,034**	**100**	-7
Big game..	11,288	81	10,911	84	-3*
Small game......................................	6,945	50	5,434	42	-22
Migratory bird...................................	3,073	22	2,956	23	-4*
Other animal....................................	1,521	11	1,047	8	-31
Days, total	**256,676**	**100**	**228,368**	**100**	-11*
Big game..	153,784	60	153,191	67	0
Small game......................................	75,117	29	60,142	26	-20
Migratory bird...................................	26,501	10	29,310	13	11*
Other animal....................................	24,522	10	19,207	8	-22*
Hunting expenditures, total (2001 dollars)	**$23,293,156**	**100**	**$20,611,025**	**100**	-12*
Trips	5,825,510	25	5,252,391	25	-10*
Equipment.......................................	12,738,229	55	10,361,495	50	-19*
Hunting equipment..............................	6,236,625	27	4,561,708	22	-27
Auxiliary equipment............................	1,393,423	6	1,202,845	6	-14*
Special equipment..............................	5,108,181	22	4,596,942	22	-10*
Other	4,729,416	20	4,997,139	24	6*

* Not different from zero at the 5 percent level.

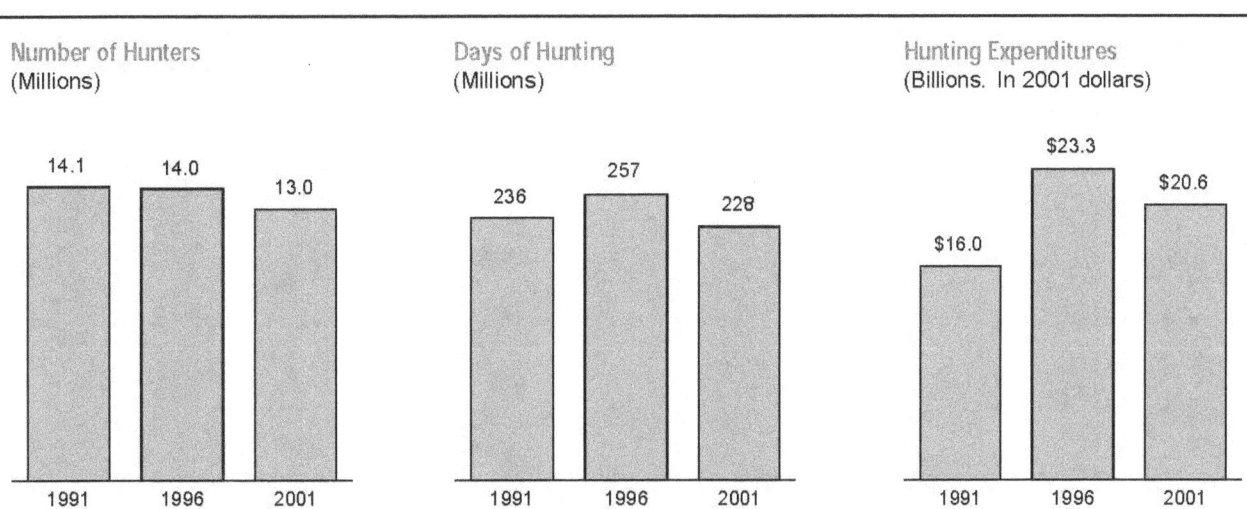

Number of Hunters
(Millions)

14.1   14.0   13.0

1991   1996   2001

Days of Hunting
(Millions)

236   257   228

1991   1996   2001

Hunting Expenditures
(Billions. In 2001 dollars)

$16.0 $23.3 $20.6

1991   1996   2001

Wildlife Watching

Wildlife-Watching Highlights

Wildlife-watching (formerly called nonconsumptive) activities including observing, feeding, and photographing wildlife continue to be popular in the United States. These activities are categorized as residential (within a mile of one's home) or nonresidential (at least one mile away from home).

The 2001 Survey collected information only on wildlife-watching activities in which the primary objective was to observe, feed, or photograph wildlife. Secondary or incidental participation such as observing wildlife while pleasure driving was not included in the Survey.

During 2001, 66.1 million U.S. residents, 31 percent of the U.S. population 16 years old and older, participated in a myriad of wildlife-watching activities. People who took an interest in wildlife around their homes (residential) numbered 63 million, while those who took trips away from their homes to watch wildlife (nonresidential) numbered close to 22 million people.

Wild Bird Observers

Of all the wildlife watching in the United States, bird watching attracted the biggest following. Forty-six million people observed birds around the home and on trips in 2001. A large majority, 88 percent (40 million), observed wild birds around the home while 40 percent, 18 million, took birdwatching trips.

Birders varied in their ability to identify different bird species. Seventy-four percent, 34 million, of these 46 million birders could identify 1 to 20 different types of birds; 13 percent, 6 million birders, could identify 21 to 40 types of birds; and 8 percent, almost 4 million birders, could identify 41 or more types of birds.

Over 2.3 million wild bird enthusiasts kept birding life lists in 2001. Participants keeping these lists—a tally of bird species seen by a birder during his or her lifetime—comprised 5 percent of all wild bird observers.

Wildlife-Watching Participants— by Activity

(In millions)

Total wildlife-watching participants	**66.1**
Nonresidential	**21.8**
Observed wildlife	20.1
Photographed wildlife . .	9.4
Fed wildlife	7.1
Residential	**62.9**
Fed wildlife	54.0
Observed wildlife	42.1
Photographed wildlife . .	13.9
Maintained plantings or natural areas	13.1
Visited public parks or areas	11.0

Detail does not add to total because of multiple responses and nonresponse.
Source: Table 36.

Wildlife-Watching Participants
(In millions)

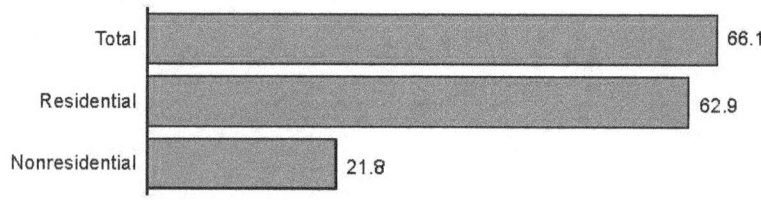

Total	66.1
Residential	62.9
Nonresidential	21.8

Wildlife-Watching Expenditures

Wildlife watching generated heavy spending. In 2001, 79 percent of all wildlife watchers 16 years old and older spent $38.4 billion, an average of $738 per spender. These expenditures represent 35 percent of the total dollars spent for all wildlife-related recreation.

Wildlife watchers spent nearly $8.2 billion on trips pursuing their activities. Food and lodging accounted for $4.8 billion, transportation expenses totaled $2.6 billion, and other trip costs, such as land use fees and equipment rental, amounted to $748 million for the year.

These recreationists purchased $23.5 billion worth of equipment. They spent $7.4 billion on wildlife-watching equipment, including binoculars, cameras, bird food, and special clothing.

Expenditures for auxiliary equipment—tents, backpacking equipment, etc.—totaled almost $717 million for the year. Participants spent over $15.5 billion on special equipment, including big ticket items such as off-road vehicles, campers, and boats.

Also for the year, wildlife watchers spent $332 million on magazines and books; $920 million on membership dues and contributions; $4.8 billion on land leasing and ownership; and $699 million on plantings for the benefit of wildlife.

Wildlife-Watching Expenditures

Total wildlife-watching expenditures	**$38.4 billion**
Total trip-related	**$8.2 billion**
Food and lodging	$4.8 billion
Transportation	$2.6 billion
Other trip costs	$0.7 billion
Total equipment expenditures	**$23.5 billion**
Wildlife-watching equipment	$7.4 billion
Auxiliary equipment	$0.7 billion
Special equipment	$15.5 billion
Total other expenditures	**$6.7 billion**
Magazines, books	$0.3 billion
Membership dues and contributions	$0.9 billion
Land leasing and ownership	$4.8 billion
Plantings	$0.7 billion

Source: Table 43.

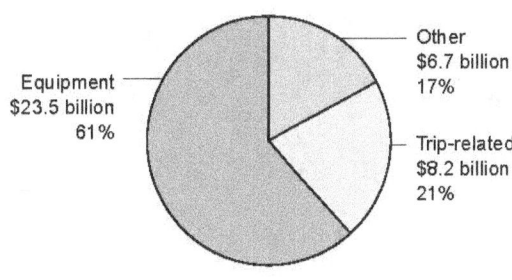

Wildlife-Watching Expenditures
(Total expenditures: $38.4 billion)

Other $6.7 billion 17%
Trip-related $8.2 billion 21%
Equipment $23.5 billion 61%

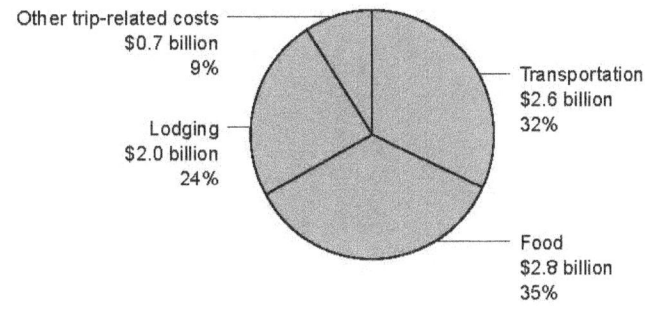

Trip-Related Expenditures
(Total expenditures: $8.2 billion)

Other trip-related costs $0.7 billion 9%
Transportation $2.6 billion 32%
Lodging $2.0 billion 24%
Food $2.8 billion 35%

Residential (Around the Home) Activities Highlights

In 2001 residential participants 16 years old and older numbered 62.9 million— 95 percent of all wildlife-watching recreationists. The most popular activity, feeding birds and other wildlife, appealed to almost 54 million people, 86 percent of all residential wildlife watchers. More than 42 million people observed wildlife, representing 67 percent of all residential participants.

Nearly 14 million (22 percent) recreationists photographed wildlife around their homes. Close in number were the 13 million who maintained plantings or natural areas for the benefit of wildlife. They represented 21 percent of all residential participants. Lastly, 11 million individuals visited public areas including parks within a mile of their homes to wildlife watch. They comprised 17 percent of all residential participants.

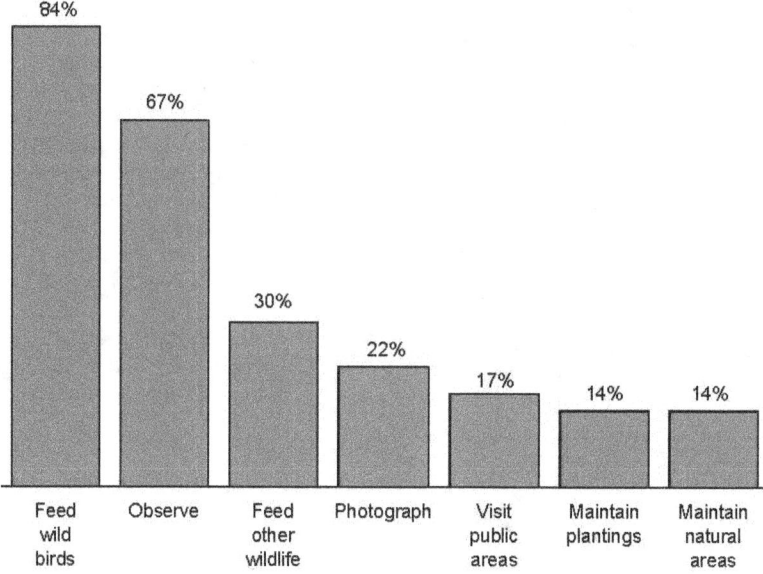

Percent of Total Residential Participants—by Activity
(Total: 62.9 million participants)

Residential Participants	
(In millions)	
Total participants	**62.9**
Feed wild birds	52.6
Observe wildlife	42.1
Feed other wildlife	18.8
Photograph wildlife	13.9
Visit public areas	11.0
Maintain plantings	8.7
Maintain natural areas	8.7

Detail does not add to total because of multiple responses and nonresponse.
Source: Table 39.

Wildlife Fed, Observed, or Photographed by Residential Participants

Of the 54 million people feeding wildlife around their homes in 2001, 97 percent (52.6 million) fed wild birds while 35 percent (18.8 million) fed other wildlife.

Of the 42.1 million participants who reported observing wildlife around their homes, 40.3 million observed birds. Observing mammals was popular among 34.6 million participants. Insects and spiders attracted the attention of 13.8 million people; 9.8 million observed amphibians or reptiles; and 7.9 million people reported observing fish or other wildlife.

Almost 14 million people photographed wildlife around their homes. The largest number, 3.9 million—28 percent of all wildlife photographers—spent 2 to 3 days taking wildlife pictures during the year. Seventeen percent (2.3 million) spent 6 to 10 days; 16 percent (2.2 million), 4 to 5 days; 15 percent (2.1 million), 1 day; 13 percent (1.8 million), 21 or more days; and 10 percent (1.3 million), 11 to 20 days.

Residential Participation by Geographic Region

In 2001, 212 million people 16 years old and older lived in the United States. Of those individuals, 30 percent fed, observed, or photographed wildlife around their homes. The participation rates of these residential participants varied from region to region.

Participation rates for around the home wildlife watching ranged from 24 percent for residents in the West South Central Region to 41 percent for those in the West North Central Region. The New England, East North Central, East South Central, and Mountain Regions also had participation rates above the national average of 30 percent.

New England's participation rate was 36 percent. The East South Central reported a participation rate of 34 percent. Following closely was East North Central with a 33 percent participation rate and the Mountain Region with a 32 percent participation rate. Both the Middle Atlantic and South Atlantic Regions had participation rates of 28 percent, while the Pacific Region's was 25 percent.

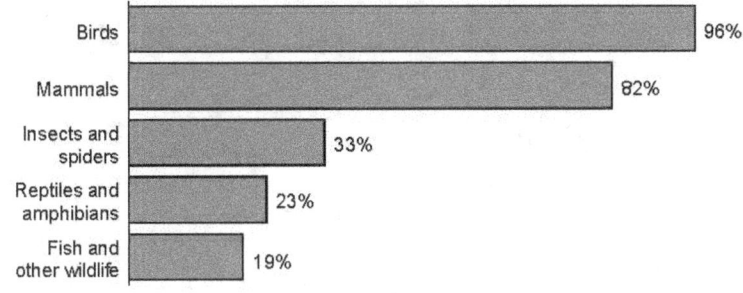

Percent of Residential Wildlife Observers—
by Type of Wildlife Observed
(Total wildlife observers: 42.1 million)

Type	Percent
Birds	96%
Mammals	82%
Insects and spiders	33%
Reptiles and amphibians	23%
Fish and other wildlife	19%

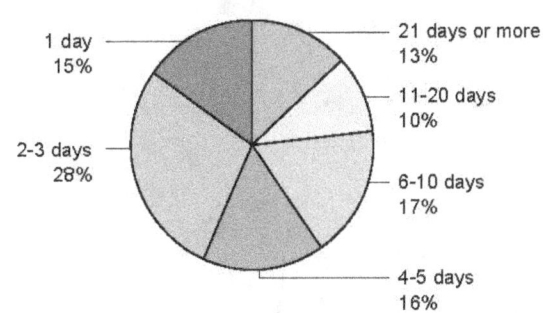

Days Spent Photographing Wildlife
(Total wildlife photographers: 13.9 million)

1 day 15%
21 days or more 13%
11-20 days 10%
6-10 days 17%
4-5 days 16%
2-3 days 28%

Residential Wildlife-Watching Participation
(National participation rate: 30%)

Mountain 32%
West North Central 41%
East North Central 33%
New England 36%
Pacific 25%
Middle Atlantic 28%
South Atlantic 28%
East South Central 34%
West South Central 24%

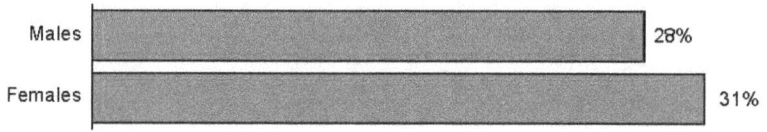

Percent of U.S. Males and Females Who Participated

Males — 28%
Females — 31%

Percent of Residential Participants—by Gender

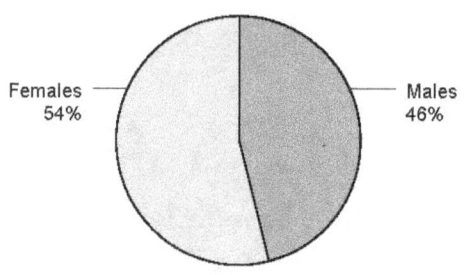

Females 54%
Males 46%

Percent of Residential Participants—by Age

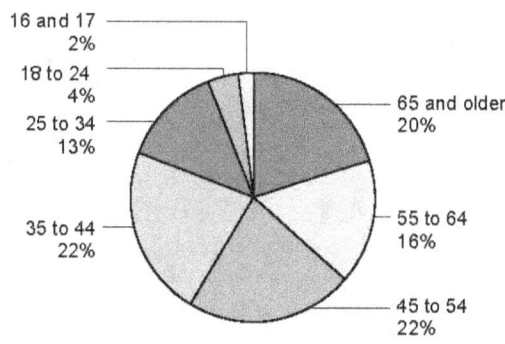

16 and 17 — 2%
18 to 24 — 4%
25 to 34 — 13%
35 to 44 — 22%
45 to 54 — 22%
55 to 64 — 16%
65 and older — 20%

Percent of U.S. Population Who Participated—by Age

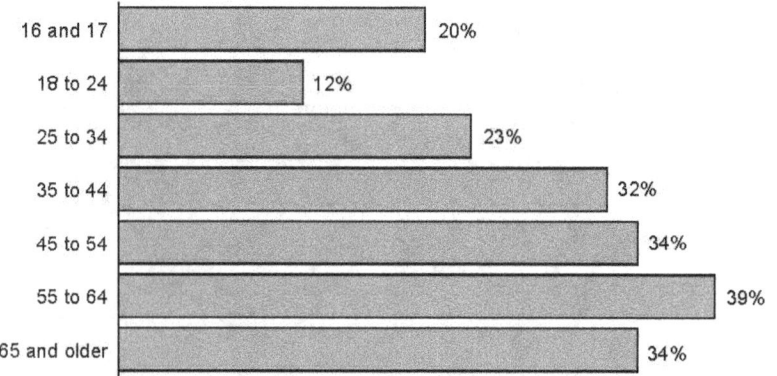

16 and 17 — 20%
18 to 24 — 12%
25 to 34 — 23%
35 to 44 — 32%
45 to 54 — 34%
55 to 64 — 39%
65 and older — 34%

Sex and Age of Residential Participants

Males and females alike enjoyed residential wildlife-watching activities. In 2001, 28 percent of American males 16 years old and older enjoyed residential activities, as did 31 percent of American females of the same age group. Of the 62.9 million residential wildlife watchers, 46 percent (28.8 million) were males, and 54 percent (34.1 million) were females.

Two age groups—the 35- to 44-year-olds (14.1 million) and the 45- to 54-year-olds (13.9 million)—each comprised 22 percent of all residential wildlife watchers. Their participation rates were 32 percent and 34 percent, respectively. Individuals 55 to 64 years old represented 16 percent of all residential participants (10.1 million) and participated at a 39 percent rate. The participation rate for the 65 years old and older group was 34 percent, accounting for 12.5 million people—20 percent of all residential participants. The 25- to 34-year-old participants totaled 8.1 million, comprised 13 percent of all residential participants, and had a participation rate of 23 percent. The participation rate for the 18 to 24-year-old group was 12 percent. They numbered 2.7 million and comprised 4 percent of all participants. Finally, the 16- and 17- year-old participants, 1.5 million, had a participation rate of 20 percent and accounted for 2 percent of all residential wildlife-watching participants.

**Residential Participants—
by Gender and Age**

(In millions)

Total, both sexes	**62.9**
Male	28.8
Female	34.1
Total, all ages	**62.9**
16 and 17	1.5
18 to 24	2.7
25 to 34	8.1
35 to 44	14.1
45 to 54	13.9
55 to 64	10.1
65 and older	12.5

Source: Table 45.

Metropolitan and Nonmetropolitan Residential Participants

In 2001, 30 percent of all U.S. residents 16 years old and older participated in wildlife watching around their homes. Seventy-five percent of these residential wildlife participants lived in metropolitan areas. Participation rates varied by population size of metropolitan areas. People living in metropolitan statistical areas (MSAs) with populations of 1,000,000 or more had a participation rate of 25 percent. These recreationists comprised 45 percent of all residential wildlife watchers. In MSAs of 250,000 to 999,999 the participation rate was 29 percent, reflecting 19 percent of all residential recreationists. Ten percent of the residential wildlife watchers lived in MSAs with a population of 50,000 to 249,999. The population of these areas had a participation rate of 39 percent.

Likewise, the participation rate for nonmetropolitan populations in the United States was 39 percent. While 19 percent of the total U.S. population lived outside metropolitan areas in 2001, they represented 25 percent of all residential wildlife watchers.

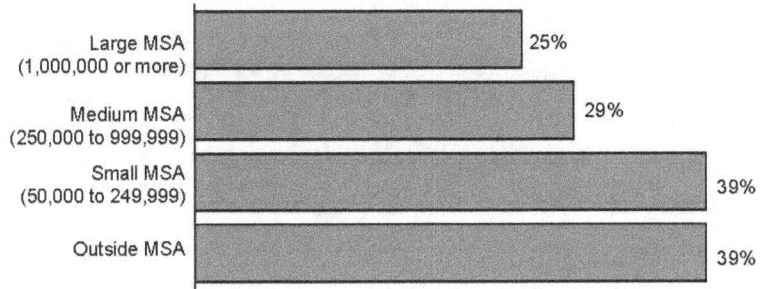

Percent of U.S. Population Who Participated—by Residence
(30% of total U.S. population participated)

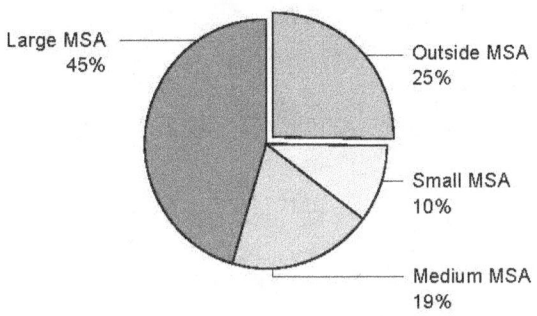

Percent of Residential Participants—by Residence
(Total residential participants: 62.9 million)

Income of Residential Participants

Individuals from all levels of household incomes engaged in residential wildlife-watching activities in 2001. Participation rates ranged from 22 percent among U.S. residents living in households earning less than $10,000 per year to 41 percent among participants living in households earning $75,000 to $99,999 annually. These groups represented 4 percent and 12 percent of all residential wildlife-watching participants, respectively.

Participants in households earning $10,000 to $19,999 a year had a participation rate of 24 percent and constituted 6 percent of all residential recreationists. The participation rate among recreationists with household incomes of $20,000 to $24,999 was 25 percent, making up 4 percent of all residential participants. People with household incomes of $25,000 to $29,999 participated at a rate of 29 percent and made up 5 percent of all residential participants. Those people with household incomes of $30,000 to $34,999 represented 6 percent of the residential participants and had a participation rate of 33 percent. Those whose incomes totaled $35,000 to $39,999 garnered a participation rate of 30 percent while representing 5 percent of all residential participants. Persons from households with incomes of $40,000 to $49,999 chalked up a participation rate of 36 percent and represented 10 percent of all residential participants. For the 18 percent of residential participants who reported annual household incomes of $50,000 to $74,999, the participation rate was 37 percent. Finally, those individuals with annual household incomes of $100,000 or more reported a participation rate of 40 percent, representing 12 percent of all residential recreationists. Eighteen percent of the residential wildlife-watching sample did not report their income.

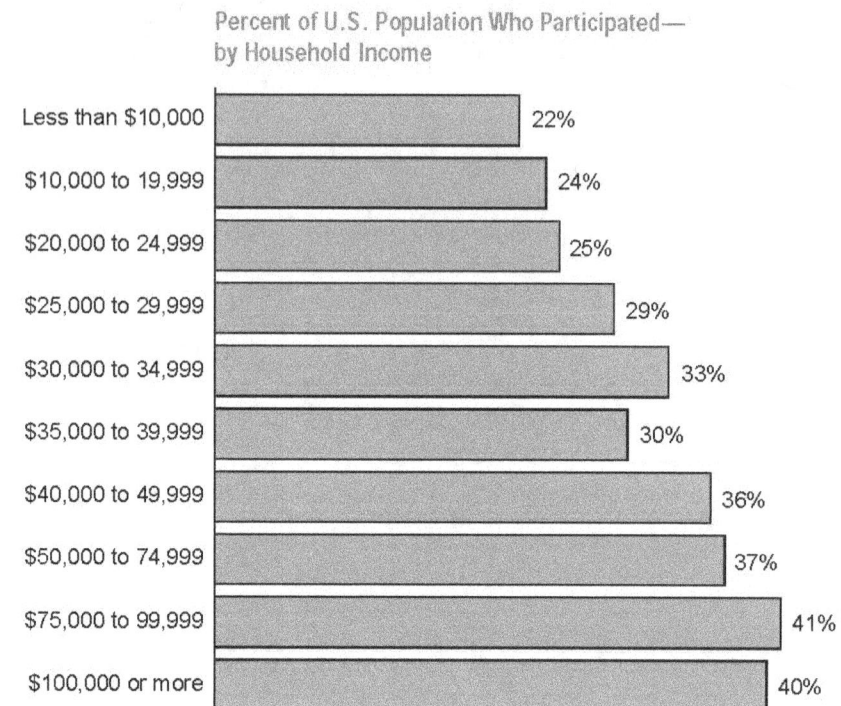

Percent of U.S. Population Who Participated—
by Household Income

Household Income	Percent
Less than $10,000	22%
$10,000 to 19,999	24%
$20,000 to 24,999	25%
$25,000 to 29,999	29%
$30,000 to 34,999	33%
$35,000 to 39,999	30%
$40,000 to 49,999	36%
$50,000 to 74,999	37%
$75,000 to 99,999	41%
$100,000 or more	40%

Education, Race, and Ethnicity of Residential Participants

Among residential participants, a wide range of educational backgrounds was recorded. The highest rate of participation was found among recreationists with 5 years or more of college, 41 percent. They made up 14 percent of all residential wildlife watchers. The lowest participation rate, 21 percent, was among people with less than 12 years of education—11 percent of all residential participants. Residential recreationists with 12 years of education, 32 percent of all residential participants, had a participation rate of 27 percent. Participants with 1 to 3 years of college had a participation rate of 31 percent, while those with 4 years of college had a participation rate of 34 percent. Those groups represented 24 percent and 19 percent of all residential wildlife watchers, respectively.

A wide variety of participation rates was found among the different races residing in the United States. Thirty-three percent of the White population engaged in residential wildlife-watching activities, 9 percent of the Black population, 8 percent of the Asian population, and 26 percent of individuals comprising the "other" race category. Of the total number of residential participants, 95 percent were White, 3 percent were Black, 1 percent was Asian, and 1 percent all other races.

Residential Participants—by Education and Race

(In millions)

Total participants	**62.9**
Education	
0-11 years	6.8
12 years	20.3
1 to 3 years of college . .	15.2
4 years of college	11.9
5 years or more	
of college	8.7
Race	
White	59.8
Black	1.9
Asian	0.6
Other	0.6

Source: Table 45.

Percent of U.S. Population Who Participated—by Education

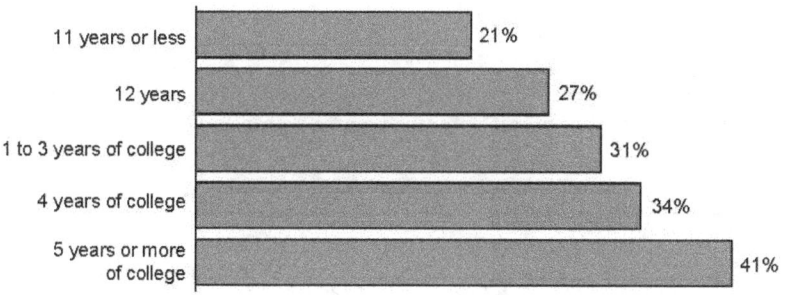

Percent of Residential Participants—by Education

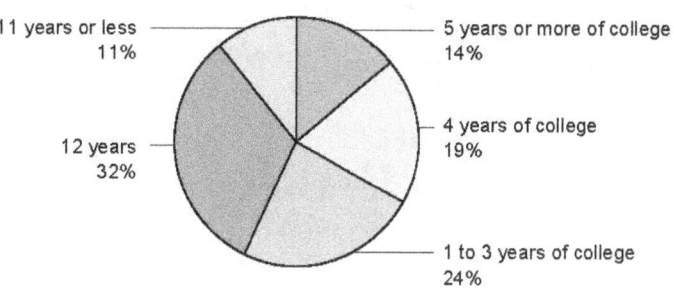

Percent of Residential Participants—by Race

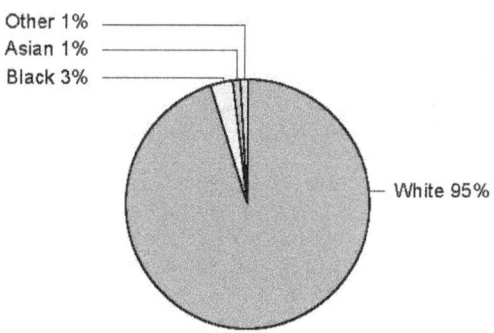

Percent of U.S. Population Who Participated—by Ethnicity

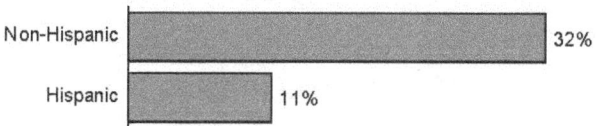

Eleven percent of the U.S. Hispanic population engaged in wildlife watching around their homes in comparison with 32 percent of the non-Hispanic population. The 60.4 million non-Hispanic participants comprised 96 percent of all residential wildlife watchers and the 2.5 million Hispanic participants, 4 percent.

Nonresidential (Away From Home) Activities Highlights

In 2001, nearly 22 million people 16 years old and older took trips away from home to feed, observe, or photograph wildlife. They comprised 33 percent of all wildlife-watching participants. Most popular with nonresidential participants was observing wildlife. Approximately 20.1 million participants, 92 percent of all nonresidential participants, observed wildlife on an average of 15 days during the year. Photographing wildlife was enjoyed by 9.4 million people, 43 percent of all nonresidential participants. They averaged 8 days per participant. Almost 7.1 million people fed wildlife on an average of 15 days and comprised 32 percent of all nonresidential recreationists.

Eighty-three percent of all nonresidential participants took trips within their resident state to participate in wildlife watching. Seventy percent took trips only in their resident state, 13 percent took trips both inside and outside their resident state, and 17 percent took trips only to other states. Altogether, 30 percent of all nonresidential participants took at least some of their trips to other states.

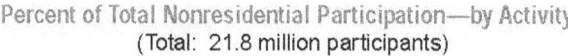

Percent of Total Nonresidential Participation—by Activity
(Total: 21.8 million participants)

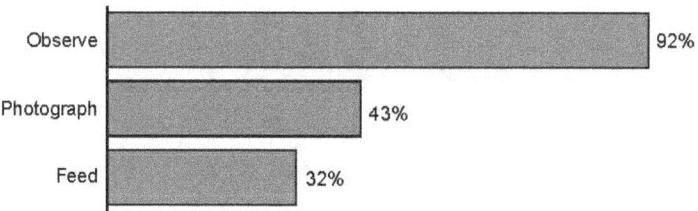

Observe	92%
Photograph	43%
Feed	32%

Percent of Nonresidential Participants— in State of Residence and Other States

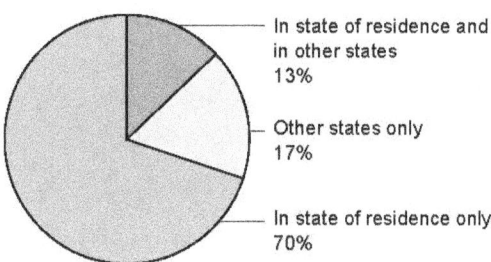

- In state of residence and in other states 13%
- Other states only 17%
- In state of residence only 70%

Nonresidential Participants	
(In millions)	
Total participants	**21.8**
Observers	20.1
Photographers	9.4
Feeders	7.1
Total days	**372**
Observing	295
Photographing	76
Feeding	103

Detail does not add to total because of multiple responses.
Source: Table 37.

U.S. Fish & Wildlife Service

Nonresidential Participants—by Type of Wildlife Observed, Fed, or Photographed

(In millions)

Total participants	**21.8**
Birds, total	**18.6**
Waterfowl	14.4
Songbirds	12.9
Birds of prey	12.5
Other water birds	10.3
Other birds	7.9
Land mammals, total	**15.5**
Small land mammals	13.0
Large land mammals	12.2
Fish	**6.3**
Marine mammals	**3.0**
Other	**9.4**
(turtles, butterflies, etc.)	

Detail does not add to total because of multiple responses.
Source: Table 40.

Wildlife Observed, Fed, or Photographed by Nonresidential Participants

In 2001, 21.8 million recreationists took trips to observe, feed, or photograph a variety of wildlife in the United States. Wild birds attracted the most, 85 percent of all nonresidential participants—18.6 million individuals. More than 14.4 million people observed waterfowl such as ducks and geese on their trips. Next on the list of favorites were songbirds which attracted 12.9 million enthusiasts and birds of prey which drew 12.5 million. Herons, pelicans, and other water birds intrigued 10.3 million recreationists. Lastly, other birds such as pheasants and turkeys attracted 7.9 million wildlife watchers while on their trips.

Land mammals such as deer, bear, and coyotes were observed, fed, or photographed by 15.5 million wildlife watchers, 71 percent of all nonresidential participants. Fish attracted the attention of 6.3 million participants, 29 percent of all nonresidential recreationists.

More than 3.0 million people, 14 percent of all nonresidential participants, observed, fed, or photographed marine mammals such as whales, seals, and dolphins. Other wildlife such as butterflies, snakes, and turtles appealed to 9.4 million people—43 percent of all nonresidential wildlife watchers.

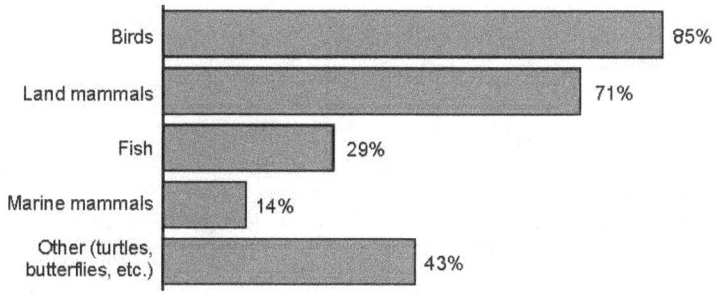

Percent of Nonresidential Participants Who Observed, Fed, or Photographed Wildlife
(Total participants: 21.8 million)

Birds	85%
Land mammals	71%
Fish	29%
Marine mammals	14%
Other (turtles, butterflies, etc.)	43%

In 2001, both public and private areas provided significant opportunities for Americans to observe, feed, or photograph wildlife on trips away from home. Over 6 million, 28 percent of all nonresidential participants, reported having visited both public and private areas. More nonresidential participants, 10.6 million or 49 percent, reported visiting only public areas to engage in their activities, while 2.5 million or 12 percent of all nonresidential participants visited only private areas.

Recreationists visited a variety of wildlife habitats on their trips. Sixty-eight percent, 14.9 million people, watched wildlife in woodlands. Lakes and streamsides also attracted a large number of visitors, 13.7 million people or 63 percent of the total. Brush-covered areas and open fields each lured 12.5 million wildlife watchers—57 percent of all trip takers. Nearly 9.1 million or 42 percent of all nonresidential participants visited wetlands, and man-made areas attracted 6.2 million recreational visitors—28 percent of all nonresidential participants. Oceansides attracted 5.2 million people accounting for 24 percent of all nonresidential recreationists. Other types of habitats drew 2.5 million nonresidential people, 12 percent of all nonresidential recreationists.

Nonresidential Participants—by Area Visited

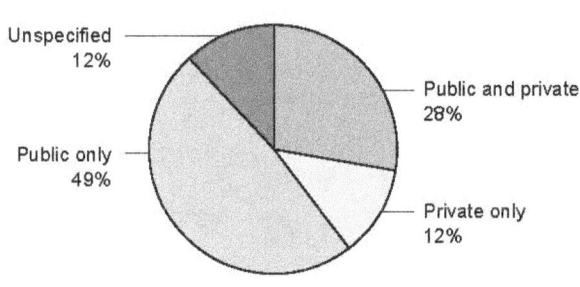

Type of Site Visited by Nonresidential Participants

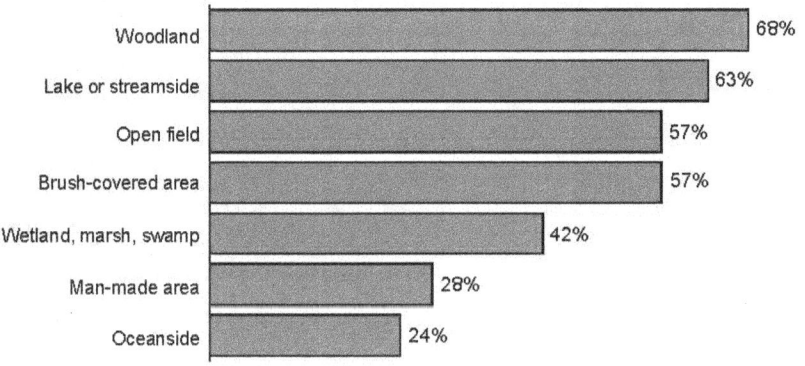

Nonresidential Participants— by Site Visited	
(In millions)	
Total participants	**21.8**
Woodland	14.9
Lake or streamside	13.7
Open field	12.5
Brush-covered area	12.5
Wetland, marsh, swamp	9.1
Man-made area	6.2
Oceanside	5.2

Detail does not add to total because of multiple responses.
Source: Table 38.

Nonresidential Participants by Geographic Division

In 2001, 212 million people 16 years old and older lived in the United States. Of those individuals, 10 percent participated in nonresidential wildlife-watching activities.

Nonresidential participation rates ranged from 8 percent in both the East South Central and West South Central Regions to 15 percent in the Mountain Region. The population of the South Atlantic had a participation rate of 9 percent. The Middle Atlantic and East North Central Regions both garnered participation rates of 10 percent. Both the New England and Pacific Regions recorded participation rates of 11 percent. The West North Central Region rounded out the list with a 14 percent participation rate.

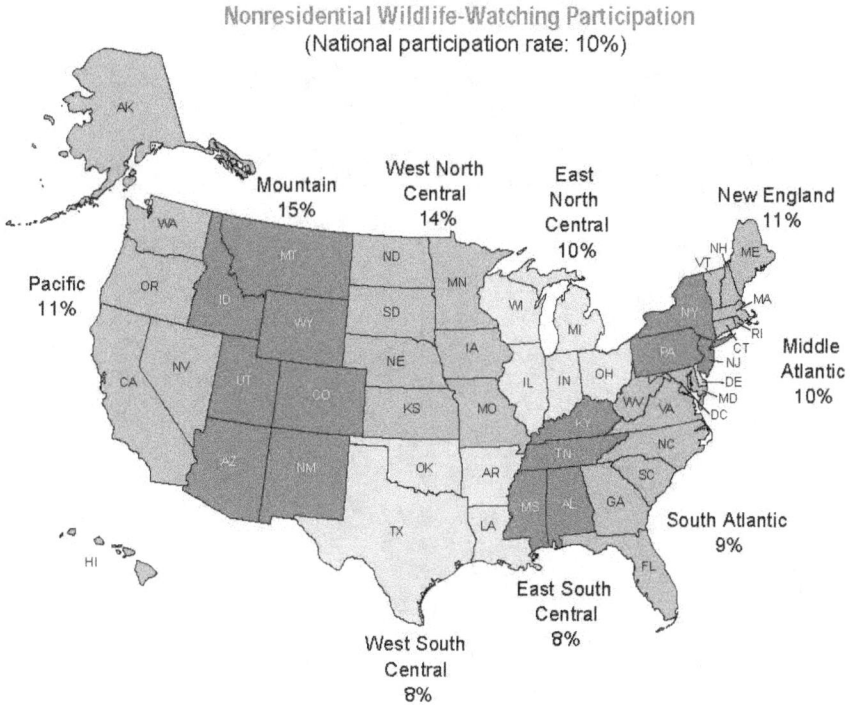

Nonresidential Wildlife-Watching Participation
(National participation rate: 10%)

Percent of U.S. Males and Females Who Participated

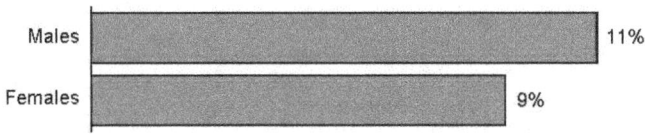

Males	11%
Females	9%

Percent of Nonresidential Participants—by Gender

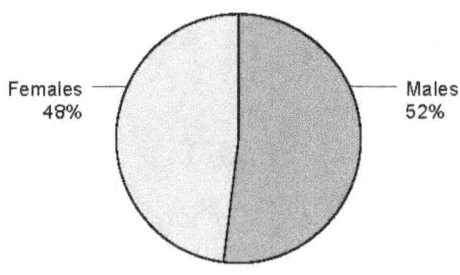

Females 48%
Males 52%

Percent of Nonresidential Participants—by Age

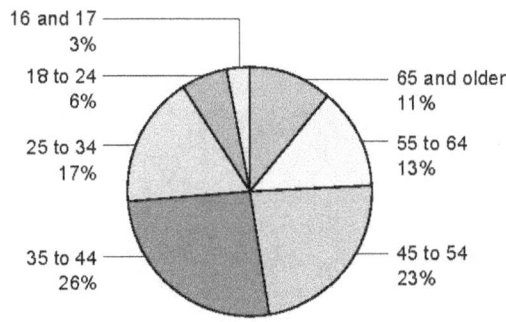

16 and 17 3%
18 to 24 6%
25 to 34 17%
35 to 44 26%
45 to 54 23%
55 to 64 13%
65 and older 11%

Percent of U.S. Population Who Participated—by Age

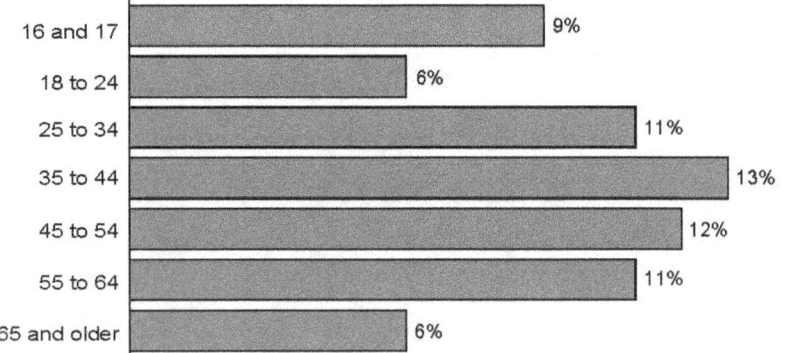

16 and 17	9%
18 to 24	6%
25 to 34	11%
35 to 44	13%
45 to 54	12%
55 to 64	11%
65 and older	6%

Sex and Age of Nonresidential Participants

Similar numbers of males and females 16 years old and older participated in nonresidential wildlife-watching activities in 2001. Eleven percent of American males and 9 percent of American females enjoyed observing, feeding, or photographing wildlife away from home. Among the 21.8 million nonresidential participants, 52 percent (11.4 million) were males, and 48 percent (10.4 million) were females.

The age group representing the most nonresidential participants, 5.7 million, was the 35- to 44- year-olds who had a participation rate of 13 percent. This group was closely followed by the 5.0 million participants in the 45- to 54-year-old age group whose participation rate was 12 percent. These two groups represented 26 percent and 23 percent of all nonresidential participants, respectively.

Both the 25- to 34-year-olds (3.8 million) and the 55- to 64-year-olds (2.9 million) had participation rates of 11 percent. They represented 17 and 13 percent of the nonresidential participants, respectively. The 16- to 17-year-olds had a 9 percent participation rate. Their 688 thousand total represented 3 percent of all nonresidential participants. Lastly, both the 18- to 24-year-olds (1.4 million) and the 65 years and older group (2.4 million) had participation rates of 6 percent. They represented 6 percent and 11 percent of all nonresidential participants, respectively.

Nonresidential Participants— by Gender and Age (In millions)	
Total, both sexes	**21.8**
Male	11.4
Female	10.4
Total, all ages	**21.8**
16 and 17	0.7
18 to 24	1.4
25 to 34	3.8
35 to 44	5.7
45 to 54	5.0
55 to 64	2.9
65 and older	2.4

Source: Table 44.

Metropolitan and Nonmetropolitan Nonresidential Participants

A substantial number of people from both urban and rural areas enjoyed wildlife-watching activities while away from home. In 2001, 10 percent of all persons living in metropolitan statistical areas (MSAs) took trips primarily to enjoy wildlife. They comprised 76 percent of all nonresidential participants. Those living in large MSAs with populations of 1,000,000 or more participated at a rate of 9 percent and represented 46 percent of all those recreationists. The participation rate for people living in medium size MSAs with populations of 250,000 to 999,999 was 10 percent—19 percent of all nonresidential participants. Smaller MSAs with populations of 50,000 to 249,999 had a participation rate of 13 percent and represented 10 percent of all nonresidential recreationists. People living outside MSAs had a participation rate of 13 percent, and accounted for 24 percent of all away-from-home wildlife watchers.

Percent of Nonresidential Participants—by Residence
(Total nonresidential participants: 21.8 million)

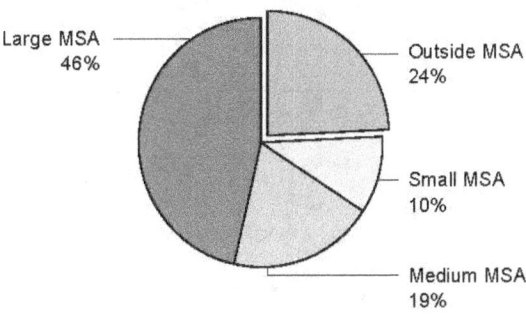

Percent of U.S. Population Who Participated—
by Residence
(10% of total U.S. population participated)

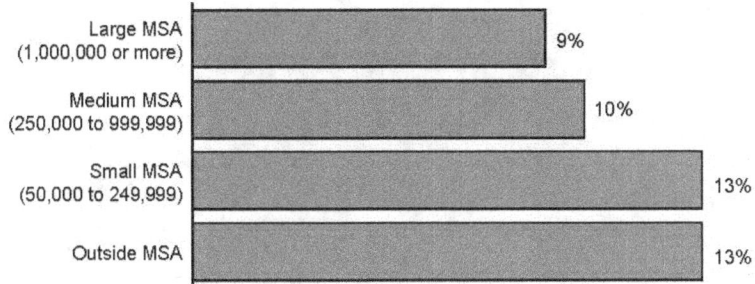

Income of Nonresidential Participants

People from households at all income levels participated in wildlife-watching recreation away from home. Participation rates ranged from 5 percent for those in households earning less than $10,000 per year (2 percent of all nonresidential participants) to 16 percent for those in households earning $75,000 to $99,999 annually (13 percent of all nonresidential participants).

Households with income levels of $50,000 to $74,999 and $100,000 or more had a 15 percent participation rate, representing 21 percent and 13 percent of all nonresidential recreationists, respectively. Others with $40,000 to $49,999 incomes showed a participation rate of 14 percent—11 percent of all nonresidential participants. Households with incomes of $30,000 to $34,999 comprised 7 percent of all nonresidential recreationists and had a 13 percent participation rate. Individuals earning $35,000 to $39,999 recorded a participation rate of 11 percent, comprising 5 percent of all nonresidential participants. Participants in the $25,000 to $29,999 household income group had a 10 percent participation rate and represented 5 percent of all nonresidential recreationists. Households at the $20,000 to $24,999 income level garnered an 8 percent participation rate and comprised 4 percent of all nonresidential wildlife recreationists. Lastly, individuals with household earnings of $10,000 to $19,999 reported a participation rate of 6 percent. They represented 4 percent of all nonresidential participants. Fifteen percent of the nonresidential wildlife watchers did not report their income.

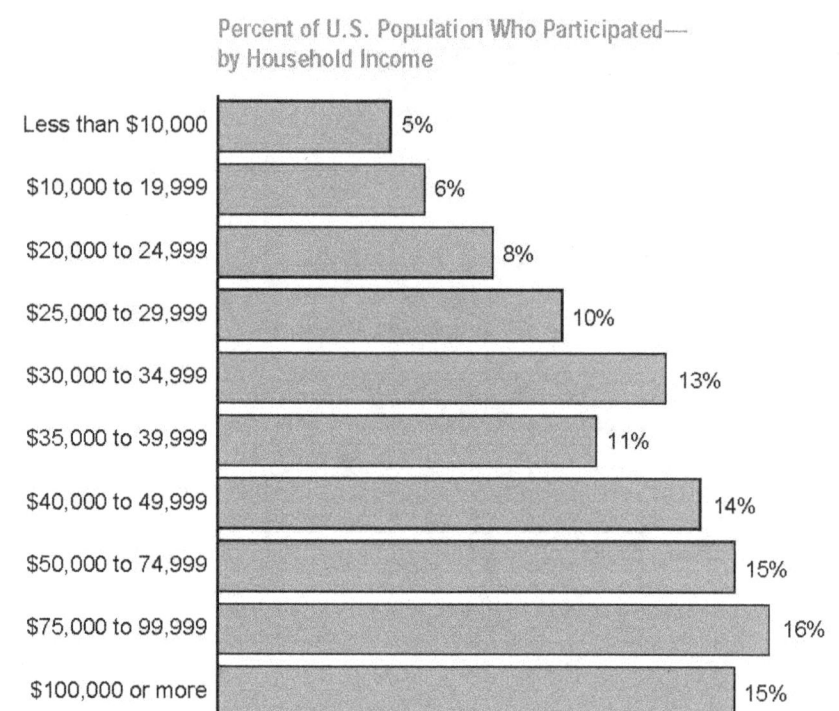

Percent of U.S. Population Who Participated—
by Household Income

Household Income	Percent
Less than $10,000	5%
$10,000 to 19,999	6%
$20,000 to 24,999	8%
$25,000 to 29,999	10%
$30,000 to 34,999	13%
$35,000 to 39,999	11%
$40,000 to 49,999	14%
$50,000 to 74,999	15%
$75,000 to 99,999	16%
$100,000 or more	15%

Education, Race, and Ethnicity of Nonresidential Participants

People of all educational levels participated in nonresidential wildlife-watching activities in 2001. Six percent of the U.S. population with 11 years of education or less participated, representing 8 percent of the nonresidential total. In contrast, 18 percent of the population with 5 years or more of college took trips to watch wildlife, representing 17 percent of all nonresidential participants. Those with 12 years of education had an 8 percent participation rate and represented 27 percent of the nonresidential total. Participants with 1 to 3 years of college participated at a rate of 12 percent, contributing 27 percent to the nonresidential total. Lastly, 13 percent of those with 4 years of college participated in nonresidential activities, making up 20 percent of all nonresidential participants.

The participation rates among races varied greatly. Eleven percent of all White individuals took trips in the United States in 2001 to participate in wildlife-watching activities. Two percent of all Black individuals participated, 2 percent of Asians, and 13 percent of individuals comprising the "other" race category. Of the total 21.8 million nonresidential participants, 95 percent were White, 2 percent Black, 1 percent Asian, and 1 percent other races.

The Hispanic and Non-Hispanic populations alike participated in nonresidential wildlife watching in 2001. Approximately 890 thousand Hispanic participants—4 percent of the U.S. Hispanic population—took trips to engage in wildlife watching. Of the Non-Hispanic population, more than 20.9 million participants took trips to wildlife watch. Their participation rate was 11 percent, and they comprised 96 percent of all nonresidential wildlife watchers.

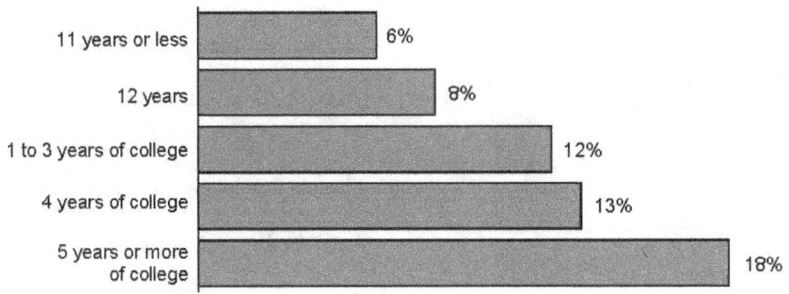

Percent of U.S. Population Who Participated—by Education
(10% of total U.S. population participated)

- 11 years or less: 6%
- 12 years: 8%
- 1 to 3 years of college: 12%
- 4 years of college: 13%
- 5 years or more of college: 18%

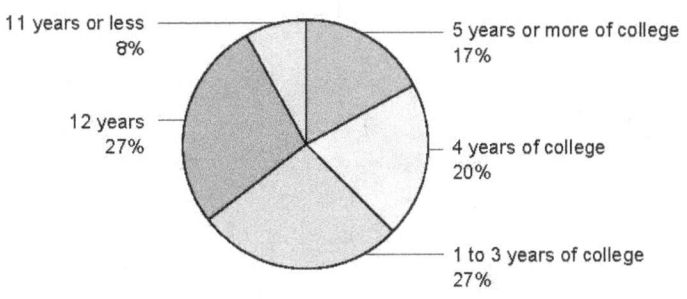

Percent of Nonresidential Participants—by Education

- 11 years or less 8%
- 5 years or more of college 17%
- 12 years 27%
- 4 years of college 20%
- 1 to 3 years of college 27%

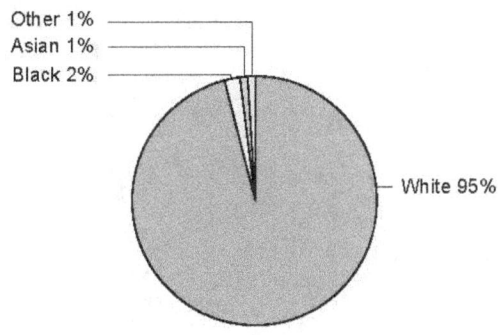

Percent of Nonresidential Participants—by Race

- Other 1%
- Asian 1%
- Black 2%
- White 95%

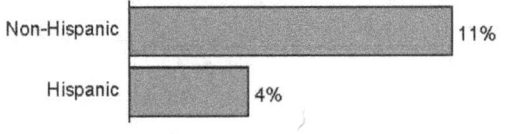

Percent of U.S. Population Who Participated—by Ethnicity

- Non-Hispanic: 11%
- Hispanic: 4%

1991-2001 Comparison of Wildlife-Watching Participants

Comparing the results from the last three surveys finds different trends for the various types of wildlife watching. The number of wildlife watchers decreased 17 percent from 1991 to 1996 and increased 5 percent from 1996 to 2001, with 76 million participants in 1991, 63 million in 1996, and 66 million in 2001. Residential wildlife watching, the preeminent type of wildlife watching, lead this trend with an 18 percent drop from 1991 to 1996 and a 4 percent increase[1] from 1996 to 2001.

---

[1]The percent change is not significant at the 0.05 level.

The overall tendency upward from 1996 to 2001 was not followed by wildlife observing and photographing, which decreased by 5 percent and 13 percent, respectively (although these are not significant differences at the 95 percent confidence level). Feeding wildlife and visiting public parks maintained their 1996 participation levels.

Unlike residential wildlife watching, nonresidential wildlife watching dropped throughout the '90s and early '00s with a 21 percent drop from 1991 to 1996 and an 8 percent drop[1] from 1996 to 2001. Days afield by participants tended upward, particularly observers and feeders, although the increase is not statistically significant.

Trip-related and equipment expenditures for wildlife watching increased 21 percent from 1991 to 1996 and 16 percent[1] from 1996 to 2001, making an overall increase of 41 percent from 1991 to 2001. This increase was the result of equipment purchases, primarily special equipment (big ticket items such as off-road vehicles and campers). Equipment purchases nearly doubled from 1991 to 2001, going up 90 percent. Trip-related expenditures by nonresidential participants tended downward from 1991 to 2001, with $9.7 billion spent in 1991 and $8.2 billion in 2001.

1991-2001 Wildlife Watching Participants, Days, and Expenditures[1]

(U.S. population 16 years old and older. Numbers in thousands)

	1991		2001		1991-2001
	Number	Percent	Number	Percent	percent change
Wildlife watching, total	**76,111**	**100**	**66,105**	**100**	**-13**
Residential	73,904	97	62,928	95	-15
Observe wildlife	54,653	72	42,111	64	-23
Photograph wildlife	16,990	22	13,937	21	-18
Feed wild birds or other wildlife	65,423	86	53,988	82	-17
Visit public parks or areas	15,525	20	10,981	17	-29
Maintain plantings or natural areas	13,601	18	13,072	20	-4*
Nonresidential	29,999	39	21,823	33	-27
Observe wildlife	28,812	38	20,080	30	-30
Photograph wildlife	14,225	19	9,427	14	-34
Feed wildlife	13,306	17	7,077	11	-47
Days, nonresidential	342,406	100	372,006	100	9*
Observing wildlife	296,456	87	295,345	79	0
Photographing wildlife	81,600	24	76,324	21	-6*
Feeding wildlife	102,104	30	103,307	28	1*
Wildlife-watching expenditures, total (2001 dollars)	**$24,002,990**	**100**	**$33,730,868**	**100**	**41**
Trips	9,722,954	41	8,162,439	24	-16*
Equipment	12,422,925	52	23,616,982	70	90
Wildlife-watching equipment	7,411,773	31	6,850,971	20	-8*
Auxiliary equipment	454,807	2	716,900	2	58*
Special equipment	4,556,348	19	16,049,111	48	252
Other	1,857,110	8	1,951,447	6	5*

[1] All 2001 expenditures are adjusted to make them comparable to 1991 estimates.

* Not different from zero at the 5 percent level.

1996-2001 Wildlife Watching Participants, Days, and Expenditures[1]

(U.S. population 16 years old and older. Numbers in thousands)

	1996		2001		1996-2001 percent change
	Number	Percent	Number	Percent	
Wildlife watching, total	**62,868**	**100**	**66,105**	**100**	**5**
Residential......................	60,751	97	62,928	95	4*
Observe wildlife..................	44,063	70	42,111	64	-4*
Photograph wildlife...............	16,021	25	13,937	21	-13*
Feed wild birds or other wildlife..................	54,122	86	53,988	82	0
Visit public parks or areas......................	11,011	18	10,981	17	0
Maintain plantings or natural areas................	13,401	21	13,072	20	-2*
Nonresidential....................	23,652	38	21,823	33	-8*
Observe wildlife..................	22,878	36	20,080	30	-12
Photograph wildlife...............	12,038	19	9,427	14	-22
Feed wildlife.....................	9,976	16	7,077	11	-29
Days, nonresidential..............................	313,790	100	372,006	100	19*
Observing wildlife	278,683	89	295,345	79	6*
Photographing wildlife............	79,342	25	76,324	21	-4*
Feeding wildlife	89,606	29	103,307	28	15*
Wildlife-watching expenditures, total (2001 dollars) ...	**$29,062,524**	**100**	**$33,730,868**	**100**	**16***
Trips	10,250,604	35	8,162,439	24	-20*
Equipment.......................	16,785,440	58	23,616,982	70	41
Wildlife-watching equipment......................	8,783,405	30	6,850,971	20	-22*
Auxiliary equipment..............................	853,374	3	716,900	2	-16*
Special equipment...............................	7,148,661	25	16,049,111	48	125
Other...........................	2,026,480	7	1,951,447	6	-4*

[1] All 2001 expenditures are adjusted to make them comparable to 1991 estimates.

* Not different from zero at the 5 percent level.

Number of Wildlife-Watching Participants (Millions)

Days of Nonresidential Activity (Millions)

Wildlife-Watching Expenditures (Billions. In 2001 dollars)

Tables

Guide to Statistical Tables

Purpose and Coverage of Tables

The statistical tables of this report were designed to meet a wide range of needs for those interested in wildlife-related recreation. Special terms used in these tables are defined in Appendix A.

The tables are based on responses to the 2001 Survey which was designed to collect data about participation in wildlife-related recreation. To have taken part in the Survey, a respondent must have been a U.S. resident (a resident of one of the 50 states or the District of Columbia). No one residing outside the United States (including U.S. citizens) was eligible for interviewing. Therefore, reported state and national totals do not include participation by those who were not U.S. residents or who were residing outside the United States.

Comparability With Previous Surveys

The numbers reported can be compared with those in the 1991 and 1996 Survey Reports. The methodology used in 2001 was similar to that used in 1996 and 1991. These results should not be directly compared to results from surveys earlier than 1991 since there were major changes in methodology. These changes were made to improve accuracy in the information provided. Trends further back than 1991 are presented in Appendix B. These trends were developed using parts of the Surveys that were comparable.

Coverage of an Individual Table

Since the Survey covers many activities in various places by participants of different ages, all table titles, headnotes, stubs, and footnotes are designed to identify and articulate each item being reported in the table. For example, the title of Table 1 shows that data about anglers and hunters, their days of participation, and their number of trips are being reported by type of activity. By contrast, the title of Table 3 indicates that it contains data on freshwater anglers and the days they fished for different species of fish.

Percentages Reported in the Tables

Percentages are reported in the tables for the convenience of the user. When exclusive groups are being reported, the base of a percentage is apparent from its context because the percents add to 100 percent (plus or minus a rounding error). For example, Table 1 reports the number of trips taken by big game hunters (57 percent), those taken by small game hunters (23 percent), those taken by migratory bird hunters (12 percent), and those taken by sportspersons hunting other animals (8 percent). These comprise 100 percent because they are exclusive categories.

Percents should not add to 100 when nonexclusive groups are being reported. Using Table 1 as an example again, note that adding the percentages associated with total number of big game hunters (84 percent), total small game hunters (42 percent), total migratory bird hunters (23 percent), and total hunters of other animals (8 percent) will not yield total hunters (100 percent) because respondents could hunt for more than one type of game.

When the base of the percentage is not apparent in context, it is identified in a footnote. For example, Table 6 reports 3 percentages with different bases: one for the number of hunters, one for the number of trips, and one for days of hunting. Footnotes are used to clarify the bases of the reported percentages.

Footnotes to the Tables

Footnotes are used to clarify the information or items that are being reported in a table. Symbols in the body of a table indicate important footnotes. These symbols are used in the tables to refer to the same footnote each time they appear:

*   Estimate based on a small sample size.
...   Sample size too small to report data reliably.
W   Less than .5 dollars.
Z   Less than .5 percent.
X   Not applicable.
NA Not available.

Estimates based upon fewer than 10 responses are regarded as being based on a sample size that is too small for reliable reporting. An estimate based upon at least 10 but fewer than 30 responses is treated as an estimate based on a small sample size. Other footnotes appear, as necessary, to qualify or clarify the estimates reported in the tables. In addition, these two important footnotes appear frequently:

- Detail does not add to total because of multiple responses.

- Detail does not add to total because of multiple responses and nonresponse.

"Multiple responses" is a term used to reflect the fact that individuals or their characteristics fall into more than one category. Using Table 2 as an example, those who fished in saltwater and freshwater appear in both of these totals. Yet each angler is represented only once in the "Total, all fishing" column. Similarly, in Table 6 those who hunt for big game and small game are counted only once as a hunter in the "Total, all hunting" column. Therefore, totals may be smaller than the sum of subcategories when multiple responses exist.

"Nonresponse" exists because the Survey questions were answered voluntarily and some respondents did not or could not answer all the questions. The effect of nonresponses is illustrated in Table 12, where the total for fishing and hunting expenditures is greater than the sum of fishing expenditures plus hunting expenditures. This occurs because some respondents did not specify either "hunting" or "fishing" as the primary purpose of the purchase. As a result, it is known that the expenditures were for fishing and/or hunting, but it is not known whether they were primarily for fishing or primarily for hunting, which was the basis for putting them in the individual fishing and hunting expenditure tables. In this case, totals are greater than the sum of subcategories when nonresponses have occurred.

Table 1. Anglers and Hunters 16 Years Old and Older, Days of Participation, and Trips by Type of Fishing and Hunting: 2001

(Population 16 years old and older. Numbers in thousands)

Type of fishing and hunting	Participants		Days of participation		Trips	
	Number	Percent	Number	Percent	Number	Percent
Total sportspersons	37,805	100	785,762	100	636,787	100
FISHING						
Total, all fishing	34,071	100	557,394	100	436,662	100
Total, all freshwater........................	28,439	83	466,984	84	365,076	84
Freshwater, except Great Lakes...............	27,913	82	443,247	80	349,188	80
Great Lakes	1,847	5	23,138	4	15,888	4
Saltwater................................	9,051	27	90,838	16	71,586	16
HUNTING						
Total, all hunting	13,034	100	228,368	100	200,125	100
Big game	10,911	84	153,191	67	114,445	57
Small game..............................	5,434	42	60,142	26	46,450	23
Migratory bird...........................	2,956	23	29,310	13	24,155	12
Other animals............................	1,047	8	19,207	8	15,074	8

Note: Detail does not add to total because of multiple responses.

Table 2. Anglers, Trips, and Days of Fishing by Type of Fishing: 2001

(Population 16 years old and older. Numbers in thousands)

| Anglers, trips, and days of fishing | Total, all fishing | | Freshwater | | | | | | Saltwater | |
			Total, all freshwater		Freshwater, except Great Lakes		Great Lakes			
	Number	Percent	Number	Percent	Number	Percent	Number	Percent	Number	Percent
ANGLERS										
Total in U.S.	34,071	100	28,439	100	27,913	100	1,847	100	9,051	100
In state of residence........	31,218	92	26,389	93	25,832	93	1,610	87	6,914	76
In other states.............	7,880	23	5,680	20	5,555	20	348	19	2,661	29
TRIPS										
Total in U.S.	436,662	100	365,076	100	349,188	100	15,888	100	71,586	100
In state of residence........	406,741	93	343,463	94	328,529	94	14,934	94	63,278	88
In other states.............	29,921	7	21,613	6	20,659	6	954	6	8,308	12
DAYS OF FISHING										
Total days in U.S............	557,394	100	466,984	100	443,247	100	23,138	100	90,838	100
In state of residence........	501,321	90	426,451	91	403,656	91	21,048	91	75,670	83
In other states.............	56,965	10	41,589	9	39,591	9	2,090	9	15,168	17
Average days per angler	16	(X)	16	(X)	16	(X)	13	(X)	10	(X)

(X) Not applicable.

Note: Detail for participants does not add to total because of multiple responses. Percents shown are based on the respective "Total in U.S." rows.

Table 3. Freshwater Anglers and Days of Fishing by Type of Fish: 2001

(Population 16 years old and older. Numbers in thousands. Excludes Great Lakes fishing)

Type of fish	Anglers		Days of fishing		Average days per angler
	Number	Percent	Number	Percent	
Total, all types of fish	**27,913**	**100**	**443,247**	**100**	**16**
Black bass (largemouth, smallmouth, etc.)	10,708	38	159,847	36	15
White bass, striped bass and striped bass hybrids.	4,946	18	61,889	14	13
Panfish.	7,910	28	103,294	23	13
Crappie.	6,657	24	95,109	21	14
Catfish and bullheads	7,517	27	103,664	23	14
Walleye	3,218	12	46,338	10	14
Sauger	174	1	2,176	(Z)	13
Northern pike, pickerel, muskie, muskie hybrids	2,060	7	27,290	6	13
Trout.	7,819	28	83,325	19	11
Salmon.	1,368	5	15,053	3	11
Steelhead	536	2	6,698	2	12
Anything[1]	4,741	17	46,257	10	10
Another type of freshwater fish	1,537	6	17,277	4	11

(Z) Less than 0.5 percent.

[1] Respondent fished for no specific species and identified "Anything" from a list of categories of fish.

Note: Detail does not add to total because of multiple responses.

Table 4. Great Lakes Anglers and Days of Fishing by Type of Fish: 2001

(Population 16 years old and older. Numbers in thousands)

Type of fish	Anglers		Days of fishing		Average days per angler
	Number	Percent	Number	Percent	
Total, all types of fish	**1,847**	**100**	**23,138**	**100**	**13**
Black bass (largemouth, smallmouth, etc.)	589	32	6,355	27	11
Walleye, sauger.	571	31	5,521	24	10
Northern pike, pickerel, muskie, muskie hybrids	140	8	...	...	...
Perch.	693	38	6,597	29	10
Salmon.	516	28	3,985	17	8
Steelhead	338	18	3,698	16	11
Lake trout	346	19	3,605	16	10
Other trout.	239	13	2,355	10	10
Anything[1]	217	12	1,994	9	9
Another type of Great Lakes fish.	157	8	1,769	8	11

... Sample size too small to report data reliably.

[1] Respondent fished for no specific species and identified "Anything" from a list of categories of fish.

Note: Detail does not add to total because of multiple responses.

Table 5. Saltwater Anglers and Days of Fishing by Type of Fish: 2001

(Population 16 years old and older. Numbers in thousands)

Type of fish	Anglers		Days of fishing		Average days per angler
	Number	Percent	Number	Percent	
Total, all types of fish	**9,051**	**100**	**90,838**	**100**	**10**
Salmon...	722	8	4,873	5	7
Striped bass.......................................	1,716	19	17,211	19	10
Flatfish (flounder, halibut)	2,269	25	21,111	23	9
Bluefish...	1,139	13	11,667	13	10
Red drum (redfish)	1,721	19	18,489	20	11
Sea trout (weakfish)	1,487	16	17,140	19	12
Mackerel	609	7	5,879	6	10
Shellfish...	585	6	3,571	4	6
Anything[1]...	3,110	34	25,240	28	8
Another type of saltwater fish	3,025	33	33,720	37	11

[1] Respondent fished for no specific species and identified "Anything" from a list of categories of fish.

Note: Detail does not add to total because of multiple responses.

Table 6. Hunters, Trips, and Days of Hunting by Type of Hunting: 2001

(Population 16 years old and older. Numbers in thousands)

Hunters, trips, and days of hunting	Total, all hunting		Big game		Small game		Migratory bird		Other animals	
	Number	Percent	Number	Percent	Number	Percent	Number	Percent	Number	Percent
HUNTERS										
Total in U.S.	**13,034**	**100**	**10,911**	**100**	**5,434**	**100**	**2,956**	**100**	**1,047**	**100**
In state of residence........	12,375	95	10,365	95	5,093	94	2,766	94	1,004	96
In other states.............	2,079	16	1,467	13	672	12	410	14	102	10
TRIPS										
Total in U.S.	**200,125**	**100**	**114,445**	**100**	**46,450**	**100**	**24,155**	**100**	**15,074**	**100**
In state of residence........	189,499	95	108,154	95	44,394	96	22,569	93	14,382	95
In other states.............	10,626	5	6,291	5	2,056	4	1,586	7	692	5
DAYS OF HUNTING										
Total days in U.S............	**228,368**	**100**	**153,191**	**100**	**60,142**	**100**	**29,310**	**100**	**19,207**	**100**
In state of residence........	209,880	92	138,809	91	55,386	92	26,672	91	18,156	95
In other states.............	20,891	9	14,386	9	4,756	8	2,638	9	1,051	5
Average days per hunter	18	(X)	14	(X)	11	(X)	10	(X)	18	(X)

(X) Not applicable.

Note: Detail does not add to total because of multiple responses. Percents shown are based on the respective "Total in U.S." rows.

Table 7. Hunters and Days of Hunting by Type of Game: 2001

(Population 16 years old and older. Numbers in thousands)

Type of game	Hunters		Days of hunting		Average days per hunter
	Number	Percent	Number	Percent	
Total, all big game..................................	**10,911**	**100**	**153,191**	**100**	**14**
Deer..	10,272	94	133,457	87	13
Elk..	910	8	6,402	4	7
Bear..	360	3	3,334	2	9
Wild turkey................................	2,504	23	23,165	15	9
Other big game............................	527	5	5,010	3	10
Total, all small game.............................	**5,434**	**100**	**60,142**	**100**	**11**
Rabbit, hare................................	2,099	39	22,768	38	11
Quail...	991	18	7,926	13	8
Grouse/prairie chicken	1,010	19	9,169	15	9
Squirrel.....................................	2,119	39	22,333	37	11
Pheasant....................................	1,723	32	12,769	21	7
Other small game	505	9	5,200	9	10
Total, all migratory birds........................	**2,956**	**100**	**29,310**	**100**	**10**
Geese..	1,000	34	10,508	36	11
Ducks..	1,589	54	18,290	62	12
Doves..	1,450	49	9,041	31	6
Other migratory bird......................	210	7	1,523	5	7
Total, all other animals (fox, raccoon, groundhog, etc.)...	**1,047**	**100**	**19,207**	**100**	**18**

Note: Detail does not add to total because of multiple responses.

Table 8. Selected Characteristics of Anglers and Hunters: 2001

(Population 16 years old and older. Numbers in thousands)

Characteristic	U.S. population		Sportspersons (fished or hunted)			Fished only		
	Number	Percent	Number	Percent who participated	Percent	Number	Percent who participated	Percent
Total persons	**212,298**	**100**	**37,805**	**18**	**100**	**24,771**	**12**	**100**
Population Density of Residence								
Urban	157,943	74	22,435	14	59	16,562	10	67
Rural	54,355	26	15,370	28	41	8,209	15	33
Population Size of Residence								
Metropolitan statistical area (MSA)	171,147	81	26,564	16	70	18,815	11	76
1,000,000 or more	112,984	53	14,739	13	39	11,050	10	45
250,000 to 999,999	41,469	20	7,638	18	20	5,229	13	21
50,000 to 249,999	16,693	8	4,186	25	11	2,536	15	10
Outside MSA	41,151	19	11,241	27	30	5,956	14	24
Census Geographic Division								
New England	10,575	5	1,504	14	4	1,119	11	5
Middle Atlantic	29,806	14	3,810	13	10	2,176	7	9
East North Central	34,082	16	6,400	19	17	3,979	12	16
West North Central	14,430	7	4,239	29	11	2,529	18	10
South Atlantic	39,286	19	6,957	18	18	5,082	13	21
East South Central	12,976	6	2,865	22	8	1,702	13	7
West South Central	23,337	11	4,924	21	13	2,936	13	12
Mountain	13,308	6	2,757	21	7	1,737	13	7
Pacific	34,498	16	4,349	13	12	3,512	10	14
Age								
16 to 17 years	7,709	4	1,497	19	4	913	12	4
18 to 24 years	22,234	10	3,303	15	9	2,053	9	8
25 to 34 years	35,333	17	7,136	20	19	4,724	13	19
35 to 44 years	44,057	21	9,966	23	26	6,416	15	26
45 to 54 years	40,541	19	7,826	19	21	5,005	12	20
55 to 64 years	25,601	12	4,629	18	12	3,179	12	13
65 years and older	36,823	17	3,447	9	9	2,481	7	10
Sex								
Male, total	101,916	48	28,462	28	75	16,618	16	67
16 to 17 years	4,106	2	1,170	28	3	644	16	3
18 to 24 years	11,326	5	2,540	22	7	1,421	13	6
25 to 34 years	17,206	8	5,179	30	14	3,010	17	12
35 to 44 years	21,346	10	7,381	35	20	4,138	19	17
45 to 54 years	19,626	9	5,861	30	16	3,296	17	13
55 to 64 years	12,201	6	3,587	29	9	2,264	19	9
65 years and older	16,105	8	2,743	17	7	1,844	11	7
Female, total	110,381	52	9,343	8	25	8,153	7	33
16 to 17 years	3,603	2	327	9	1	269	7	1
18 to 24 years	10,908	5	764	7	2	632	6	3
25 to 34 years	18,127	9	1,958	11	5	1,714	9	7
35 to 44 years	22,711	11	2,585	11	7	2,278	10	9
45 to 54 years	20,915	10	1,965	9	5	1,709	8	7
55 to 64 years	13,400	6	1,042	8	3	915	7	4
65 years and older	20,718	10	703	3	2	638	3	3
Ethnicity								
Hispanic	21,910	10	1,743	8	5	1,314	6	5
Non-Hispanic	190,388	90	36,063	19	95	23,457	12	95
Race								
White	181,129	85	35,300	19	93	22,733	13	92
Black	21,708	10	1,666	8	4	1,370	6	6
Asian	7,141	3	365	5	1	332	5	1
All others	2,320	1	474	20	1	336	14	1
Annual Household Income								
Less than $10,000	10,594	5	978	9	3	731	7	3
$10,000 to $19,999	15,272	7	1,831	12	5	1,306	9	5
$20,000 to $24,999	10,902	5	1,659	15	4	1,094	10	4
$25,000 to $29,999	11,217	5	2,000	18	5	1,238	11	5
$30,000 to $34,999	11,648	5	2,349	20	6	1,519	13	6
$35,000 to $39,999	9,816	5	2,186	22	6	1,414	14	6
$40,000 to $49,999	16,896	8	4,116	24	11	2,548	15	10
$50,000 to $74,999	31,383	15	7,893	25	21	4,979	16	20
$75,000 to $99,999	17,762	8	4,413	25	12	2,888	16	12
$100,000 or more	19,202	9	4,521	24	12	3,254	17	13
Not reported	57,606	27	5,858	10	15	3,801	7	15
Education								
11 years or less	32,820	15	4,705	14	12	2,934	9	12
12 years	73,719	35	13,309	18	35	8,335	11	34
1 to 3 years college	49,491	23	9,980	20	26	6,569	13	27
4 years college	34,803	16	5,994	17	16	4,181	12	17
5 years or more college	21,464	10	3,817	18	10	2,752	13	11

See footnotes at end of table.

(Population 16 years old and older. Numbers in thousands)

Characteristic	Hunted only			Fished and hunted		
	Number	Percent who participated	Percent	Number	Percent who participated	Percent
Total persons	3,734	2	100	9,300	4	100
Population Density of Residence						
Urban	1,510	1	40	4,363	3	47
Rural...........................	2,224	4	60	4,938	9	53
Population Size of Residence						
Metropolitan statistical area (MSA)	2,173	1	58	5,576	3	60
1,000,000 or more...............	997	1	27	2,693	2	29
250,000 to 999,999.............	708	2	19	1,701	4	18
50,000 to 249,999..............	469	3	13	1,182	7	13
Outside MSA....................	1,561	4	42	3,724	9	40
Census Geographic Division						
New England....................	103	1	3	283	3	3
Middle Atlantic	559	2	15	1,074	4	12
East North Central	741	2	20	1,680	5	18
West North Central..............	403	3	11	1,307	9	14
South Atlantic	506	1	14	1,369	3	15
East South Central	322	2	9	842	6	9
West South Central..............	549	2	15	1,440	6	15
Mountain.......................	314	2	8	706	5	8
Pacific.........................	238	1	6	599	2	6
Age						
16 to 17 years	179	2	5	405	5	4
18 to 24 years	373	2	10	878	4	9
25 to 34 years	559	2	15	1,854	5	20
35 to 44 years	920	2	25	2,631	6	28
45 to 54 years	886	2	24	1,935	5	21
55 to 64 years	461	2	12	989	4	11
65 years and older	356	1	10	609	2	7
Sex						
Male, total......................	3,304	3	88	8,541	8	92
16 to 17 years..................	155	4	4	371	9	4
18 to 24 years..................	309	3	8	809	7	9
25 to 34 years..................	475	3	13	1,694	10	18
35 to 44 years..................	811	4	22	2,432	11	26
45 to 54 years..................	801	4	21	1,764	9	19
55 to 64 years..................	421	3	11	902	7	10
65 years and older..............	332	2	9	567	4	6
Female, total	430	(Z)	12	759	1	8
16 to 17 years..................	*24	*1	*1	*34	*1	*(Z)
18 to 24 years..................	*64	*1	*2	68	1	1
25 to 34 years..................	85	(Z)	2	160	1	2
35 to 44 years..................	109	(Z)	3	199	1	2
45 to 54 years..................	85	(Z)	2	171	1	2
55 to 64 years..................	*40	*(Z)	*1	86	1	1
65 years and older..............	...	...	...	*41	*(Z)	*(Z)
Ethnicity						
Hispanic	179	1	5	250	1	3
Non-Hispanic....................	3,555	2	95	9,050	5	97
Race						
White	3,599	2	96	8,968	5	96
Black	*66	*(Z)	*2	230	1	2
Asian	...	...	...	...	...	...
All others	46	2	1	92	4	1
Annual Household Income						
Less than $10,000	100	1	3	147	1	2
$10,000 to $19,999................	183	1	5	342	2	4
$20,000 to $24,999................	185	2	5	380	3	4
$25,000 to $29,999................	238	2	6	525	5	6
$30,000 to $34,999................	258	2	7	572	5	6
$35,000 to $39,999................	248	3	7	525	5	6
$40,000 to $49,999................	420	2	11	1,148	7	12
$50,000 to $74,999................	780	2	21	2,134	7	23
$75,000 to $99,999................	384	2	10	1,141	6	12
$100,000 or more.................	301	2	8	966	5	10
Not reported.....................	637	1	17	1,420	2	15
Education						
11 years or less	577	2	15	1,194	4	13
12 years........................	1,477	2	40	3,497	5	38
1 to 3 years college	911	2	24	2,501	5	27
4 years college..................	472	1	13	1,342	4	14
5 years or more college...........	298	1	8	767	4	8

* Estimate based on a small sample size.   ... Sample size too small to report data reliably.   (Z) Less than 0.5 percent.

Note: Percent who participated shows the percent of each row's population who participated in the activity named by the column. Percent columns show the percent of each column's participants who are described by the row heading.

Table 9. Selected Characteristics of Anglers by Type of Fishing: 2001

(Population 16 years old and older. Numbers in thousands)

Characteristic	U.S. population		Total, all fishing			Total freshwater		
	Number	Percent	Number	Percent who participated	Percent	Number	Percent who participated	Percent
Total persons	**212,298**	**100**	**34,071**	**16**	**100**	**28,439**	**13**	**100**
Population Density of Residence								
Urban........................	157,943	74	20,925	13	61	16,731	11	59
Rural	54,355	26	13,146	24	39	11,707	22	41
Population Size of Residence								
Metropolitan statistical area (MSA)...	171,147	81	24,391	14	72	19,563	11	69
1,000,000 or more	112,984	53	13,743	12	40	10,525	9	37
250,000 to 999,999	41,469	20	6,930	17	20	5,738	14	20
50,000 to 249,999	16,693	8	3,718	22	11	3,299	20	12
Outside MSA...................	41,151	19	9,680	24	28	8,876	22	31
Census Geographic Division								
New England..................	10,575	5	1,402	13	4	1,031	10	4
Middle Atlantic	29,806	14	3,250	11	10	2,220	7	8
East North Central..............	34,082	16	5,659	17	17	5,197	15	18
West North Central	14,430	7	3,836	27	11	3,749	26	13
South Atlantic	39,286	19	6,451	16	19	4,631	12	16
East South Central.............	12,976	6	2,543	20	7	2,356	18	8
West South Central	23,337	11	4,375	19	13	3,661	16	13
Mountain.....................	13,308	6	2,443	18	7	2,401	18	8
Pacific.......................	34,498	16	4,111	12	12	3,193	9	11
Age								
16 to 17 years	7,709	4	1,318	17	4	1,165	15	4
18 to 24 years	22,234	10	2,931	13	9	2,624	12	9
25 to 34 years	35,333	17	6,577	19	19	5,559	16	20
35 to 44 years	44,057	21	9,047	21	27	7,612	17	27
45 to 54 years	40,541	19	6,940	17	20	5,576	14	20
55 to 64 years	25,601	12	4,168	16	12	3,382	13	12
65 years and older	36,823	17	3,090	8	9	2,520	7	9
Sex								
Male	101,916	48	25,159	25	74	21,126	21	74
Female.......................	110,381	52	8,912	8	26	7,313	7	26
Ethnicity								
Hispanic......................	21,910	10	1,564	7	5	1,097	5	4
Non-Hispanic..................	190,388	90	32,507	17	95	27,342	14	96
Race								
White........................	181,129	85	31,701	18	93	26,613	15	94
Black........................	21,708	10	1,600	7	5	1,305	6	5
Asian........................	7,141	3	342	5	1	203	3	1
All others....................	2,320	1	428	18	1	317	14	1
Annual Household Income								
Less than $10,000	10,594	5	878	8	3	776	7	3
$10,000 to $19,999	15,272	7	1,648	11	5	1,431	9	5
$20,000 to $24,999	10,902	5	1,474	14	4	1,251	11	4
$25,000 to $29,999	11,217	5	1,763	16	5	1,570	14	6
$30,000 to $34,999	11,648	5	2,091	18	6	1,807	16	6
$35,000 to $39,999	9,816	5	1,939	20	6	1,656	17	6
$40,000 to $49,999	16,896	8	3,696	22	11	3,194	19	11
$50,000 to $74,999	31,383	15	7,113	23	21	6,030	19	21
$75,000 to $99,999	17,762	8	4,029	23	12	3,248	18	11
$100,000 or more..............	19,202	9	4,220	22	12	3,225	17	11
Not reported..................	57,606	27	5,221	9	15	4,250	7	15
Education								
11 years or less	32,820	15	4,128	13	12	3,605	11	13
12 years......................	73,719	35	11,832	16	35	10,103	14	36
1 to 3 years college	49,491	23	9,069	18	27	7,464	15	26
4 years college.................	34,803	16	5,522	16	16	4,402	13	15
5 years or more college	21,464	10	3,520	16	10	2,864	13	10

See footnotes at end of table.

(Population 16 years old and older. Numbers in thousands)

Characteristic	Freshwater, except Great Lakes			Great Lakes			Saltwater		
	Number	Percent who participated	Percent	Number	Percent who participated	Percent	Number	Percent who participated	Percent
Total persons	**27,913**	**13**	**100**	**1,847**	**1**	**100**	**9,051**	**4**	**100**
Population Density of Residence									
Urban..........................	16,353	10	59	1,252	1	68	6,558	4	72
Rural	11,560	21	41	595	1	32	2,494	5	28
Population Size of Residence									
Metropolitan statistical area (MSA)...	19,136	11	69	1,472	1	80	7,736	5	85
1,000,000 or more	10,220	9	37	966	1	52	4,930	4	54
250,000 to 999,999	5,638	14	20	375	1	20	1,975	5	22
50,000 to 249,999	3,278	20	12	131	1	7	831	5	9
Outside MSA...................	8,777	21	31	375	1	20	1,315	3	15
Census Geographic Division									
New England...................	1,030	10	4	*16	*(Z)	*1	707	7	8
Middle Atlantic	2,113	7	8	384	1	21	1,201	4	13
East North Central...............	4,790	14	17	1,303	4	71	298	1	3
West North Central	3,749	26	13	*56	*(Z)	*3	122	1	1
South Atlantic	4,629	12	17	*33	*(Z)	*2	3,265	8	36
East South Central...............	2,356	18	8	...	...	...	363	3	4
West South Central	3,661	16	13	...	...	...	1,320	6	15
Mountain......................	2,393	18	9	*28	*(Z)	*2	126	1	1
Pacific........................	3,193	9	11	...	...	...	1,650	5	18
Age									
16 to 17 years	1,145	15	4	*93	*1	*5	284	4	3
18 to 24 years	2,576	12	9	*110	*(Z)	*6	676	3	7
25 to 34 years	5,452	15	20	380	1	21	1,638	5	18
35 to 44 years	7,492	17	27	523	1	28	2,356	5	26
45 to 54 years	5,469	13	20	354	1	19	2,015	5	22
55 to 64 years	3,310	13	12	262	1	14	1,221	5	13
65 years and older	2,469	7	9	125	(Z)	7	861	2	10
Sex									
Male	20,729	20	74	1,535	2	83	6,956	7	77
Female........................	7,184	7	26	311	(Z)	17	2,096	2	23
Ethnicity									
Hispanic.......................	1,081	5	4	...	...	...	681	3	8
Non-Hispanic...................	26,832	14	96	1,810	1	98	8,370	4	92
Race									
White.........................	26,165	14	94	1,681	1	91	8,174	5	90
Black..........................	1,233	6	4	137	1	7	481	2	5
Asian.........................	198	3	1	...	...	...	197	3	2
All others.....................	317	14	1	...	...	...	199	9	2
Annual Household Income									
Less than $10,000	755	7	3	...	...	...	135	1	1
$10,000 to $19,999	1,413	9	5	*62	*(Z)	*3	338	2	4
$20,000 to $24,999	1,223	11	4	*62	*1	*3	279	3	3
$25,000 to $29,999	1,539	14	6	*63	*1	*3	319	3	4
$30,000 to $34,999	1,743	15	6	160	1	9	479	4	5
$35,000 to $39,999	1,640	17	6	*57	*1	*3	502	5	6
$40,000 to $49,999	3,152	19	11	224	1	12	906	5	10
$50,000 to $74,999	5,920	19	21	375	1	20	1,909	6	21
$75,000 to $99,999	3,205	18	11	221	1	12	1,149	6	13
$100,000 or more................	3,146	16	11	258	1	14	1,626	8	18
Not reported....................	4,178	7	15	331	1	18	1,409	2	16
Education									
11 years or less	3,539	11	13	206	1	11	897	3	10
12 years.......................	9,842	13	35	714	1	39	2,748	4	30
1 to 3 years college.............	7,362	15	26	457	1	25	2,497	5	28
4 years college.................	4,346	12	16	252	1	14	1,815	5	20
5 years or more college...........	2,824	13	10	217	1	12	1,093	5	12

* Estimate based on a small sample size.   ... Sample size too small to report data reliably.   (Z) Less than 0.5 percent.

Note: Percent who participated shows the percent of each row's population who participated in the activity named by the column (the percent of those living in urban areas who fished in the Great Lakes, etc.). Percent columns show the percent of each column's participants who are described by the row heading (the percent of those who fished in the Great Lakes who lived in urban areas, etc.).

Table 10. Selected Characteristics of Hunters by Type of Hunting: 2001

(Population 16 years old and older. Numbers in thousands)

Characteristic	U.S. population Number	U.S. population Percent	Total, all hunting Number	Total, all hunting Percent who participated	Total, all hunting Percent	Big game Number	Big game Percent who participated	Big game Percent
Total persons	**212,298**	**100**	**13,034**	**6**	**100**	**10,911**	**5**	**100**
Population Density of Residence								
Urban.........................	157,943	74	5,873	4	45	4,630	3	42
Rural	54,355	26	7,161	13	55	6,281	12	58
Population Size of Residence								
Metropolitan statistical area (MSA)...	171,147	81	7,749	5	59	6,319	4	58
1,000,000 or more	112,984	53	3,690	3	28	2,971	3	27
250,000 to 999,999	41,469	20	2,409	6	18	1,999	5	18
50,000 to 249,999	16,693	8	1,650	10	13	1,350	8	12
Outside MSA...................	41,151	19	5,285	13	41	4,591	11	42
Census Geographic Division								
New England...................	10,575	5	386	4	3	353	3	3
Middle Atlantic	29,806	14	1,633	5	13	1,538	5	14
East North Central...............	34,082	16	2,421	7	19	2,102	6	19
West North Central	14,430	7	1,710	12	13	1,320	9	12
South Atlantic	39,286	19	1,875	5	14	1,601	4	15
East South Central...............	12,976	6	1,164	9	9	967	7	9
West South Central	23,337	11	1,988	9	15	1,575	7	14
Mountain......................	13,308	6	1,020	8	8	824	6	8
Pacific........................	34,498	16	837	2	6	630	2	6
Age								
16 to 17 years	7,709	4	584	8	4	492	6	5
18 to 24 years	22,234	10	1,251	6	10	1,052	5	10
25 to 34 years	35,333	17	2,413	7	19	1,985	6	18
35 to 44 years	44,057	21	3,551	8	27	3,003	7	28
45 to 54 years	40,541	19	2,821	7	22	2,370	6	22
55 to 64 years	25,601	12	1,450	6	11	1,236	5	11
65 years and older	36,823	17	965	3	7	772	2	7
Sex								
Male	101,916	48	11,845	12	91	9,923	10	91
Female........................	110,381	52	1,190	1	9	987	1	9
Ethnicity								
Hispanic.......................	21,910	10	428	2	3	322	1	3
Non-Hispanic...................	190,388	90	12,606	7	97	10,589	6	97
Race								
White.........................	181,129	85	12,568	7	96	10,586	6	97
Black.........................	21,708	10	297	1	2	193	1	2
Asian.........................	7,141	3	*32	*(Z)	*(Z)	*23	*(Z)	*(Z)
All others.....................	2,320	1	138	6	1	108	5	1
Annual Household Income								
Less than $10,000	10,594	5	247	2	2	203	2	2
$10,000 to $19,999	15,272	7	525	3	4	441	3	4
$20,000 to $24,999	10,902	5	565	5	4	499	5	5
$25,000 to $29,999	11,217	5	763	7	6	638	6	6
$30,000 to $34,999	11,648	5	830	7	6	738	6	7
$35,000 to $39,999	9,816	5	773	8	6	666	7	6
$40,000 to $49,999	16,896	8	1,569	9	12	1,375	8	13
$50,000 to $74,999	31,383	15	2,915	9	22	2,433	8	22
$75,000 to $99,999	17,762	8	1,525	9	12	1,305	7	12
$100,000 or more...............	19,202	9	1,267	7	10	919	5	8
Not reported...................	57,606	27	2,057	4	16	1,695	3	16
Education								
11 years or less	32,820	15	1,771	5	14	1,492	5	14
12 years.......................	73,719	35	4,973	7	38	4,401	6	40
1 to 3 years college...............	49,491	23	3,412	7	26	2,812	6	26
4 years college..................	34,803	16	1,814	5	14	1,420	4	13
5 years or more college	21,464	10	1,065	5	8	785	4	7

See footnotes at end of table.

Table 10. **Selected Characteristics of Hunters by Type of Hunting: 2001**—Continued

(Population 16 years old and older. Numbers in thousands)

Characteristic	Small game			Migratory bird			Other animals		
	Number	Percent who participated	Percent	Number	Percent who participated	Percent	Number	Percent who participated	Percent
Total persons	**5,434**	**3**	**100**	**2,956**	**1**	**100**	**1,047**	**(Z)**	**100**
Population Density of Residence									
Urban..........................	2,467	2	45	1,652	1	56	316	(Z)	30
Rural	2,968	5	55	1,304	2	44	731	1	70
Population Size of Residence									
Metropolitan statistical area (MSA)...	3,171	2	58	1,956	1	66	478	(Z)	46
1,000,000 or more	1,466	1	27	903	1	31	215	(Z)	21
250,000 to 999,999	980	2	18	653	2	22	159	(Z)	15
50,000 to 249,999	724	4	13	400	2	14	105	1	10
Outside MSA...................	2,263	6	42	1,001	2	34	569	1	54
Census Geographic Division									
New England..................	158	1	3	44	(Z)	1	28	(Z)	3
Middle Atlantic	664	2	12	191	1	6	211	1	20
East North Central..............	997	3	18	274	1	9	168	(Z)	16
West North Central	903	6	17	456	3	15	156	1	15
South Atlantic.................	745	2	14	416	1	14	141	(Z)	13
East South Central..............	527	4	10	308	2	10	105	1	10
West South Central	762	3	14	784	3	27	111	(Z)	11
Mountain	399	3	7	266	2	9	80	1	8
Pacific........................	279	1	5	218	1	7	48	(Z)	5
Age									
16 to 17 years	283	4	5	157	2	5	61	1	6
18 to 24 years	592	3	11	279	1	9	118	1	11
25 to 34 years	1,020	3	19	657	2	22	152	(Z)	14
35 to 44 years	1,489	3	27	874	2	30	279	1	27
45 to 54 years	1,148	3	21	594	1	20	266	1	25
55 to 64 years	540	2	10	234	1	8	131	1	13
65 years and older	361	1	7	161	(Z)	5	*39	*(Z)	*4
Sex									
Male	5,114	5	94	2,815	3	95	1,005	1	96
Female........................	320	(Z)	6	142	(Z)	5	*42	*(Z)	*4
Ethnicity									
Hispanic.......................	123	1	2	150	1	5	*40	*(Z)	*4
Non-Hispanic...................	5,311	3	98	2,806	1	95	1,007	1	96
Race									
White.........................	5,153	3	95	2,872	2	97	1,017	1	97
Black.........................	206	1	4	*42	*(Z)	*1	*21	*(Z)	*2
Asian.........................	...	...	...	...	...	...	...	...	...
All others.....................	50	2	1	*34	*1	*1	...	...	...
Annual Household Income									
Less than $10,000	94	1	2	*33	*(Z)	*1	...	...	...
$10,000 to $19,999	215	1	4	54	(Z)	2	41	(Z)	4
$20,000 to $24,999	249	2	5	68	1	2	*45	*(Z)	*4
$25,000 to $29,999	328	3	6	126	1	4	55	(Z)	5
$30,000 to $34,999	338	3	6	117	1	4	*76	*1	*7
$35,000 to $39,999	356	4	7	188	2	6	*53	*1	*5
$40,000 to $49,999	625	4	11	272	2	9	160	1	15
$50,000 to $74,999	1,218	4	22	784	2	27	220	1	21
$75,000 to $99,999	643	4	12	391	2	13	141	1	13
$100,000 or more...............	587	3	11	470	2	16	67	(Z)	6
Not reported....................	781	1	14	453	1	15	180	(Z)	17
Education									
11 years or less	779	2	14	357	1	12	161	(Z)	15
12 years......................	1,968	3	36	790	1	27	413	1	39
1 to 3 years college..............	1,359	3	25	904	2	31	254	1	24
4 years college.................	798	2	15	544	2	18	176	1	17
5 years or more college...........	530	2	10	362	2	12	*42	*(Z)	*4

* Estimate based on a small sample size.　　... Sample size too small to report data reliably.　　(Z) Less than 0.5 percent.

Note: Percent who participated shows the percent of each row's population who participated in the activity named by the column (the percent of those living in urban areas who hunted big game, etc.). Percent columns show the percent of each column's participants who are described by the row heading (the percent of big game hunters who lived in urban areas, etc.).

Table 11. Persons With Disabilities Who Participated in Fishing and Hunting: 2001

(Population 16 years old and older. Numbers in thousands)

Fishing and hunting	Participants		Days of participation		Trips	
	Number	Percent	Number	Percent	Number	Percent
Total sportspersons	**37,805**	**100**	**785,762**	**100**	**636,787**	**100**
Total disabled sportspersons	2,080	100	54,705	100	42,950	100
Mobility impaired	1,681	81	46,043	84	35,165	82
Hearing impaired.........................	210	10	5,142	9	3,453	8
Sight impaired	135	7	3,412	6	3,681	9
Mentally impaired	239	11	4,278	8	3,874	9
Total anglers................................	**34,071**	**100**	**557,394**	**100**	**436,662**	**100**
Total disabled anglers	1,866	100	41,402	100	33,000	100
Mobility impaired	1,507	81	34,421	83	26,194	79
Hearing impaired.........................	185	10	3,941	10	2,617	8
Sight impaired	129	7	3,127	8	3,467	11
Mentally impaired	200	11	3,062	7	3,176	10
Total hunters................................	**13,034**	**100**	**228,368**	**100**	**200,125**	**100**
Total disabled hunters	678	100	13,303	100	9,950	100
Mobility impaired	570	84	11,622	87	8,971	90
Hearing impaired.........................	*87	*13	*1,202	*9	*836	*8
Sight impaired	*31	*5	*285	*2	*214	*2
Mentally impaired	76	11	1,215	9	*698	*7

* Estimate based on a small sample size.

Note: Detail does not add to total because of multiple responses and nonresponse.

Table 12. Summary of Expenditures for Fishing and Hunting: 2001

(Population 16 years old and older)

Expenditure item	Expenditures		Spenders		
	Amount (thousands of dollars)	Average per sportsman (dollars)	Number (thousands)	Percent of sportspersons	Average per spender (dollars)
Total, all items	**69,976,330**	**1,851**	**35,919**	**95**	**1,948**
TRIP-RELATED EXPENDITURES					
Total trip-related	**19,908,392**	**527**	**33,338**	**88**	**597**
Food and lodging, total............................	**8,330,938**	**220**	**29,380**	**78**	**284**
Food....................................	6,121,645	162	29,180	77	210
Lodging.................................	2,209,293	58	7,778	21	284
Transportation, total	**5,305,077**	**140**	**29,234**	**77**	**181**
Public...................................	586,422	16	1,651	4	355
Private	4,718,654	125	28,888	76	163
Other trip costs[1]	**6,272,377**	**166**	**26,802**	**71**	**234**
EQUIPMENT EXPENDITURES					
Fishing equipment....................................	4,640,715	123	21,493	57	216
Hunting equipment	4,866,399	129	10,579	28	460
Auxiliary equipment[2]	2,627,686	70	10,866	29	242
Special equipment[3]	28,819,402	762	3,947	10	7,301
OTHER EXPENDITURES					
Books, magazines	307,981	8	7,628	20	40
Membership dues and contributions....................	515,282	14	5,220	14	99
Land leasing and ownership...........................	7,128,486	189	2,329	6	3,061
Licenses, stamps, tags, and permits	1,161,988	31	24,201	64	48

[1] Other trip costs include guide fees, pack trip or package fees, public and private land use fees, equipment rental, boating costs (which include launching, mooring, storage, maintenance, insurance, pumpout fees, and fuel), bait, ice, and heating and cooking fuel.

[2] Auxiliary equipment includes camping equipment, binoculars, special fishing and hunting clothing, etc.

[3] Special equipment includes boats, campers, cabins, trail bikes, etc.

Note: Detail does not add to total because of multiple responses. Detail in subsequent tables may not add to totals shown here because of nonresponse to individual questions.

Table 13. Expenditures for Fishing: 2001

(Population 16 years old and older)

Expenditure item	Expenditures		Spenders		
	Amount (thousands of dollars)	Average per angler (dollars)	Number (thousands)	Percent of anglers	Average per spender (dollars)
Total, all items	**35,632,257**	**1,046**	**31,950**	**94**	**1,115**
TRIP-RELATED EXPENDITURES					
Total trip-related	**14,656,000**	**430**	**29,645**	**87**	**494**
Food and lodging, total	**5,880,997**	**173**	**25,603**	**75**	**230**
Food	4,141,250	122	25,406	75	163
Lodging	1,739,747	51	6,473	19	269
Transportation, total	**3,515,756**	**103**	**25,146**	**74**	**140**
Public	400,429	12	1,254	4	319
Private..	3,115,328	91	24,816	73	126
Other trip costs, total	**5,259,247**	**154**	**25,658**	**75**	**205**
Guide fees, pack trip or package fees..................	686,903	20	2,587	8	266
Public land use fees..............................	121,274	4	3,565	10	34
Private land use fees	92,961	3	1,283	4	72
Equipment rental	253,514	7	1,992	6	127
Boating costs[1].................................	2,630,429	77	8,265	24	318
Bait..	1,105,350	32	21,757	64	51
Ice...	290,917	9	12,481	37	23
Heating and cooking fuel	77,899	2	3,334	10	23
EQUIPMENT EXPENDITURES					
Fishing equipment, total	**4,617,612**	**136**	**21,228**	**62**	**218**
Rods, reels, poles, and rodmaking components	1,900,343	56	11,712	34	162
Lines and leaders................................	460,079	14	13,647	40	34
Artificial lures, flies, baits, and dressing for flies or lines.....	800,467	23	14,966	44	53
Hooks, sinkers, swivels, and other items attached to a line, except lures and baits	343,525	10	15,497	45	22
Tackle boxes....................................	133,093	4	4,169	12	32
Creels, stringers, fish bags, landing nets, and gaff hooks	101,937	3	3,480	10	29
Minnow traps, seines, and bait containers	52,816	2	3,031	9	17
Depth finders, fish finders, and other electronic fishing devices	457,054	13	1,098	3	416
Ice fishing equipment	82,876	2	644	2	129
Other fishing equipment	285,423	8	2,990	9	95
Auxiliary equipment, total	**721,049**	**21**	**4,347**	**13**	**166**
Camping equipment...............................	340,382	10	2,054	6	166
Binoculars, field glasses, telescopes, etc.................	30,050	1	367	1	82
Special fishing clothing, rubber boots, waders, and foul weather gear................................	243,608	7	2,248	7	108
Processing and taxidermy costs.......................	34,992	1	151	(Z)	232
Other...	72,016	2	551	2	131
Special equipment[2]................................	**11,624,862**	**341**	**2,319**	**7**	**5,013**
OTHER EXPENDITURES					
Magazines, books.................................	117,501	3	3,437	10	34
Membership dues and contributions.......................	102,762	3	1,614	5	64
Land leasing and ownership	3,152,594	93	794	2	3,972
Licenses, stamps, tags, and permits, total..................	639,876	19	20,184	59	32
Licenses	597,210	18	19,972	59	30
Stamps, tags, and permits	42,666	1	3,588	11	12

(Z) Less than 0.5 percent.

[1] Boating costs include launching, mooring, storage, maintenance, insurance, pumpout fees, and fuel.

[2] Special equipment includes boats, campers, cabins, trail bikes, etc.

Note: Detail does not add to total because of multiple responses. Detail in Tables 14 to 17 may not add to totals shown here because of multiple responses and nonresponse.

Table 14. Trip and Equipment Expenditures for Freshwater Fishing: 2001

(Population 16 years old and older)

Expenditure item	Expenditures		Spenders		
	Amount (thousands of dollars)	Average per angler (dollars)	Number (thousands)	Percent of anglers	Average per spender (dollars)
Total, all items	**21,348,370**	**751**	**26,132**	**92**	**817**
TRIP-RELATED EXPENDITURES					
Total trip-related	**10,169,234**	**358**	**25,352**	**89**	**401**
Food and lodging, total	**4,338,368**	**153**	**21,629**	**76**	**201**
Food	3,144,549	111	21,449	75	147
Lodging	1,193,818	42	5,294	19	225
Transportation, total	**2,782,609**	**98**	**21,524**	**76**	**129**
Public	221,099	8	779	3	284
Private..	2,561,510	90	21,352	75	120
Other trip costs, total	**3,048,257**	**107**	**21,753**	**76**	**140**
Guide fees, pack trip or package fees..............	255,966	9	1,186	4	216
Public land use fees............................	94,769	3	3,082	11	31
Private land use fees	73,299	3	1,048	4	70
Equipment rental	147,863	5	1,417	5	104
Boating costs[1]................................	1,397,420	49	6,483	23	216
Bait..	805,230	28	18,747	66	43
Ice...	203,803	7	10,323	36	20
Heating and cooking fuel	69,907	2	3,117	11	22
EQUIPMENT EXPENDITURES					
Fishing equipment, total	**3,162,930**	**111**	**17,057**	**60**	**185**
Rods, reels, poles, and rodmaking components	1,280,446	45	8,996	32	142
Lines and leaders...............................	320,810	11	10,575	37	30
Artificial lures, flies, baits, and dressing for flies or lines.....	614,032	22	12,013	42	51
Hooks, sinkers, swivels, and other items attached to a line, except lures and baits	238,934	8	12,013	42	20
Tackle boxes..................................	94,609	3	3,027	11	31
Creels, stringers, fish bags, landing nets, and gaff hooks	67,335	2	2,567	9	26
Minnow traps, seines, and bait containers	34,625	1	2,228	8	16
Depth finders, fish finders, and other electronic fishing devices	235,975	8	741	3	319
Ice fishing equipment	81,610	3	623	2	131
Other fishing equipment	194,554	7	2,027	7	96
Auxiliary equipment, total	**536,406**	**19**	**3,338**	**12**	**161**
Camping equipment............................	296,953	10	1,711	6	174
Binoculars, field glasses, telescopes, etc.................	17,924	1	226	1	79
Special fishing clothing, rubber boots, waders, and foul weather gear................................	173,625	6	1,642	6	106
Processing and taxidermy costs.......................	19,828	1	95	(Z)	209
Other...	28,076	1	383	1	73
Special equipment[2]................................	**7,479,801**	**263**	**1,695**	**6**	**4,413**

(Z) Less than 0.5 percent.

[1] Boating costs include launching, mooring, storage, maintenance, insurance, pumpout fees, and fuel.
[2] Special equipment includes boats, campers, cabins, trail bikes, etc.

Note: Detail does not add to total because of multiple responses.

Table 15. Trip and Equipment Expenditures for Freshwater Fishing Except Great Lakes: 2001

(Population 16 years old and over)

Expenditure item	Expenditures		Spenders		
	Amount (thousands of dollars)	Average per angler (dollars)	Number (thousands)	Percent of anglers	Average per spender (dollars)
Total, all items	**19,972,014**	**716**	**25,543**	**92**	**782**
TRIP-RELATED EXPENDITURES					
Total trip-related	**9,392,904**	**337**	**24,771**	**89**	**379**
Food and lodging, total	**4,028,437**	**144**	**21,079**	**76**	**191**
Food	2,923,180	105	20,904	75	140
Lodging	1,105,257	40	5,072	18	218
Transportation, total	**2,624,595**	**94**	**20,977**	**75**	**125**
Public	209,056	7	741	3	282
Private..	2,415,539	87	20,801	75	116
Other trip costs, total	**2,739,872**	**98**	**21,173**	**76**	**129**
Guide fees, pack trip or package fees................	236,495	8	1,061	4	223
Public land use fees...............................	90,904	3	2,944	11	31
Private land use fees	67,731	2	997	4	68
Equipment rental	128,813	5	1,297	5	99
Boating costs[1]...................................	1,194,849	43	6,153	22	194
Bait..	761,793	27	18,230	65	42
Ice...	192,022	7	10,042	36	19
Heating and cooking fuel	67,266	2	3,027	11	22
EQUIPMENT EXPENDITURES					
Fishing equipment, total	**2,959,515**	**106**	**16,458**	**59**	**180**
Rods, reels, poles, and rodmaking components	1,171,010	42	8,610	31	136
Lines and leaders.................................	305,802	11	10,186	36	30
Artificial lures, flies, baits, and dressing for flies or lines.....	585,275	21	11,573	41	51
Hooks, sinkers, swivels, and other items attached to a line, except lures and baits	228,785	8	11,597	42	20
Tackle boxes.....................................	91,603	3	2,925	10	31
Creels, stringers, fish bags, landing nets, and gaff hooks	63,898	2	2,442	9	26
Minnow traps, seines, and bait containers	33,064	1	2,149	8	15
Depth finders, fish finders, and other electronic fishing devices	228,855	8	725	3	316
Ice fishing equipment	77,867	3	591	2	132
Other fishing equipment	173,356	6	1,963	7	88
Auxiliary equipment, total	**498,449**	**18**	**3,171**	**11**	**157**
Camping equipment................................	278,991	10	1,668	6	167
Binoculars, field glasses, telescopes, etc..................	17,875	1	226	1	79
Special fishing clothing, rubber boots, waders, and foul weather gear..................................	159,143	6	1,528	5	104
Processing and taxidermy costs........................	14,994	1	73	(Z)	206
Other...	27,445	1	374	1	73
Special equipment[2]...................................	**7,121,146**	**255**	**1,588**	**6**	**4,483**

(Z) Less than 0.5 percent.

[1] Boating costs include launching, mooring, storage, maintenance, insurance, pumpout fees, and fuel.
[2] Special equipment includes boats, campers, cabins, trail bikes, etc.

Note: Detail does not add to total because of multiple responses.

Table 16. Trip and Equipment Expenditures for Great Lakes Fishing: 2001

(Population 16 years old and older)

Expenditure item	Expenditures		Spenders		
	Amount (thousands of dollars)	Average per angler (dollars)	Number (thousands)	Percent of anglers	Average per spender (dollars)
Total, all items	1,274,435	690	1,699	92	750
TRIP-RELATED EXPENDITURES					
Total trip-related	776,330	420	1,670	90	465
Food and lodging, total	309,931	168	1,403	76	221
Food	221,370	120	1,392	75	159
Lodging	88,561	48	357	19	248
Transportation, total	158,014	86	1,398	76	113
Public	*12,043	*7	*57	*3	*210
Private	145,971	79	1,372	74	106
Other trip costs, total	308,385	167	1,451	79	213
Guide fees, pack trip or package fees	19,471	11	156	8	125
Public land use fees	3,865	2	165	9	23
Private land use fees	*5,568	*3	*62	*3	*90
Equipment rental	19,050	10	135	7	141
Boating costs[1]	202,571	110	501	27	404
Bait	43,437	24	1,150	62	38
Ice	11,781	6	572	31	21
Heating and cooking fuel	2,641	1	128	7	21
EQUIPMENT EXPENDITURES					
Fishing equipment, total	175,213	95	681	37	257
Rods, reels, poles, and rodmaking components	93,223	50	337	18	277
Lines and leaders	13,001	7	345	19	38
Artificial lures, flies, baits, and dressing for flies or lines.....	23,637	13	410	22	58
Hooks, sinkers, swivels, and other items attached to a line, except lures and baits	8,751	5	372	20	24
Tackle boxes	*2,385	*1	*89	*5	*27
Creels, stringers, fish bags, landing nets, and gaff hooks	*2,749	*1	*105	*6	*26
Minnow traps, seines, and bait containers	*737	*(W)	*50	*3	*15
Depth finders, fish finders, and other electronic fishing devices	...	...	...	...	...
Ice fishing equipment	...	...	...	...	...
Other fishing equipment	*20,807	*11	*58	*3	*358
Auxiliary equipment, total	33,201	18	132	7	251
Camping equipment	...	...	...	...	...
Binoculars, field glasses, telescopes, etc	...	...	...	...	...
Special fishing clothing, rubber boots, waders, and foul weather gear	*12,549	*7	*105	*6	*120
Processing and taxidermy costs	...	...	...	...	...
Other	...	...	...	...	...
Special equipment[2]	*289,691	*157	*72	*4	*4,046

* Estimate based on a small sample size.   ... Sample size too small to report data reliably.   (W) Less than 0.5 dollar.

[1] Boating costs include launching, mooring, storage, maintenance, insurance, pumpout fees, and fuel.
[2] Special equipment includes boats, campers, cabins, trail bikes, etc.

Note: Detail does not add to total because of multiple responses.

Table 17. Trip and Equipment Expenditures for Saltwater Fishing: 2001

(Population 16 years old and older)

Expenditure item	Expenditures		Spenders		
	Amount (thousands of dollars)	Average per angler (dollars)	Number (thousands)	Percent of anglers	Average per spender (dollars)
Total, all items	**8,388,962**	**927**	**8,115**	**90**	**1,034**
TRIP-RELATED EXPENDITURES					
Total trip-related	4,486,766	496	7,980	88	562
Food and lodging, total	1,542,629	170	6,998	77	220
Food...	996,701	110	6,937	77	144
Lodging	545,928	60	1,614	18	338
Transportation, total	733,148	81	6,440	71	114
Public...	179,330	20	560	6	320
Private...	553,818	61	6,127	68	90
Other trip costs, total	2,210,990	244	6,886	76	321
Guide fees, pack trip or package fees...................	430,937	48	1,533	17	281
Public land use fees..............................	26,505	3	589	7	45
Private land use fees	19,662	2	272	3	72
Equipment rental	105,651	12	616	7	171
Boating costs[1]...................................	1,233,009	136	2,328	26	530
Bait...	300,121	33	5,038	56	60
Ice..	87,114	10	3,460	38	25
Heating and cooking fuel	7,992	1	376	4	21
EQUIPMENT EXPENDITURES					
Fishing equipment, total	987,392	109	3,470	38	285
Rods, reels, poles, and rodmaking components	433,774	48	1,827	20	237
Lines and leaders..................................	99,376	11	2,144	24	46
Artificial lures, flies, baits, and dressing for flies or lines.....	119,012	13	1,923	21	62
Hooks, sinkers, swivels, and other items attached to a line, except lures and baits	70,585	8	2,381	26	30
Tackle boxes......................................	21,725	2	711	8	31
Creels, stringers, fish bags, landing nets, and gaff hooks	25,618	3	589	7	44
Minnow traps, seines, and bait containers	12,434	1	526	6	24
Depth finders, fish finders, and other electronic fishing devices	138,316	15	252	3	548
Other fishing equipment	66,552	7	582	6	114
Auxiliary equipment, total	103,125	11	647	7	159
Camping equipment.................................	20,736	2	142	2	146
Binoculars, field glasses, telescopes, etc..................	5,850	1	91	1	65
Special fishing clothing, rubber boots, waders, and foul weather gear.................................	47,180	5	388	4	122
Processing and taxidermy costs.......................	*13,983	*2	*42	*(Z)	*336
Other..	15,375	2	127	1	121
Special equipment[2].................................	2,811,679	311	395	4	7,125

* Estimate based on a small sample.   (Z) Less than 0.5 percent.

[1] Boating costs include launching, mooring, storage, maintenance, insurance, pumpout fees, and fuel.
[2] Special equipment includes boats, campers, cabins, trail bikes, etc.

Note: Detail does not add to total because of multiple responses.

U.S. Fish & Wildlife Service

Table 18. Expenditures for Hunting: 2001

(Population 16 years old and older)

Expenditure item	Expenditures		Spenders		
	Amount (thousands of dollars)	Average per hunter (dollars)	Number (thousands)	Percent of hunters	Average per spender (dollars)
Total, all items	20,611,025	1,581	12,585	97	1,638
TRIP-RELATED EXPENDITURES					
Total trip-related	5,252,391	403	11,280	87	466
Food and lodging, total	2,449,942	188	10,073	77	243
Food	1,980,395	152	10,057	77	197
Lodging	469,547	36	1,701	13	276
Transportation, total	1,789,320	137	10,502	81	170
Public	185,994	14	452	3	411
Private	1,603,326	123	10,421	80	154
Other trip costs, total	1,013,129	78	3,479	27	291
Guide fees, pack trip or package fees................	377,233	29	573	4	659
Public land use fees...............................	53,499	4	630	5	85
Private land use fees	370,858	28	919	7	403
Equipment rental	36,395	3	262	2	139
Boating costs[1]...................................	85,912	7	556	4	154
Heating and cooking fuel	89,232	7	1,930	15	46
EQUIPMENT EXPENDITURES					
Hunting equipment, total	4,561,709	350	9,516	73	479
Guns and rifles....................................	1,966,867	151	2,888	22	681
Rifles	907,470	70	1,579	12	575
Shotguns.....................................	676,619	52	1,262	10	536
Muzzleloaders, primitive firearms..............	105,507	8	390	3	271
Pistols, handguns.............................	277,270	21	567	4	489
Bows, arrows, archery equipment...................	462,097	35	1,892	15	244
Telescopic sights	307,033	24	1,272	10	241
Decoys and game calls	139,686	11	2,168	17	64
Ammunition.......................................	651,896	50	8,451	65	77
Hand loading equipment	139,919	11	945	7	148
Hunting dogs and associated costs	604,616	46	892	7	678
Other..	289,595	22	2,201	17	132
Auxiliary equipment, total	1,202,845	92	4,584	35	262
Camping equipment................................	113,661	9	638	5	178
Binoculars, field glasses, telescopes, etc.	153,862	12	1,168	9	132
Special hunting clothing, rubber boots, waders, and foul weather gear...............................	463,990	36	2,977	23	156
Processing and taxidermy costs.....................	385,947	30	1,470	11	263
Other..	85,385	7	310	2	275
Special equipment[2].................................	4,596,942	353	573	4	8,020
OTHER EXPENDITURES					
Magazines, books...................................	84,530	6	1,835	14	46
Membership dues and contributions	243,678	19	2,054	16	119
Land leasing and ownership	3,975,892	305	1,680	13	2,367
Licenses, stamps, tags, and permits, total..................	693,038	53	10,403	80	67
Licenses	572,242	44	9,985	77	57
Federal duck stamps	29,524	2	1,968	15	15
Other stamps, tags, and permits	91,273	7	2,868	22	32

[1] Boating costs include launching, mooring, storage, maintenance, insurance, pumpout fees, and fuel.

[2] Special equipment includes boats, campers, cabins, trail bikes, etc.

Note: Detail does not add to total because of multiple responses. Detail in Tables 19-22 may not add to totals shown here because of multiple responses and nonresponse.

Table 19. Trip and Equipment Expenditures for Big Game Hunting: 2001

(Population 16 years old and older)

Expenditure item	Expenditures		Spenders		
	Amount (thousands of dollars)	Average per hunter (dollars)	Number (thousands)	Percent of hunters	Average per spender (dollars)
Total, all items	**10,087,930**	**925**	**9,962**	**91**	**1,013**
TRIP-RELATED EXPENDITURES					
Total trip-related	**3,565,342**	**327**	**9,378**	**86**	**380**
Food and lodging, total	**1,687,863**	**155**	**8,349**	**77**	**202**
Food	1,377,078	126	8,334	76	165
Lodging	310,785	28	1,262	12	246
Transportation, total	**1,128,366**	**103**	**8,719**	**80**	**129**
Public	91,700	8	285	3	321
Private..	1,036,666	95	8,645	79	120
Other trip costs, total	**749,113**	**69**	**2,671**	**24**	**280**
Guide fees, pack trip or package fees....................	298,823	27	343	3	870
Public land use fees...............................	38,104	3	430	4	89
Private land use fees	271,648	25	681	6	399
Equipment rental	22,393	2	182	2	123
Boating costs[1]	50,703	5	208	2	244
Heating and cooking fuel	67,441	6	1,695	16	40
EQUIPMENT EXPENDITURES					
Hunting equipment, total	**2,218,798**	**203**	**6,622**	**61**	**335**
Guns and rifles..................................	921,215	84	1,611	15	572
Rifles.......................................	600,793	55	1,026	9	586
Shotguns....................................	141,970	13	349	3	407
Muzzleloaders, primitive firearms...................	94,685	9	352	3	269
Pistols, handguns..............................	83,768	8	150	1	557
Bows, arrows, archery equipment.....................	439,302	40	1,743	16	252
Telescopic sights	242,892	22	982	9	247
Decoys and game calls	44,511	4	1,185	11	38
Ammunition....................................	264,359	24	4,913	45	54
Hand loading equipment	69,814	6	621	6	112
Hunting dogs and associated costs	73,815	7	105	1	701
Other..	162,892	15	1,373	13	119
Auxiliary equipment, total	**935,142**	**86**	**3,551**	**33**	**263**
Camping equipment...............................	87,188	8	513	5	170
Binoculars, field glasses, telescopes, etc...............	115,090	11	879	8	131
Special hunting clothing, rubber boots, waders, and foul weather gear................................	313,551	29	2,104	19	149
Processing and taxidermy costs........................	349,914	32	1,364	13	256
Other..	69,400	6	208	2	333
Special equipment[2]................................	**3,368,648**	**309**	**465**	**4**	**7,251**

[1] Boating costs include launching, mooring, storage, maintenance, insurance, pumpout fees, and fuel.
[2] Special equipment includes boats, campers, cabins, trail bikes, etc.

Note: Detail does not add to total because of multiple responses.

U.S. Fish & Wildlife Service

Table 20. Trip and Equipment Expenditures for Small Game Hunting: 2001

(Population 16 years old and older)

Expenditure item	Expenditures		Spenders		
	Amount (thousands of dollars)	Average per hunter (dollars)	Number (thousands)	Percent of hunters	Average per spender (dollars)
Total, all items	**1,816,199**	**334**	**4,556**	**84**	**399**
TRIP-RELATED EXPENDITURES					
Total trip-related	**909,006**	**167**	**4,255**	**78**	**214**
Food and lodging, total	437,891	81	3,635	67	120
Food..	340,049	63	3,633	67	94
Lodging	97,842	18	418	8	234
Transportation, total	347,605	64	3,844	71	90
Public..	29,638	5	113	2	263
Private.......................................	317,967	59	3,801	70	84
Other trip costs, total	123,510	23	799	15	155
Guide fees, pack trip or package fees..................	43,269	8	182	3	238
Public land use fees.............................	3,022	1	115	2	26
Private land use fees	52,627	10	229	4	229
Equipment rental...............................	*6,862	*1	*71	*1	*96
Boating costs[1]................................	9,734	2	99	2	98
Heating and cooking fuel	7,996	1	317	6	25
EQUIPMENT EXPENDITURES					
Hunting equipment, total	660,440	122	2,003	37	330
Guns and rifles................................	281,413	52	570	10	493
Rifles	50,827	9	196	4	259
Shotguns................................	204,787	38	361	7	568
Muzzleloaders, primitive firearms.........	...	...	...	...	...
Pistols, handguns........................	25,799	5	56	1	461
Bows, arrows, archery equipment....................	...	...	...	...	...
Telescopic sights	19,764	4	95	2	209
Decoys and game calls	7,699	1	175	3	44
Ammunition...................................	91,204	17	1,404	26	65
Hand loading equipment	16,284	3	106	2	153
Hunting dogs and associated costs	214,635	39	401	7	536
Other..	27,769	5	186	3	149
Auxiliary equipment, total	63,361	12	385	7	165
Camping equipment.............................	*15,219	*3	*56	*1	*271
Binoculars, field glasses, telescopes, etc.............	*2,889	*1	*51	*1	*56
Special hunting clothing, rubber boots, waders, and					
foul weather gear............................	31,916	6	273	5	117
Processing and taxidermy costs.....................	*8,002	*1	*40	*1	*202
Other..	*5,335	*1	*24	*(Z)	*221
Special equipment[2]..................................	*183,393	*34	*21	*(Z)	*8,631

* Estimate based on a small sample size.   ... Sample size too small to report data reliably.   (Z) Less than 0.5 percent.

[1] Boating costs include launching, mooring, storage, maintenance, insurance, pumpout fees, and fuel.
[2] Special equipment includes boats, campers, cabins, trail bikes, etc.

Note: Detail does not add to total because of multiple responses.

Table 21. Trip and Equipment Expenditures for Migratory Bird Hunting: 2001

(Population 16 years old and older)

Expenditure item	Expenditures		Spenders		
	Amount (thousands of dollars)	Average per hunter (dollars)	Number (thousands)	Percent of hunters	Average per spender (dollars)
Total, all items	**1,388,581**	**470**	**2,533**	**86**	**548**
TRIP-RELATED EXPENDITURES					
Total trip-related	**656,943**	**222**	**2,398**	**81**	**274**
Food and lodging, total	**280,369**	**95**	**2,085**	**71**	**134**
Food	227,972	77	2,084	71	109
Lodging	52,397	18	237	8	221
Transportation, total	**246,548**	**83**	**2,155**	**73**	**114**
Public	64,655	22	112	4	576
Private	181,892	62	2,112	71	86
Other trip costs, total	**130,027**	**44**	**671**	**23**	**194**
Guide fees, pack trip or package fees	35,071	12	124	4	282
Public land use fees	8,949	3	128	4	70
Private land use fees	45,996	16	115	4	400
Equipment rental	*2,402	*1	*35	*1	*68
Boating costs[1]	24,738	8	326	11	76
Heating and cooking fuel	12,871	4	200	7	64
EQUIPMENT EXPENDITURES					
Hunting equipment, total	**533,561**	**180**	**1,396**	**47**	**382**
Guns and rifles	204,601	69	301	10	679
Rifles	...	...	...	...	...
Shotguns	178,211	60	269	9	662
Muzzleloaders, primitive firearms	...	...	...	...	...
Pistols, handguns	...	...	...	...	...
Bows, arrows, archery equipment	...	...	...	...	...
Telescopic sights	...	...	...	...	...
Decoys and game calls	60,731	21	523	18	116
Ammunition	118,125	40	1,070	36	110
Hand loading equipment	*5,759	*2	*25	*1	*228
Hunting dogs and associated costs	120,570	41	222	7	544
Other	21,107	7	191	6	110
Auxiliary equipment, total	**67,585**	**23**	**263**	**9**	**257**
Camping equipment	...	...	...	...	...
Binoculars, field glasses, telescopes, etc.	*5,887	*2	*19	*1	*307
Special hunting clothing, rubber boots, waders, and foul weather gear	49,416	17	207	7	239
Processing and taxidermy costs	*9,981	*3	*45	*2	*224
Other	...	...	...	...	...
Special equipment[2]	***130,491**	***44**	***37**	***1**	***3,527**

* Estimate based on a small sample size.   ... Sample size too small to report data reliably.

[1] Boating costs include launching, mooring, storage, maintenance, insurance, pumpout fees, and fuel.
[2] Special equipment includes boats, campers, cabins, trail bikes, etc.

Note: Detail does not add to total because of multiple responses.

Table 22. Trip and Equipment Expenditures for Hunting Other Animals: 2001

(Population 16 years old and older)

Expenditure item	Expenditures		Spenders		
	Amount (thousands of dollars)	Average per hunter (dollars)	Number (thousands)	Percent of hunters	Average per spender (dollars)
Total, all items	243,760	233	648	62	376
TRIP-RELATED EXPENDITURES					
Total trip-related	121,101	116	545	52	222
Food and lodging, total	43,820	42	427	41	103
Food..	35,297	34	426	41	83
Lodging	*8,523	*8	*33	*3	*259
Transportation, total	66,802	64	487	46	137
Public..	...	...	...	...	...
Private...	66,802	64	487	46	137
Other trip costs, total	10,479	10	57	5	183
Guide fees, pack trip or package fees....................	...	...	...	...	...
Public land use fees...........................	...	...	...	...	...
Private land use fees	...	...	...	...	...
Equipment rental	...	...	...	...	...
Boating costs[1].....................................	...	...	...	...	...
Heating and cooking fuel	*923	*1	*30	*3	*30
EQUIPMENT EXPENDITURES					
Hunting equipment, total	84,759	81	239	23	354
Guns and rifles.......................................	*21,071	*20	*41	*4	*515
Rifles..	*18,355	*18	*32	*3	*574
Shotguns...	...	...	...	...	...
Muzzleloaders, primitive firearms....................	...	...	...	...	...
Pistols, handguns.................................	...	...	...	...	...
Bows, arrows, archery equipment....................	...	...	...	...	...
Telescopic sights	*5,432	*5	*29	*3	*188
Decoys and game calls	2,724	3	45	4	61
Ammunition...	9,735	9	142	14	69
Hand loading equipment	*2,080	*2	*20	*2	*105
Hunting dogs and associated costs	*40,570	*39	*27	*3	*1,494
Other..	...	...	...	...	...
Auxiliary equipment, total	*6,137	*6	*32	*3	*193
Camping equipment...................................	...	...	...	...	...
Binoculars, field glasses, telescopes, etc...............	...	...	...	...	...
Special hunting clothing, rubber boots, waders, and foul weather gear.................................	*2,521	*2	*23	*2	*109
Processing and taxidermy costs........................	...	...	...	...	...
Other..	...	...	...	...	...
Special equipment[2]...................................	...	...	...	...	...

* Estimate based on a small sample size.   ... Sample size too small to report data reliably.

[1] Boating costs include launching, mooring, storage, maintenance, insurance, pumpout fees, and fuel.
[2] Special equipment includes boats, campers, cabins, trail bikes, etc.

Note: Detail does not add to total because of multiple responses.

Table 23. Special Equipment Expenditures for Fishing and Hunting: 2001

(Population 16 years old and older)

Special equipment item	Expenditures		Spenders		
	Amount (thousands of dollars)	Average per sportsperson (dollars)	Number (thousands)	Percent of sportspersons	Average per spender (dollars)
Total, all items	**28,819,402**	**762**	**3,947**	**10**	**7,301**
Motor boat (other than bass boat)......................	3,414,855	90	569	2	6,001
Bass boat	1,305,835	35	199	1	6,558
Canoe, other nonmotor boat	232,607	6	375	1	620
Boat motor, trailer or hitch, and other boat accessories.......	1,358,130	36	1,191	3	1,140
Travel or tent trailer, pickup, camper, van, motor home, recreational vehicle (RV), house trailer	13,299,315	352	992	3	13,404
Cabin...	3,161,500	84	93	(Z)	34,046
Trail bike, dune buggy, 4x4 vehicle, 4-wheeler, snowmobile ..	5,734,891	152	735	2	7,801
Other...	312,270	8	876	2	357

(Z) Less than 0.5 percent.

Note: Detail does not add to total because of multiple responses.

Table 24. Anglers and Hunters Who Purchased Licenses or Were Exempt: 2001

(Population 16 years old and older. Numbers in thousands)

Sportspersons	Anglers		Hunters	
	Number	Percent	Number	Percent
Total sportspersons	**34,071**	**100**	**13,034**	**100**
Total license purchasers[1].................................	**21,396**	**63**	**10,688**	**82**
Sportspersons purchasing licenses:				
In state of residence.................................	20,004	59	10,192	78
In other states.................................	3,781	11	1,539	12
Total exempt from purchasing licenses......................	**4,284**	**13**	**1,689**	**13**
Sportspersons exempt from license purchase:				
In state of residence.................................	3,959	12	1,557	12
In other states.................................	608	2	209	2
Other[2]	**10,268**	**30**	**1,453**	**11**
Not reported	**448**	**1**	**155**	**1**

[1] Includes persons who had licenses bought for them. Does not include persons who purchased licenses and did not fish or hunt in 2001.

[2] Includes persons engaged in activities requiring no licenses or exemptions and those who failed to buy a license for activities requiring a license.

Note: Detail does not add to total because of multiple responses and nonresponse. Respondents could have been licensed in one state and exempt in another.

Table 25. Selected Characteristics of Anglers and Hunters Who Purchased Licenses: 2001

(Population 16 years old and older. Numbers in thousands)

Characteristic	Anglers Total Number	Total Percent	Purchased a license[1] Number	Purchased a license[1] Percent	Did not purchase a license[2] Number	Did not purchase a license[2] Percent	Hunters Total Number	Total Percent	Purchased a license[1] Number	Purchased a license[1] Percent	Did not purchase a license[2] Number	Did not purchase a license[2] Percent
Total persons	34,071	100	21,396	63	12,675	37	13,034	100	10,688	82	2,346	18
Population Density of Residence												
Urban	20,925	100	13,207	63	7,718	37	5,873	100	4,848	83	1,025	17
Rural.....................	13,146	100	8,190	62	4,957	38	7,161	100	5,840	82	1,322	18
Population Size of Residence												
Metropolitan statistical area												
(MSA)...................	24,391	100	15,049	62	9,341	38	7,749	100	6,291	81	1,458	19
1,000,000 or more.........	13,743	100	8,297	60	5,445	40	3,690	100	2,957	80	732	20
250,000 to 999,999.......	6,930	100	4,291	62	2,640	38	2,409	100	1,979	82	430	18
50,000 to 249,999.........	3,718	100	2,461	66	1,257	34	1,650	100	1,354	82	296	18
Outside MSA..............	9,680	100	6,347	66	3,334	34	5,285	100	4,397	83	888	17
Census Geographic Division												
New England.............	1,402	100	743	53	659	47	386	100	340	88	46	12
Middle Atlantic	3,250	100	1,785	55	1,466	45	1,633	100	1,488	91	145	9
East North Central	5,659	100	3,720	66	1,939	34	2,421	100	2,122	88	300	12
West North Central..........	3,836	100	2,830	74	1,006	26	1,710	100	1,424	83	286	17
South Atlantic	6,451	100	3,255	50	3,196	50	1,875	100	1,329	71	547	29
East South Central	2,543	100	1,538	60	1,006	40	1,164	100	889	76	275	24
West South Central..........	4,375	100	2,694	62	1,681	38	1,988	100	1,535	77	453	23
Mountain.................	2,443	100	1,895	78	548	22	1,020	100	906	89	114	11
Pacific...................	4,111	100	2,937	71	1,174	29	837	100	656	78	181	22
Age												
16 to 17 years	1,318	100	692	53	626	47	584	100	489	84	95	16
18 to 24 years	2,931	100	1,814	62	1,117	38	1,251	100	1,018	81	233	19
25 to 34 years	6,577	100	4,254	65	2,324	35	2,413	100	2,030	84	382	16
35 to 44 years	9,047	100	5,928	66	3,119	34	3,551	100	2,988	84	563	16
45 to 54 years	6,940	100	4,613	66	2,327	34	2,821	100	2,402	85	419	15
55 to 64 years	4,168	100	2,712	65	1,456	35	1,450	100	1,195	82	255	18
65 years and older	3,090	100	1,384	45	1,706	55	965	100	565	59	400	41
Sex												
Male......................	25,159	100	16,715	66	8,445	34	11,845	100	9,837	83	2,008	17
Female	8,912	100	4,682	53	4,231	47	1,190	100	851	72	339	28
Ethnicity												
Hispanic	1,564	100	774	49	790	51	428	100	315	73	114	27
Non-Hispanic..............	32,507	100	20,623	63	11,885	37	12,606	100	10,373	82	2,233	18
Race												
White	31,701	100	20,130	64	11,572	37	12,568	100	10,404	83	2,164	17
Black	1,600	100	811	51	789	49	297	100	184	62	112	38
Asian	342	100	214	62	128	38	*32	*100	...	...	...	...
All others	428	100	242	57	186	43	138	100	70	51	68	49
Annual Household Income												
Less than $10,000	878	100	458	52	420	48	247	100	188	76	59	24
$10,000 to $19,999..........	1,648	100	899	55	749	45	525	100	372	71	153	29
$20,000 to $24,999..........	1,474	100	832	56	641	44	565	100	405	72	160	28
$25,000 to $29,999..........	1,763	100	1,101	62	661	38	763	100	603	79	159	21
$30,000 to $34,999..........	2,091	100	1,426	68	665	32	830	100	683	82	147	18
$35,999 to $39,999..........	1,939	100	1,354	70	586	30	773	100	677	88	96	12
$40,000 to $49,999..........	3,696	100	2,495	68	1,200	32	1,569	100	1,328	85	241	15
$50,000 to $74,999..........	7,113	100	4,698	66	2,415	34	2,915	100	2,497	86	418	14
$75,000 to $99,999..........	4,029	100	2,533	63	1,497	37	1,525	100	1,272	83	253	17
$100,000 or more..........	4,220	100	2,611	62	1,609	38	1,267	100	1,018	80	249	20
Not reported.	5,221	100	2,989	57	2,232	43	2,057	100	1,646	80	411	20
Education												
11 years or less	4,128	100	2,350	57	1,779	43	1,771	100	1,421	80	350	20
12 years..................	11,832	100	7,551	64	4,281	36	4,973	100	4,138	83	836	17
1 to 3 years college	9,069	100	5,843	64	3,226	36	3,412	100	2,775	81	637	19
4 years college.............	5,522	100	3,447	62	2,075	38	1,814	100	1,481	82	332	18
5 or more years college........	3,520	100	2,205	63	1,314	37	1,065	100	873	82	192	18
Days of Participation												
1 to 5 days	14,251	100	7,125	50	7,033	49	4,104	100	2,932	71	1,127	27
6 to 10 days...............	6,092	100	3,916	64	2,090	34	2,665	100	2,237	84	393	15
11 to 25 days..............	7,066	100	5,236	74	1,771	25	3,555	100	3,134	88	399	11
26 days or more............	6,316	100	5,049	80	1,194	19	2,615	100	2,343	90	260	10

* Estimate based on a small sample size.   ... Sample size too small to report data reliably.

[1] Includes persons who purchased a license in 2001 in any state. Respondents could have been licensed in one state and exempt in another.
[2] Includes those persons who did not purchase a license in any state in 2001 and those who did not specify a license purchase in 2001.

Table 26. Freshwater Anglers and Days of Fishing by Type of Water: 2001

(Population 16 years old and older. Numbers in thousands. Excludes Great Lakes fishing)

Type of water	Anglers		Days of fishing	
	Number	Percent	Number	Percent
Total, all types of water	**27,913**	**100**	**443,247**	**100**
Lakes, reservoirs, and ponds................................	23,611	85	317,834	72
Rivers or streams...	12,324	44	141,049	32

Note: Detail does not add to total because of multiple responses and nonresponse.

Table 27. Great Lakes Anglers and Days of Fishing by Great Lake: 2001

(Population 16 years old and older. Numbers in thousands)

Great Lake	Anglers		Days of fishing	
	Number	Percent	Number	Percent
Total, all Great Lakes	**1,847**	**100**	**23,138**	**100**
Lake Ontario, including the Niagara River	241	13	3,560	15
Lake Erie, including the Detroit River........................	645	35	7,748	33
Lake Huron, including St. Mary's River System...............	155	8	1,171	5
Lake Michigan...	561	30	4,836	21
Lake Superior...	*93	*5	*601	*3
Lake St. Clair, including the St. Clair River	*96	*5	*524	*2
St. Lawrence River	*111	*6	*905	*4
Tributaries to the Great Lakes...............................	284	15	3,331	14

* Estimate based on a small sample size.

Note: Detail does not add to total because of multiple responses and nonresponse.

Table 28. Hunters and Days of Hunting on Public and Private Land by Type of Hunting: 2001

(Population 16 years old and older. Numbers in thousands)

Hunters and days of hunting	Total, all hunting		Big game		Small game		Migratory bird		Other animals	
	Number	Percent	Number	Percent	Number	Percent	Number	Percent	Number	Percent
HUNTERS										
Total, all land	**13,034**	**100**	**10,911**	**100**	**5,434**	**100**	**2,956**	**100**	**1,047**	**100**
Public land, total	**5,156**	**40**	**3,998**	**37**	**1,972**	**36**	**1,045**	**35**	**287**	**27**
Public land only.............	1,879	14	1,815	17	935	17	576	19	104	10
Public and private land	3,277	25	2,183	20	1,037	19	469	16	184	18
Private land, total.............	**10,724**	**82**	**8,748**	**80**	**4,345**	**80**	**2,255**	**76**	**904**	**86**
Private land only	7,447	57	6,565	60	3,308	61	1,787	60	720	69
Private and public land	3,277	25	2,183	20	1,037	19	469	16	184	18
DAYS OF HUNTING										
Total, all land	**228,368**	**100**	**153,191**	**100**	**60,142**	**100**	**29,310**	**100**	**19,207**	**100**
Public land[1]	60,454	26	36,070	24	16,170	27	9,126	31	3,227	17
Private land[2].................	169,795	74	110,283	72	42,382	70	19,707	67	16,076	84

[1] Days of hunting on public land includes both days spent solely on public land and those spent on public and private land.
[2] Days of hunting on private land includes both days spent solely on private land and those spent on private and public land.

Note: Detail does not add to total because of multiple responses and nonresponse.

U.S. Fish & Wildlife Service

Table 29. Hunters and Days of Hunting on Public Land by Selected Characteristic: 2001

(Population 16 years old and older. Numbers in thousands)

Characteristic	Total hunters, public and private land	Hunters on public land[1] — Number	Hunters on public land — Percent of total hunters	Hunters on public land — Percent of hunters using public land	Total days, public and private land	Days on public land[2] — Number	Days on public land — Percent of total days	Days on public land — Percent of days on public land
Total persons......................	13,034	5,156	40	100	228,368	60,454	26	100
Population Density of Residence								
Urban............................	5,873	2,592	44	50	84,455	29,225	35	48
Rural............................	7,161	2,564	36	50	143,913	31,229	22	52
Population Size of Residence								
Metropolitan statistical area (MSA)....	7,749	3,177	41	62	121,857	34,888	29	58
1,000,000 or more................	3,690	1,565	42	30	55,646	16,096	29	27
250,000 to 999,999..............	2,409	1,027	43	20	40,180	11,373	28	19
50,000 to 249,999..............	1,650	585	35	11	26,031	7,420	29	12
Outside MSA......................	5,285	1,978	37	38	106,511	25,566	24	42
Census Geographic Division								
New England......................	386	169	44	3	7,488	1,758	23	3
Middle Atlantic...................	1,633	761	47	15	30,060	9,538	32	16
East North Central.................	2,421	771	32	15	39,820	8,690	22	14
West North Central................	1,710	655	38	13	27,186	7,109	26	12
South Atlantic....................	1,875	529	28	10	39,043	7,077	18	12
East South Central.................	1,164	349	30	7	25,482	4,156	16	7
West South Central................	1,988	493	25	10	35,116	5,745	16	10
Mountain.........................	1,020	871	85	17	12,995	9,641	74	16
Pacific...........................	837	559	67	11	11,179	6,739	60	11
Age								
16 to 17 years....................	584	241	41	5	11,420	2,469	22	4
18 to 24 years....................	1,251	445	36	9	23,862	6,341	27	10
25 to 34 years....................	2,413	971	40	19	44,765	11,835	26	20
35 to 44 years....................	3,551	1,460	41	28	62,185	17,488	28	29
45 to 54 years....................	2,821	1,098	39	21	47,579	11,846	25	20
55 to 64 years....................	1,450	630	43	12	25,236	7,549	30	12
65 years and older................	965	310	32	6	13,321	2,926	22	5
Sex								
Male............................	11,845	4,826	41	94	214,300	57,647	27	95
Female..........................	1,190	329	28	6	14,068	2,808	20	5
Ethnicity								
Hispanic.........................	428	205	48	4	5,139	2,027	39	3
Non-Hispanic.....................	12,606	4,950	39	96	223,228	58,427	26	97
Race								
White............................	12,568	4,974	40	96	221,019	58,946	27	98
Black............................	297	95	32	2	5,383	706	13	1
Asian............................	*32	...	...	...	*332	...	...	...
All others.......................	138	75	55	1	1,634	698	43	1
Annual Household Income								
Less than $10,000.................	247	50	20	1	4,525	553	12	1
$10,000 to $19,999...............	525	209	40	4	8,889	2,609	29	4
$20,000 to $24,999...............	565	194	34	4	10,747	2,820	26	5
$25,000 to $29,999...............	763	267	35	5	15,600	2,733	18	5
$30,000 to $34,999...............	830	398	48	8	14,532	5,222	36	9
$35,000 to $39,999...............	773	337	44	7	15,387	3,421	22	6
$40,000 to $49,999...............	1,569	632	40	12	26,000	7,185	28	12
$50,000 to $74,999...............	2,915	1,132	39	22	52,593	14,380	27	24
$75,000 to $99,999...............	1,525	689	45	13	25,935	8,088	31	13
$100,000 or more.................	1,267	522	41	10	17,879	4,644	26	8
Not reported......................	2,057	726	35	14	36,283	8,798	24	15
Education								
11 years or less..................	1,771	676	38	13	36,091	7,768	22	13
12 years.........................	4,973	1,911	38	37	97,298	25,983	27	43
1 to 3 years college................	3,412	1,379	40	27	53,206	15,434	29	26
4 years college...................	1,814	759	42	15	27,554	7,548	27	12
5 or more years college............	1,065	430	40	8	14,219	3,721	26	6

* Estimate based on a small sample size.   ... Sample size too small to report data reliably.
[1] Hunters on public land include those who hunted on both public and private land.
[2] Days of hunting on public land includes both days spent solely on public land and those spent on public and private land.

Note: Percent of total hunters and percent of total days are based on the total hunters and total days columns for each row. Percent of hunters using public land and percent of days on public land are based on the total number of hunters on public land and total number of days on public land, respectively.

Table 30. Hunters and Days of Hunting on Private Land by Selected Characteristic: 2001

(Population 16 years old and older. Numbers in thousands)

Characteristic	Hunters				Days of hunting			
		Hunters on private land[1]				Days on private land[2]		
	Total hunters, public and private land	Number	Percent of total hunters	Percent of hunters using private land	Total days, public and private land	Number	Percent of total days	Percent of days on private land
Total persons.....................	**13,034**	**10,724**	**82**	**100**	**228,368**	**169,795**	**74**	**100**
Population Density of Residence								
Urban	5,873	4,510	77	42	84,455	55,262	65	33
Rural............................	7,161	6,213	87	58	143,913	114,533	80	67
Population Size of Residence								
Metropolitan statistical area (MSA)	7,749	6,201	80	58	121,857	86,632	71	51
1,000,000 or more	3,690	2,835	77	26	55,646	38,278	69	23
250,000 to 999,999	2,409	1,964	82	18	40,180	29,310	73	17
50,000 to 249,999	1,650	1,401	85	13	26,031	19,043	73	11
Outside MSA.....................	5,285	4,523	86	42	106,511	83,163	78	49
Census Geographic Division								
New England	386	326	85	3	7,488	5,871	78	3
Middle Atlantic	1,633	1,334	82	12	30,060	21,599	72	13
East North Central.................	2,421	2,111	87	20	39,820	30,142	76	18
West North Central	1,710	1,507	88	14	27,186	20,551	76	12
South Atlantic...................	1,875	1,669	89	16	39,043	32,012	82	19
East South Central.................	1,164	1,101	95	10	25,482	21,731	85	13
West South Central	1,988	1,790	90	17	35,116	28,702	82	17
Mountain	1,020	443	43	4	12,995	4,579	35	3
Pacific...........................	837	444	53	4	11,179	4,608	41	3
Age								
16 to 17 years	584	468	80	4	11,420	9,145	80	5
18 to 24 years	1,251	1,041	83	10	23,862	18,323	77	11
25 to 34 years	2,413	2,047	85	19	44,765	33,186	74	20
35 to 44 years	3,551	2,890	81	27	62,185	45,072	72	27
45 to 54 years	2,821	2,311	82	22	47,579	35,631	75	21
55 to 64 years	1,450	1,166	80	11	25,236	18,170	72	11
65 years and older	965	801	83	7	13,321	10,267	77	6
Sex								
Male...........................	11,845	9,766	82	91	214,300	158,552	74	93
Female	1,190	957	80	9	14,068	11,243	80	7
Ethnicity								
Hispanic	428	293	68	3	5,139	2,581	50	2
Non-Hispanic....................	12,606	10,431	83	97	223,228	167,213	75	98
Race								
White	12,568	10,377	83	97	221,019	164,095	74	97
Black..........................	297	248	84	2	5,383	4,641	86	3
Asian..........................	*32	...	...	...	*332	...	...	...
All others......................	138	80	58	1	1,634	924	57	1
Annual Household Income								
Less than $10,000	247	203	82	2	4,525	3,806	84	2
$10,000 to $19,999	525	395	75	4	8,889	6,591	74	4
$20,000 to $24,999	565	471	83	4	10,747	7,963	74	5
$25,000 to $29,999	763	659	86	6	15,600	11,962	77	7
$30,000 to $34,999	830	624	75	6	14,532	9,427	65	6
$35,000 to $39,999	773	655	85	6	15,387	11,985	78	7
$40,000 to $49,999	1,569	1,252	80	12	26,000	18,762	72	11
$50,000 to $74,999	2,915	2,409	83	22	52,593	38,304	73	23
$75,000 to $99,999	1,525	1,221	80	11	25,935	18,776	72	11
$100,000 or more.................	1,267	1,103	87	10	17,879	13,215	74	8
Not reported.....................	2,057	1,733	84	16	36,283	29,005	80	17
Education								
11 years or less	1,771	1,453	82	14	36,091	28,140	78	17
12 years	4,973	4,055	82	38	97,298	71,278	73	42
1 to 3 years college.................	3,412	2,752	81	26	53,206	38,875	73	23
4 years college...................	1,814	1,546	85	14	27,554	21,035	76	12
5 or more years college.............	1,065	917	86	9	14,219	10,467	74	6

* Estimate based on a small sample size.   ... Sample size too small to report data reliably.
[1] Hunters on private land include those who hunted on both private and public land.
[2] Days of hunting on private land includes both days spent solely on private land and those spent on private and public land.
Note: Percent of total hunters and percent of total days are based on the total hunters and total days columns for each row. Percent of hunters using private land and percent of days on private land are based on the total number of hunters on private land and total number of days on private land, respectively.

Table 31. Anglers Fishing From Boats and Days of Participation by Type of Fishing: 2001

(Population 16 years old and older. Numbers in thousands)

Participants and days of fishing	Total, all fishing		Freshwater, excludes Great Lakes		Great Lakes		Saltwater	
	Number	Percent	Number	Percent	Number	Percent	Number	Percent
Total anglers.........................	34,071	100	27,913	100	1,847	100	9,051	100
Anglers fishing from boats	19,481	57	14,787	53	1,193	65	6,261	69
Total days of fishing	557,394	100	443,247	100	23,138	100	90,838	100
Days fishing from boats	258,159	46	190,976	43	12,044	52	55,139	61

Note: Detail does not add to total because of multiple responses and nonresponses.

Table 32. Participation in Ice Fishing and Fly-Fishing: 2001

(Population 16 years old and older. Numbers in thousands)

Anglers and days	Number	Percent
Total anglers...	34,071	100
Ice anglers	2,332	7
Fly-anglers	4,192	12
Total days of fishing..	557,394	100
Days of ice fishing..	20,819	4
Days of fly-fishing..	39,758	7

Note: Detail does not add to total because of multiple responses.

Table 33. Hunters Using Bows and Arrows, Muzzleloaders, and Other Primitive Firearms for Hunting: 2001

(Population 16 years old and older. Numbers in thousands)

Hunters	Number	Percent
Total hunters...	13,034	100
Hunters using bow and arrow..	3,070	24
Hunters using muzzleloader or other primitive firearm................................	2,050	16
Total days of hunting...	228,368	100
With bow and arrow	38,705	17
With muzzleloader or other primitive firearm	12,841	6

Note: Detail does not add to total because of multiple responses.

Table 34. Land Owned or Leased for the Primary Purpose of Fishing or Hunting: 2001

(Population 16 years of age or older. Numbers in thousands)

Fishing and hunting	Number	Percent
LAND OWNERSHIP		
Sportspersons Owning Land		
Total sportspersons	**1,752**	**100**
Anglers..	849	48
Hunters..	1,061	61
Acres Owned		
Total acres owned..	**141,769**	**100**
Acres for fishing	23,985	17
Acres for hunting...	117,784	83
Expenditures for Land Owned		
Total expenditures	**6,343,397**	**100**
For fishing	2,992,008	47
For hunting..	3,351,389	53
LAND LEASING		
Sportspersons Leasing Land		
Total sportspersons	**1,151**	**100**
Anglers..	200	17
Hunters..	982	85
Acres Leased		
Total acres leased..	**226,585**	**100**
Acres for fishing	1,310	1
Acres for hunters	225,275	99
Expenditures for Land Leased		
Total expenditures	**785,088**	**100**
For fishing	160,586	20
For hunting..	624,503	80

Note: Detail does not add to total because of multiple responses and nonresponse.

U.S. Fish & Wildlife Service

Table 35. Why Anglers and Hunters Did Not Participate More in 2001

(Population 16 years old and older. Numbers in thousands)

Reason	Number	Percent
ANGLERS		
Total anglers	**34,071**	**100**
Anglers who did not fish as much in 2001 as they would have liked to	19,114	56
Reasons:		
Not enough time	10,778	32
Family or work obligations	10,289	30
School	836	2
Not enough money/cost too much	1,198	4
Personal health or disability	1,359	4
No one to fish with	649	2
Not enough places to fish/not enough access	232	1
Fishing places too crowded	79	(Z)
Did not know where to go	*65	*(Z)
Catch limits too restrictive	*32	*(Z)
Length of fishing season too restrictive	*26	*(Z)
Not enough fish	185	1
Fear of traveling due to terrorist attack	...	...
Weather	499	1
Pollution or litter	*46	*(Z)
Other	271	1
HUNTERS		
Total hunters	**13,034**	**100**
Hunters who did not hunt as much in 2001 as they would have liked to	8,278	64
Reasons:		
Not enough time	3,952	30
Family or work obligations	4,653	36
School	488	4
Not enough money/cost too much	542	4
Personal health or disability	614	5
No one to hunt with	225	2
Not enough places to hunt/not enough access	162	1
Hunting places too crowded	*49	*(Z)
Did not know where to go	*62	*(Z)
Bag limits too restrictive	*32	*(Z)
Length of hunting season too restrictive	198	2
Did not draw a special license in lottery	65	1
Not enough game	134	1
Fear of traveling due to terrorist attack	...	...
Weather	237	2
Pollution or litter	...	...
Other	128	1

* Estimate based on a small sample size.   ... Sample size too small to report data reliably.   (Z) Less than 0.5 percent.

Note: Detail does not add to total because of multiple responses and nonresponse.

Table 36. Wildlife-Watching Participants by Type of Activity: 2001

(Population 16 years old and older. Numbers in thousands)

Activity	Number	Percent	Activity	Number	Percent
Total participants	**66,105**	**100**	Residential (around the home)	62,928	95
			Observe wildlife	42,111	64
Nonresidential (away from home)	21,823	33	Photograph wildlife	13,937	21
Observe wildlife	20,080	30	Feed wildlife	53,988	82
Photograph wildlife	9,427	14	Visit public parks or areas[1]	10,981	17
Feed wildlife	7,077	11	Maintain plantings or natural areas	13,072	20

[1] Includes visits only to parks or publicly held areas within one mile of home.

Note: Detail does not add to total because of multiple responses.

Table 37. Participants, Trips, and Days of Participation in Nonresidential (Away From Home) Wildlife-Watching Activities: 2001

(Population 16 years old and older. Numbers in thousands)

Participants, trips, and days of participation	Number	Percent	Participants, trips, and days of participation	Number	Percent
PARTICIPANTS			**DAYS**		
Total participants	**21,823**	**100**	Total days	372,006	100
Observe wildlife	20,080	92	Observing wildlife	295,345	79
Photograph wildlife	9,427	43	Photographing wildlife	76,324	21
Feed wildlife	7,077	32	Feeding wildlife	103,307	28
TRIPS			Average days per participant	17	(X)
Total trips	**230,631**	**100**	Observing wildlife	15	(X)
Average days per trip	2	(X)	Photographing wildlife	8	(X)
			Feeding wildlife	15	(X)

(X) Not applicable.

Note: Detail does not add to total because of multiple responses and nonresponse.

Table 38. Nonresidential (Away From Home) Wildlife-Watching Participants by Area or Site Visited: 2001

(Population 16 years old and older. Numbers in thousands)

Area or site visited	Number	Percent	Area or site visited	Number	Percent
AREA			**SITE**		
Total, all areas............	**21,823**	**100**	**Total, all sites**.............	**21,823**	**100**
Public only	10,616	49	Oceanside	5,192	24
Private only..............	2,529	12	Lake and streamside.......	13,699	63
Public and private........	6,051	28	Marsh, wetland, swamp	9,091	42
Not reported	2,627	12	Woodland	14,859	68
			Brush-covered area.......	12,476	57
			Open field.............	12,468	57
			Man-made area...........	6,167	28
			Other...................	2,536	12

Note: Detail does not add to total because of multiple responses and nonresponse.

Table 39. Participation in Residential (Around the Home) Wildlife-Watching Activities: 2001

(Population 16 years old and older. Numbers in thousands)

Activity	Number	Percent	Activity	Number	Percent
Total residential participants.......	**62,928**	**100**	**PHOTOGRAPH WILDLIFE**		
Observe wildlife..............	42,111	67			
Visit public parks or other public			**Participants photographing:**		
areas[1].........................	10,981	17	Total, 1 day or more...........	13,937	100
Photograph wildlife	13,937	22	1 day........................	2,106	15
Feed wildlife.................	53,988	86	2 to 3 days	3,889	28
Maintain natural areas	8,671	14	4 to 5 days	2,200	16
Maintain plantings	8,732	14	6 to 10 days	2,335	17
			11 to 20 days	1,336	10
OBSERVE WILDLIFE			21 days or more	1,797	13
Participants observing:					
			FEED WILDLIFE		
Total, all wildlife..............	42,111	100	**Participants feeding:**		
Birds	40,306	96	Total, all wildlife..............	53,988	100
Land mammals, all............	34,641	82	Wild birds...................	52,558	97
Large mammals	17,481	42	Other wildlife	18,793	35
Small mammals	32,747	78			
Amphibians or reptiles.........	9,773	23	**MAINTAIN NATURAL AREAS**		
Insects or spiders	13,835	33			
Fish or other wildlife	7,932	19	**Participants maintaining:**		
			Total, all acreages..............	8,671	100
Participants observing:			1 acre or less................	5,425	63
			2 to 10 acres.................	2,239	26
Total, 1 day or more...........	42,111	100	11 to 50 acres................	676	8
1 to 10 days	8,176	19	More than 50 acres............	202	2
11 to 20 days	3,551	8			
21 to 50 days	5,640	13	**MAINTAIN PLANTINGS**		
51 to 100 days	6,520	15			
101 to 200 days	5,735	14	**Participants maintaining**		
201 days or more	11,376	27	plantings.....................	8,732	100
VISIT PUBLIC PARKS OR OTHER AREAS[1]			**Participants spending:**		
			Less than $25	4,400	50
Participants visiting:			$25 to $75....................	1,931	22
			More than $75	1,920	22
Total, 1 day or more...........	10,981	100			
1 to 5 days	5,553	51	Average expenditure per		
6 to 10 days	1,693	15	participant for plantings...........	80	(X)
11 days or more	3,527	32			

(X) Not applicable.

[1] Includes visits only to parks or publicly held areas within 1 mile of home.

Note: Detail does not add to total because of multiple responses and nonresponse.

Table 40. **Nonresidential (Away From Home) Wildlife-Watching Participants by Wildlife Observed, Photographed, or Fed and Place: 2001**

(Population 16 years old and older. Numbers in thousands)

Wildlife observed, photographed, or fed	Total participants		Participation by place					
			Total		In state of residence		In other states	
	Number	Percent	Number	Percent	Number	Percent	Number	Percent
Total, all wildlife	21,823	100	21,823	100	18,041	83	6,570	30
Total birds..........................	18,580	85	18,580	100	16,150	87	5,855	32
Songbirds...........................	12,878	59	12,878	100	11,182	87	3,860	30
Birds of prey	12,495	57	12,495	100	10,596	85	4,060	32
Waterfowl..........................	14,432	66	14,432	100	12,384	86	4,258	30
Other water birds (shorebirds, herons, pelicans, etc.)	10,314	47	10,314	100	8,474	82	3,229	31
Other birds (pheasants, turkeys, road runners, etc.)	7,907	36	7,907	100	6,640	84	2,248	28
Total land mammals	15,506	71	15,506	100	13,207	85	4,844	31
Large land mammals (deer, bear, etc.)...	12,226	56	12,226	100	10,047	82	3,784	31
Small land mammals (squirrel, prairie dog, etc.)	12,958	59	12,958	100	10,911	84	4,200	32
Fish..............................	6,330	29	6,330	100	5,019	79	2,000	32
Marine mammals.....................	3,013	14	3,013	100	1,982	66	1,233	41
Other wildlife (turtles, butterflies, etc.)	9,409	43	9,409	100	7,929	84	3,071	33

Note: Detail does not add to total because of multiple responses. Column showing percent of total participants is based on the "Total, all wildlife" number. Participation by place percent columns are based on the total number of participants for each type of wildlife.

Table 41. **Wild Bird Observers and Days of Observation: 2001**

(Population 16 years old and older. Numbers in thousands)

Observers and days of observation	Number	Percent
OBSERVERS		
Total bird observers...	45,951	100
Residential (around the home) observers	40,306	88
Nonresidential (away from home) observers	18,342	40
DAYS		
Total days observing birds	5,467,841	100
Residential (around the home)	5,159,259	94
Nonresidential (away from home).....................................	308,583	6

Note: Detail does not add to total because of multiple responses.

Table 42. **Number of Participants Who Can Identify Wild Birds by Sight or Sound and Who Keep Birding Life Lists: 2001**

(Population 16 years old and older. Numbers in thousands)

Participants	Number	Percent
Total bird observers...	45,951	100
Observers who can identify:		
1-20 bird species...	33,980	74
21-40 bird species..	5,934	13
41 or more species..	3,887	8
Observers who keep birding life lists...................................	2,315	5

Note: Detail does not add to total because of nonresponse.

Table 43. Expenditures for Wildlife Watching: 2001

(Population 16 years old and older)

Expenditure item	Expenditures (thousands of dollars)	Spenders		
		Number (thousands)	Percent of wildlife-watching participants[1]	Average per spender (dollars)
Total, all items[2]	**38,414,488**	**52,083**	**79**	**738**
TRIP-RELATED EXPENDITURES				
Total trip-related	**8,162,439**	**18,224**	**84**	**448**
Food and lodging, total..................................	**4,818,843**	**15,365**	**70**	**314**
Food...	2,835,868	15,263	70	186
Lodging	1,982,975	5,648	26	351
Transportation, total	**2,595,542**	**17,091**	**78**	**152**
Public...	702,231	1,986	9	354
Private	1,893,311	16,495	76	115
Other trip costs, total	**748,054**	**6,350**	**29**	**118**
Guide fees, pack trip or package fees........................	113,034	1,209	6	94
Public land use fees...	114,813	3,879	18	30
Private land use fees..	50,430	869	4	58
Equipment rental	105,198	1,156	5	91
Boating costs[3]	326,461	1,056	5	309
Heating and cooking fuel	38,118	1,586	7	24
EQUIPMENT AND OTHER EXPENSES				
Total..	**30,252,049**	**47,939**	**73**	**631**
Wildlife-watching equipment, total	**7,353,977**	**45,802**	**69**	**161**
Binoculars, spotting scopes..................................	507,387	4,683	7	108
Cameras, video cameras, special lenses, and other photographic equipment	1,656,755	4,454	7	372
Film and developing	910,423	13,528	20	67
Bird food, total	2,604,692	38,435	58	68
Commercially prepared and packaged wild bird food..........	2,034,825	35,738	54	57
Other bulk foods used to feed wild birds....................	569,867	12,742	19	45
Feed for other wildlife......................................	503,006	9,595	15	52
Nest boxes, bird houses, feeders, baths	732,671	15,888	24	46
Day packs, carrying cases, and special clothing	323,043	2,949	4	110
Other wildlife-watching equipment (such as field guides and maps)...	116,000	3,688	6	31
Auxiliary equipment, total	**716,900**	**3,807**	**6**	**188**
Tents, tarps...	185,552	1,956	3	95
Frame packs and backpacking equipment	129,382	1,091	2	119
Other camping equipment	266,382	1,966	3	136
Other auxiliary equipment (such as blinds)	135,583	308	(Z)	441
Special equipment, total	**15,468,716**	**1,410**	**2**	**10,971**
Off-the-road vehicle...	6,677,688	543	1	12,300
Travel or tent trailer, pickup, camper, van, motor home, house trailer, recreational vehicle (RV)	6,272,294	413	1	15,196
Boats, boat accessories	996,463	464	1	2,150
Cabins...	...	...	...	...
Other..	*572,396	*75	*(Z)	*7,614
Magazines, books..	331,955	8,297	13	40
Land leasing and ownership.................................	4,761,010	555	1	8,585
Membership dues and contributions..........................	920,183	7,746	12	119
Plantings..	699,309	5,649	9	124

* Estimate based on a small sample size.   ... Sample size too small to report data reliably.   (Z) Less than 0.5 percent.

[1] Percent of wildlife-watching participants column is based on nonresidential participants for trip-related expenditures. For equipment and other expenditures the percent of wildlife-watching participants is based on total participants.

[2] Information on trip-related expenditures was collected for nonresidential participants only. Equipment and other expenditures are based on information collected from both nonresidential and residential participants.

[3] Boating costs include launching, mooring, storage, maintenance, insurance, pumpout fees, and fuel.

Note: Detail does not add to total because of multiple responses and nonresponse.

Table 44. Selected Characteristics of Participants in Nonresidential (Away From Home) Wildlife-Watching Activities: 2001

(Population 16 years old and older. Numbers in thousands)

Characteristic	U.S. population Number	U.S. population Percent	Total wildlife-watching participants Number	Total wildlife-watching participants Percent who participated	Total wildlife-watching participants Percent	Total nonresidential participants Number	Total nonresidential participants Percent who participated	Total nonresidential participants Percent
Total persons....................	212,298	100	66,105	31	100	21,823	10	100
Population Density of Residence								
Urban.	157,943	74	42,214	27	64	14,838	9	68
Rural.	54,355	26	23,891	44	36	6,986	13	32
Population Size of Residence								
Metropolitan statistical area (MSA).......	171,147	81	49,414	29	75	16,536	10	76
1,000,000 or more.	112,984	53	29,724	26	45	10,126	9	46
250,000 to 999,999.	41,469	20	12,880	31	19	4,191	10	19
50,000 to 249,999.	16,693	8	6,811	41	10	2,218	13	10
Outside MSA	41,151	19	16,691	41	25	5,287	13	24
Census Geographic Division								
New England.	10,575	5	3,875	37	6	1,155	11	5
Middle Atlantic	29,806	14	8,740	29	13	2,849	10	13
East North Central	34,082	16	11,631	34	18	3,571	10	16
West North Central.	14,430	7	6,206	43	9	2,059	14	9
South Atlantic	39,286	19	11,395	29	17	3,469	9	16
East South Central	12,976	6	4,514	35	7	1,086	8	5
West South Central.	23,337	11	5,747	25	9	1,822	8	8
Mountain	13,308	6	4,619	35	7	2,019	15	9
Pacific	34,498	16	9,377	27	14	3,793	11	17
Age								
16 to 17 years	7,709	4	1,678	22	3	688	9	3
18 to 24 years	22,234	10	3,051	14	5	1,364	6	6
25 to 34 years	35,333	17	8,869	25	13	3,770	11	17
35 to 44 years	44,057	21	14,939	34	23	5,701	13	26
45 to 54 years	40,541	19	14,491	36	22	4,991	12	23
55 to 64 years	25,601	12	10,326	40	16	2,929	11	13
65 years and older	36,823	17	12,752	35	19	2,381	6	11
Sex								
Male, total	101,916	48	30,695	30	46	11,387	11	52
16 to 17 years	4,106	2	864	21	1	424	10	2
18 to 24 years	11,326	5	1,559	14	2	812	7	4
25 to 34 years	17,206	8	3,969	23	6	1,801	10	8
35 to 44 years	21,346	10	6,951	33	11	2,840	13	13
45 to 54 years	19,626	9	6,772	35	10	2,623	13	12
55 to 64 years	12,201	6	4,802	39	7	1,549	13	7
65 years and older	16,105	8	5,778	36	9	1,338	8	6
Female, total	110,381	52	35,409	32	54	10,436	9	48
16 to 17 years	3,603	2	814	23	1	263	7	1
18 to 24 years	10,908	5	1,493	14	2	551	5	3
25 to 34 years	18,127	9	4,899	27	7	1,969	11	9
35 to 44 years	22,711	11	7,987	35	12	2,862	13	13
45 to 54 years	20,915	10	7,719	37	12	2,367	11	11
55 to 64 years	13,400	6	5,523	41	8	1,380	10	6
65 years and older	20,718	10	6,974	34	11	1,044	5	5
Ethnicity								
Hispanic.	21,910	10	2,699	12	4	890	4	4
Non-Hispanic	190,388	90	63,406	33	96	20,933	11	96
Race								
White.	181,129	85	62,781	35	95	20,823	11	95
Black.	21,708	10	2,029	9	3	529	2	2
Asian.	7,141	3	654	9	1	178	2	1
All others.	2,320	1	641	28	1	294	13	1
Annual Household Income								
Less than $10,000	10,594	5	2,387	23	4	491	5	2
$10,000 to $19,999.	15,272	7	3,837	25	6	867	6	4
$20,000 to $24,999.	10,902	5	2,879	26	4	854	8	4
$25,000 to $29,999.	11,217	5	3,461	31	5	1,109	10	5
$30,000 to $34,999.	11,648	5	4,069	35	6	1,459	13	7
$35,000 to $39,999.	9,816	5	3,142	32	5	1,109	11	5
$40,000 to $49,999.	16,896	8	6,402	38	10	2,365	14	11
$50,000 to $74,999.	31,383	15	12,359	39	19	4,585	15	21
$75,000 to $99,999.	17,762	8	7,735	44	12	2,910	16	13
$100,000 or more.	19,202	9	8,010	42	12	2,871	15	13
Not reported	57,606	27	11,823	21	18	3,202	6	15
Education								
11 years or less	32,820	15	7,201	22	11	1,844	6	8
12 years	73,719	35	21,154	29	32	5,938	8	27
1 to 3 years college	49,491	23	16,013	32	24	5,796	12	27
4 years college.	34,803	16	12,603	36	19	4,464	13	20
5 or more years college.	21,464	10	9,133	43	14	3,781	18	17

See footnotes at end of table.

Table 44. Selected Characteristics of Participants in Nonresidential (Away From Home) Wildlife-Watching Activities: 2001—Continued

(Population 16 years old and older. Numbers in thousands)

Characteristic	Observe			Photograph			Feed		
	Number	Percent who participated	Percent	Number	Percent who participated	Percent	Number	Percent who participated	Percent
Total persons......................	20,080	9	100	9,427	4	100	7,077	3	100
Population Density of Residence									
Urban.............................	13,677	9	68	6,653	4	71	4,819	3	68
Rural.............................	6,403	12	32	2,774	5	29	2,259	4	32
Population Size of Residence									
Metropolitan statistical area (MSA).......	15,232	9	76	7,251	4	77	5,651	3	80
1,000,000 or more.................	9,343	8	47	4,642	4	49	3,447	3	49
250,000 to 999,999.................	3,866	9	19	1,720	4	18	1,392	3	20
50,000 to 249,999.................	2,024	12	10	888	5	9	812	5	11
Outside MSA	4,848	12	24	2,176	5	23	1,426	3	20
Census Geographic Division									
New England......................	1,097	10	5	480	5	5	295	3	4
Middle Atlantic....................	2,661	9	13	1,170	4	12	887	3	13
East North Central.................	3,280	10	16	1,393	4	15	1,215	4	17
West North Central.................	1,947	13	10	725	5	8	636	4	9
South Atlantic.....................	3,144	8	16	1,550	4	16	1,388	4	20
East South Central.................	1,009	8	5	430	3	5	392	3	6
West South Central.................	1,541	7	8	708	3	8	861	4	12
Mountain.........................	1,916	14	10	1,119	8	12	373	3	5
Pacific...........................	3,484	10	17	1,853	5	20	1,029	3	15
Age									
16 to 17 years.....................	636	8	3	270	4	3	249	3	4
18 to 24 years.....................	1,261	6	6	541	2	6	434	2	6
25 to 34 years.....................	3,393	10	17	1,500	4	16	1,453	4	21
35 to 44 years.....................	5,310	12	26	2,673	6	28	1,736	4	25
45 to 54 years.....................	4,673	12	23	2,508	6	27	1,570	4	22
55 to 64 years.....................	2,698	11	13	1,129	4	12	909	4	13
65 years and older..................	2,111	6	11	806	2	9	726	2	10
Sex									
Male, total	10,330	10	51	4,739	5	50	3,498	3	49
16 to 17 years	384	9	2	*156	*4	*2	*174	*4	*2
18 to 24 years	743	7	4	315	3	3	234	2	3
25 to 34 years	1,594	9	8	734	4	8	621	4	9
35 to 44 years	2,623	12	13	1,171	5	12	766	4	11
45 to 54 years	2,407	12	12	1,304	7	14	822	4	12
55 to 64 years	1,403	11	7	587	5	6	534	4	8
65 years and older	1,176	7	6	472	3	5	346	2	5
Female, total.....................	9,751	9	49	4,688	4	50	3,580	3	51
16 to 17 years	252	7	1	*115	*3	*1	*75	*2	*1
18 to 24 years	518	5	3	226	2	2	200	2	3
25 to 34 years	1,799	10	9	766	4	8	832	5	12
35 to 44 years	2,687	12	13	1,502	7	16	970	4	14
45 to 54 years	2,266	11	11	1,204	6	13	748	4	11
55 to 64 years	1,295	10	6	542	4	6	375	3	5
65 years and older	935	5	5	333	2	4	379	2	5
Ethnicity									
Hispanic..........................	806	4	4	447	2	5	345	2	5
Non-Hispanic	19,275	10	96	8,980	5	95	6,732	4	95
Race									
White.............................	19,181	11	96	8,965	5	95	6,673	4	94
Black.............................	472	2	2	*207	*1	*2	287	1	4
Asian.............................	159	2	1	*109	*2	*1	...	...	...
All others.........................	269	12	1	146	6	2	*92	*4	*1
Annual Household Income									
Less than $10,000	473	4	2	*153	*1	*2	171	2	2
$10,000 to $19,999.................	790	5	4	282	2	3	362	2	5
$20,000 to $24,999.................	783	7	4	373	3	4	382	4	5
$25,000 to $29,999.................	1,004	9	5	388	3	4	474	4	7
$30,000 to $34,999.................	1,363	12	7	586	5	6	506	4	7
$35,000 to $39,999.................	990	10	5	415	4	4	358	4	5
$40,000 to $49,999.................	2,163	13	11	1,008	6	11	674	4	10
$50,000 to $74,999.................	4,219	13	21	2,151	7	23	1,395	4	20
$75,000 to $99,999.................	2,723	15	14	1,298	7	14	992	6	14
$100,000 or more..................	2,671	14	13	1,382	7	15	787	4	11
Not reported	2,903	5	14	1,390	2	15	976	2	14
Education									
11 years or less....................	1,696	5	8	622	2	7	742	2	10
12 years..........................	5,368	7	27	2,282	3	24	2,125	3	30
1 to 3 years college.................	5,207	11	26	2,514	5	27	1,994	4	28
4 years college.....................	4,171	12	21	2,042	6	22	1,236	4	17
5 or more years college..............	3,637	17	18	1,967	9	21	981	5	14

* Estimate based on a small sample size.　　　... Sample size too small to report data reliably.

Note: Detail does not add to total because of multiple responses. Percent who participated columns show the percent of each row's population who participated in the activity named by the column. Percent columns show the percent of each column's participants who are described by the row heading.

Table 45. Selected Characteristics of Participants in Residential (Around the Home) Wildlife-Watching Activities: 2001

(Population 16 years old and older. Numbers in thousands)

Characteristic	U.S. population		Total wildlife-watching participants			Total residential participants		
	Number	Percent	Number	Percent who participated	Percent	Number	Percent who participated	Percent
Total persons	**212,298**	**100**	**66,105**	**31**	**100**	**62,928**	**30**	**100**
Population Density of Residence								
Urban	157,943	74	42,214	27	64	39,715	25	63
Rural..........................	54,355	26	23,891	44	36	23,214	43	37
Population Size of Residence								
Metropolitan statistical area (MSA)	171,147	81	49,414	29	75	46,889	27	75
1,000,000 or more...............	112,984	53	29,724	26	45	28,152	25	45
250,000 to 999,999.............	41,469	20	12,880	31	19	12,210	29	19
50,000 to 249,999..............	16,693	8	6,811	41	10	6,527	39	10
Outside MSA....................	41,151	19	16,691	41	25	16,040	39	25
Census Geographic Division								
New England...................	10,575	5	3,875	37	6	3,765	36	6
Middle Atlantic.................	29,806	14	8,740	29	13	8,452	28	13
East North Central	34,082	16	11,631	34	18	11,196	33	18
West North Central..............	14,430	7	6,206	43	9	5,938	41	9
South Atlantic	39,286	19	11,395	29	17	10,911	28	17
East South Central	12,976	6	4,514	35	7	4,390	34	7
West South Central..............	23,337	11	5,747	25	9	5,490	24	9
Mountain......................	13,308	6	4,619	35	7	4,282	32	7
Pacific........................	34,498	16	9,377	27	14	8,504	25	14
Age								
16 to 17 years	7,709	4	1,678	22	3	1,504	20	2
18 to 24 years	22,234	10	3,051	14	5	2,693	12	4
25 to 34 years	35,333	17	8,869	25	13	8,137	23	13
35 to 44 years	44,057	21	14,939	34	23	14,101	32	22
45 to 54 years	40,541	19	14,491	36	22	13,899	34	22
55 to 64 years	25,601	12	10,326	40	16	10,084	39	16
65 years and older	36,823	17	12,752	35	19	12,511	34	20
Sex								
Male, total.....................	101,916	48	30,695	30	46	28,825	28	46
16 to 17 years.................	4,106	2	864	21	1	736	18	1
18 to 24 years.................	11,326	5	1,559	14	2	1,362	12	2
25 to 34 years.................	17,206	8	3,969	23	6	3,575	21	6
35 to 44 years.................	21,346	10	6,951	33	11	6,446	30	10
45 to 54 years.................	19,626	9	6,772	35	10	6,427	33	10
55 to 64 years.................	12,201	6	4,802	39	7	4,663	38	7
65 years and older..............	16,105	8	5,778	36	9	5,616	35	9
Female, total	110,381	52	35,409	32	54	34,103	31	54
16 to 17 years.................	3,603	2	814	23	1	768	21	1
18 to 24 years.................	10,908	5	1,493	14	2	1,332	12	2
25 to 34 years.................	18,127	9	4,899	27	7	4,562	25	7
35 to 44 years.................	22,711	11	7,987	35	12	7,655	34	12
45 to 54 years.................	20,915	10	7,719	37	12	7,472	36	12
55 to 64 years.................	13,400	6	5,523	41	8	5,420	40	9
65 years and older..............	20,718	10	6,974	34	11	6,895	33	11
Ethnicity								
Hispanic	21,910	10	2,699	12	4	2,486	11	4
Non-Hispanic...................	190,388	90	63,406	33	96	60,443	32	96
Race								
White	181,129	85	62,781	35	95	59,815	33	95
Black	21,708	10	2,029	9	3	1,927	9	3
Asian	7,141	3	654	9	1	593	8	1
All others	2,320	1	641	28	1	593	26	1
Annual Household Income								
Less than $10,000	10,594	5	2,387	23	4	2,344	22	4
$10,000 to $19,999.............	15,272	7	3,837	25	6	3,728	24	6
$20,000 to $24,999.............	10,902	5	2,879	26	4	2,765	25	4
$25,000 to $29,999.............	11,217	5	3,461	31	5	3,304	29	5
$30,000 to $34,999.............	11,648	5	4,069	35	6	3,799	33	6
$35,000 to $39,999.............	9,816	5	3,142	32	5	2,950	30	5
$40,000 to $49,999.............	16,896	8	6,402	38	10	6,070	36	10
$50,000 to $74,999.............	31,383	15	12,359	39	19	11,564	37	18
$75,000 to $99,999.............	17,762	8	7,735	44	12	7,349	41	12
$100,000 or more...............	19,202	9	8,010	42	12	7,705	40	12
Not reported...................	57,606	27	11,823	21	18	11,351	20	18
Education								
11 years or less	32,820	15	7,201	22	11	6,849	21	11
12 years......................	73,719	35	21,154	29	32	20,255	27	32
1 to 3 years college	49,491	23	16,013	32	24	15,199	31	24
4 years college.................	34,803	16	12,603	36	19	11,931	34	19
5 or more years college...........	21,464	10	9,133	43	14	8,696	41	14

See footnotes at end of table.

(Population 16 years old and older. Numbers in thousands)

Characteristic	Residential participants								
	Observe			Photograph			Feed wild birds		
	Number	Percent who participated	Percent	Number	Percent who participated	Percent	Number	Percent who participated	Percent
Total persons	**42,111**	**20**	**100**	**13,937**	**7**	**100**	**52,558**	**25**	**100**
Population Density of Residence									
Urban	26,142	17	62	8,066	5	58	32,452	21	62
Rural........................	15,969	29	38	5,872	11	42	20,106	37	38
Population Size of Residence									
Metropolitan statistical area (MSA)	31,289	18	74	10,358	6	74	38,758	23	74
1,000,000 or more..............	18,749	17	45	6,036	5	43	22,722	20	43
250,000 to 999,999..............	8,294	20	20	2,673	6	19	10,539	25	20
50,000 to 249,999..............	4,246	25	10	1,649	10	12	5,497	33	10
Outside MSA..................	10,822	26	26	3,579	9	26	13,800	34	26
Census Geographic Division									
New England..................	2,650	25	6	919	9	7	3,203	30	6
Middle Atlantic	5,813	20	14	1,994	7	14	6,795	23	13
East North Central	7,554	22	18	2,344	7	17	9,896	29	19
West North Central..............	3,977	28	9	1,401	10	10	5,074	35	10
South Atlantic	7,027	18	17	2,342	6	17	9,257	24	18
East South Central	2,783	21	7	742	6	5	4,006	31	8
West South Central..............	3,654	16	9	1,014	4	7	4,831	21	9
Mountain.....................	3,065	23	7	1,137	9	8	3,211	24	6
Pacific........................	5,588	16	13	2,045	6	15	6,285	18	12
Age									
16 to 17 years	848	11	2	421	5	3	933	12	2
18 to 24 years	1,514	7	4	580	3	4	1,815	8	3
25 to 34 years	5,332	15	13	1,725	5	12	6,159	17	12
35 to 44 years	9,413	21	22	3,475	8	25	11,430	26	22
45 to 54 years	9,804	24	23	3,542	9	25	11,874	29	23
55 to 64 years	6,768	26	16	2,363	9	17	8,879	35	17
65 years and older	8,432	23	20	1,832	5	13	11,470	31	22
Sex									
Male, total....................	19,132	19	45	6,287	6	45	23,451	23	45
16 to 17 years..............	420	10	1	*157	*4	*1	501	12	1
18 to 24 years..............	823	7	2	261	2	2	818	7	2
25 to 34 years..............	2,256	13	5	864	5	6	2,672	16	5
35 to 44 years..............	4,307	20	10	1,337	6	10	5,017	24	10
45 to 54 years..............	4,400	22	10	1,626	8	12	5,370	27	10
55 to 64 years..............	3,069	25	7	1,114	9	8	4,022	33	8
65 years and older..............	3,857	24	9	928	6	7	5,051	31	10
Female, total	22,979	21	55	7,651	7	55	29,107	26	55
16 to 17 years..............	428	12	1	264	7	2	432	12	1
18 to 24 years..............	691	6	2	319	3	2	996	9	2
25 to 34 years..............	3,075	17	7	861	5	6	3,487	19	7
35 to 44 years..............	5,106	22	12	2,137	9	15	6,412	28	12
45 to 54 years..............	5,404	26	13	1,916	9	14	6,504	31	12
55 to 64 years..............	3,699	28	9	1,249	9	9	4,857	36	9
65 years and older..............	4,575	22	11	904	4	6	6,418	31	12
Ethnicity									
Hispanic	1,663	8	4	394	2	3	2,033	9	4
Non-Hispanic.................	40,447	21	96	13,543	7	97	50,525	27	96
Race									
White	40,191	22	95	13,570	7	97	50,238	28	96
Black	1,209	6	3	*141	*1	*1	1,449	7	3
Asian	315	4	1	*113	*2	*1	413	6	1
All others	396	17	1	113	5	1	459	20	1
Annual Household Income									
Less than $10,000	1,460	14	3	245	2	2	1,965	19	4
$10,000 to $19,999..............	2,436	16	6	499	3	4	3,313	22	6
$20,000 to $24,999..............	1,772	16	4	690	6	5	2,295	21	4
$25,000 to $29,999..............	2,256	20	5	666	6	5	2,769	25	5
$30,000 to $34,999..............	2,731	23	6	781	7	6	3,156	27	6
$35,000 to $39,999..............	1,886	19	4	572	6	4	2,487	25	5
$40,000 to $49,999..............	4,146	25	10	1,416	8	10	4,987	30	9
$50,000 to $74,999..............	7,827	25	19	2,973	9	21	9,561	30	18
$75,000 to $99,999..............	5,068	29	12	1,697	10	12	6,126	34	12
$100,000 or more..............	5,391	28	13	2,065	11	15	6,193	32	12
Not reported....................	7,139	12	17	2,334	4	17	9,707	17	18
Education									
11 years or less	4,253	13	10	1,011	3	7	5,763	18	11
12 years.....................	13,080	18	31	4,036	5	29	17,676	24	34
1 to 3 years college	10,335	21	25	3,630	7	26	12,479	25	24
4 years college.....................	8,001	23	19	2,838	8	20	9,654	28	18
5 or more years college..............	6,441	30	15	2,423	11	17	6,987	33	13

* Estimate based on a small sample size.
Note: Detail does not add to total because of multiple responses and nonresponse. Percent who participated columns show the percent of each row's population who participated in the activity named by the column. Percent columns show the percent of each column's participants who are described by the row heading.

Table 46. Land Owned or Leased for the Primary Purpose of Wildlife Watching: 2001

(Population 16 years of age or older)

Wildlife watching	Number (in thousands)	Average per person
Land Ownership for Wildlife Watching		
Participants owning land..	664	(X)
Acres owned..	44,144	67
Expenditures for owned land (dollars)...............................	4,459,706	6,721
Land Leasing for Wildlife Watching		
Participants leasing land...	116	(X)
Acres leased..	10,489	90
Expenditures for leased land (dollars)..............................	301,304	2,597

(X) Not applicable.

Note: Detail does not add to total because of multiple responses and nonresponse.

Table 47. Persons With Disabilities Who Participated in Wildlife Watching: 2001

(Population 16 years old and older. Numbers in thousands)

Disability	Total wildlife watching		Nonresidential		Residential	
	Number	Percent	Number	Percent	Number	Percent
Total wildlife-watching participants	**66,105**	**100**	**21,823**	**100**	**62,928**	**100**
Total disabled participants	**4,951**	**100**	**1,279**	**100**	**4,757**	**100**
Mobility impaired	3,958	80	1,038	81	3,777	79
Hearing impaired	456	9	*110	*9	447	9
Sight impaired	396	8	*50	*4	395	8
Mentally impaired	652	13	184	14	648	14

*Estimate based on a small sample size.

Note: Detail does not add to total because of multiple responses and nonresponse.

Table 48. Participation of Wildlife-Watching Participants in Fishing and Hunting: 2001

(Population 16 years old and older. Numbers in thousands)

Type of fishing and hunting	Total		Nonresidential		Residential	
	Number	Percent	Number	Percent	Number	Percent
Total participants..........................	**66,105**	**100**	**21,823**	**100**	**62,928**	**100**
Nonsportspersons...........................	44,263	67	11,739	54	43,035	68
Sportspersons...............................	21,842	33	10,084	46	19,893	32
Anglers..................................	19,712	30	9,105	42	17,991	29
Hunters.................................	8,066	12	4,005	18	7,286	12

Note: Detail does not add to total because of multiple responses and nonresponse.

Table 49. Participation of Sportspersons in Wildlife-Watching Activities: 2001

(Population 16 years old and older. Numbers in thousands)

Wildlife-watching activity	Sportspersons		Anglers		Hunters	
	Number	Percent	Number	Percent	Number	Percent
Total sportspersons	**37,805**	**100**	**34,071**	**100**	**13,034**	**100**
Sportspersons who:						
Did not engage in wildlife-watching activities.....	15,963	42	14,359	42	4,969	38
Engaged in wildlife-watching activities	21,842	58	19,712	58	8,066	62
Nonresidential	10,084	27	9,105	27	4,005	31
Residential...............................	19,893	53	17,991	53	7,286	56

Note: Detail does not add to total because of multiple responses and nonresponse.

Table 50. Participants in Wildlife-Related Recreation by Participant's State of Residence: 2001

(Population 16 years old and older. Numbers in thousands)

Participant's state of residence	Population	Total participants		Sportspersons		Wildlife-watching participants	
		Number	Percent of population	Number	Percent of population	Number	Percent of population
United States, total.....	**212,298**	**82,302**	**39**	**37,805**	**18**	**66,105**	**31**
Alabama..............	3,427	1,323	39	726	21	965	28
Alaska..............	454	320	70	205	45	241	53
Arizona..............	3,700	1,296	35	437	12	1,107	30
Arkansas..............	1,999	1,038	52	621	31	778	39
California.............	25,982	6,873	26	2,486	10	5,491	21
Colorado.............	3,215	1,518	47	679	21	1,213	38
Connecticut.............	2,536	996	39	331	13	883	35
Delaware.............	599	220	37	94	16	170	28
Florida	12,171	3,857	32	2,158	18	2,856	23
Georgia.............	6,096	1,932	32	1,136	19	1,326	22
Hawaii	916	195	21	114	12	126	14
Idaho.............	972	507	52	306	31	388	40
Illinois.............	9,244	3,148	34	1,507	16	2,492	27
Indiana	4,558	2,179	48	914	20	1,786	39
Iowa	2,201	1,212	55	580	26	983	45
Kansas	2,017	942	47	491	24	735	36
Kentucky	3,121	1,547	50	703	23	1,264	40
Louisiana	3,306	1,326	40	829	25	840	25
Maine	1,005	607	60	256	26	520	52
Maryland	4,078	1,546	38	571	14	1,311	32
Massachusetts...........	4,837	1,726	36	521	11	1,493	31
Michigan.............	7,587	2,950	39	1,325	17	2,424	32
Minnesota.............	3,688	2,388	65	1,437	39	1,993	54
Mississippi	2,111	851	40	533	25	579	27
Missouri.............	4,206	2,010	48	1,076	26	1,612	38
Montana	699	438	63	279	40	362	52
Nebraska.............	1,266	623	49	308	24	498	39
Nevada.............	1,454	439	30	194	13	334	23
New Hampshire..........	954	506	53	175	18	450	47
New Jersey.............	6,300	1,993	32	669	11	1,694	27
New Mexico.............	1,337	595	45	256	19	471	35
New York	14,201	3,990	28	1,493	11	3,524	25
North Carolina...........	5,918	2,330	39	982	17	1,884	32
North Dakota...........	483	228	47	170	35	135	28
Ohio	8,645	3,407	39	1,513	17	2,768	32
Oklahoma.............	2,587	1,308	51	730	28	1,042	40
Oregon	2,630	1,545	59	611	23	1,286	49
Pennsylvania.............	9,303	4,169	45	1,648	18	3,522	38
Rhode Island	765	280	37	96	13	242	32
South Carolina...........	3,080	1,375	45	674	22	1,079	35
South Dakota.............	559	326	58	176	31	251	45
Tennessee	4,317	2,109	49	903	21	1,706	40
Texas.............	15,445	4,515	29	2,745	18	3,088	20
Utah	1,554	736	47	468	30	572	37
Vermont	479	319	67	125	26	287	60
Virginia.............	5,471	2,535	46	970	18	2,168	40
Washington.............	4,516	2,537	56	932	21	2,234	49
West Virginia	1,447	694	48	353	24	517	36
Wisconsin.............	4,059	2,489	61	1,141	28	2,159	53
Wyoming	377	223	59	138	37	172	46

Note: Detail does not add to total because of multiple responses. U.S. totals include responses from participants residing in the District of Columbia, as described in the statistical accuracy appendix.

U.S. Fish & Wildlife Service

Table 51. Participants in Wildlife-Related Recreation by State Where Activity Took Place: 2001

(Population 16 years old and older. Numbers in thousands)

State where activity took place	Total participants		Sportspersons		Wildlife-watching participants	
	Number	Percent	Number	Percent	Number	Percent
United States, total.....	82,302	100	37,805	46	66,105	80
Alabama...............	1,557	100	1,021	66	1,016	65
Alaska.................	632	100	457	72	420	67
Arizona................	1,720	100	486	28	1,465	85
Arkansas...............	1,369	100	960	70	841	61
California..............	7,231	100	2,556	35	5,720	79
Colorado..............	2,138	100	1,077	50	1,552	73
Connecticut............	1,151	100	356	31	967	84
Delaware...............	407	100	157	39	317	78
Florida	4,860	100	3,158	65	3,240	67
Georgia...............	2,198	100	1,236	56	1,494	68
Hawaii	324	100	151	46	220	68
Idaho..................	868	100	486	56	643	74
Illinois.................	3,390	100	1,366	40	2,627	77
Indiana	2,427	100	965	40	1,866	77
Iowa	1,334	100	645	48	1,022	77
Kansas	1,091	100	563	52	807	74
Kentucky	1,834	100	901	49	1,362	74
Louisiana	1,558	100	1,059	68	935	60
Maine	975	100	449	46	778	80
Maryland	1,911	100	752	39	1,524	80
Massachusetts...........	1,988	100	632	32	1,686	85
Michigan...............	3,481	100	1,659	48	2,666	77
Minnesota..............	2,915	100	1,733	59	2,155	74
Mississippi	1,017	100	720	71	631	62
Missouri	2,494	100	1,382	55	1,826	73
Montana	871	100	463	53	687	79
Nebraska...............	768	100	382	50	565	74
Nevada	657	100	193	29	543	83
New Hampshire	892	100	295	33	766	86
New Jersey.............	2,345	100	855	36	1,895	81
New Mexico.............	884	100	379	43	671	76
New York..............	4,620	100	1,760	38	3,885	84
North Carolina	2,882	100	1,386	48	2,168	75
North Dakota	322	100	259	81	190	59
Ohio	3,658	100	1,540	42	2,897	79
Oklahoma..............	1,529	100	838	55	1,131	74
Oregon	2,051	100	761	37	1,680	82
Pennsylvania............	4,570	100	1,783	39	3,794	83
Rhode Island	399	100	181	45	298	75
South Carolina	1,666	100	922	55	1,186	71
South Dakota	518	100	349	67	358	69
Tennessee	2,671	100	1,062	40	2,084	78
Texas..................	4,949	100	2,857	58	3,240	65
Utah	1,091	100	585	54	806	74
Vermont	569	100	211	37	496	87
Virginia................	3,001	100	1,137	38	2,460	82
Washington.............	2,970	100	1,024	34	2,496	84
West Virginia	843	100	444	53	605	72
Wisconsin..............	3,165	100	1,611	51	2,442	77
Wyoming	662	100	373	56	498	75

Note: Detail does not add to total because of multiple responses. U.S. totals include responses from participants residing in the District of Columbia, as described in the statistical accuracy appendix.

Table 52. Expenditures for Wildlife-Related Recreation by State Where Spending Took Place: 2001

(Population 16 years old and older. Expenditures in thousands of dollars)

State where spending took place	Total, wildlife-associated expenditures				Fishing and hunting expenditures			
	Total	Trip related	Equipment	Other	Total	Trip related	Equipment	Other
United States, total.....	**108,390,818**	**28,070,831**	**64,493,795**	**14,826,194**	**69,976,330**	**19,908,392**	**40,954,202**	**8,113,737**
Alabama..............	2,306,670	633,611	1,297,544	375,514	1,680,270	554,080	889,908	236,282
Alaska................	1,375,057	970,931	305,843	98,283	876,192	584,698	252,505	38,989
Arizona...............	1,619,724	512,038	1,040,740	66,947	799,006	207,360	556,210	35,436
Arkansas..............	1,290,326	411,178	656,098	223,050	1,046,336	391,133	451,545	203,657
California	5,709,602	2,169,604	2,952,662	587,337	3,128,727	1,288,798	1,713,467	126,462
Colorado..............	2,000,962	908,188	924,467	168,306	1,376,560	491,454	751,639	133,467
Connecticut...........	501,940	145,547	273,575	82,819	275,976	107,537	130,757	37,682
Delaware..............	130,350	48,268	66,366	15,716	88,012	33,981	45,283	8,748
Florida	6,211,889	2,886,641	2,941,961	383,288	4,636,408	2,211,257	2,103,920	321,231
Georgia...............	1,664,546	561,262	908,864	194,420	1,128,775	437,998	544,162	146,615
Hawaii	261,476	143,877	106,095	11,504	129,857	74,820	53,613	1,425
Idaho.................	982,423	296,120	552,420	133,883	754,953	199,314	434,571	121,069
Illinois...............	1,947,646	396,329	1,387,167	164,150	1,351,405	310,711	914,582	126,112
Indiana	1,487,815	316,680	939,767	231,368	846,577	198,155	599,687	48,735
Iowa	822,961	187,677	569,455	65,829	634,570	165,610	425,984	42,975
Kansas	591,123	209,487	320,608	61,027	462,460	177,313	248,659	36,488
Kentucky	1,844,927	334,023	1,232,252	278,652	1,243,377	284,247	903,456	55,675
Louisiana	1,608,468	574,843	933,472	100,154	1,440,048	519,418	836,133	84,496
Maine	1,083,721	296,847	503,923	282,951	570,154	149,317	364,137	56,700
Maryland	1,743,481	407,769	998,859	336,854	880,794	278,077	548,263	54,455
Massachusetts..........	1,072,482	389,870	606,939	75,673	603,149	227,437	354,842	20,869
Michigan..............	2,753,176	963,736	1,603,414	186,027	2,060,419	681,757	1,248,765	129,897
Minnesota.............	2,702,571	1,089,457	1,417,149	195,965	2,171,514	973,816	1,046,667	151,031
Mississippi	973,984	286,452	593,915	93,617	670,508	250,343	350,268	69,897
Missouri	1,828,153	581,939	1,111,023	135,191	1,379,397	424,953	835,336	119,108
Montana	943,118	463,392	386,866	92,859	592,782	255,897	271,423	65,463
Nebraska..............	584,898	153,515	396,296	35,087	455,151	135,102	293,156	26,893
Nevada	680,536	168,194	472,029	40,313	430,390	98,029	298,584	33,776
New Hampshire	618,694	268,859	307,862	41,973	275,754	91,554	159,509	24,691
New Jersey............	2,230,952	583,597	1,505,798	141,557	987,108	441,555	476,286	69,267
New Mexico............	1,022,568	301,637	582,895	138,036	464,279	150,622	285,038	28,619
New York	3,523,958	808,167	1,908,322	807,469	2,116,764	559,993	1,105,658	451,113
North Carolina	2,455,216	702,566	1,525,904	226,746	1,628,333	544,043	951,343	132,948
North Dakota	351,285	120,787	206,981	23,517	324,184	111,425	191,819	20,941
Ohio	2,289,385	623,335	1,463,425	202,625	1,666,334	493,547	1,010,071	162,716
Oklahoma.............	994,527	378,388	531,070	85,069	801,279	309,177	419,613	72,489
Oregon	2,060,509	672,557	1,142,262	245,690	1,291,103	367,567	801,968	121,567
Pennsylvania...........	2,974,644	644,290	1,868,212	462,142	2,012,845	472,632	1,138,344	401,869
Rhode Island	287,955	137,708	140,653	9,593	118,319	71,069	44,388	2,862
South Carolina	1,337,821	502,654	753,025	82,141	1,081,448	413,609	603,575	64,265
South Dakota	561,563	252,812	255,317	53,434	469,605	199,256	231,749	38,600
Tennessee	1,716,100	589,981	975,315	150,804	1,267,557	383,253	762,864	121,441
Texas.................	5,354,194	1,655,981	2,854,256	843,957	4,071,251	1,427,201	1,909,402	734,648
Utah	1,375,152	436,607	775,842	162,704	819,442	260,746	497,853	60,843
Vermont	385,651	138,974	145,806	100,870	181,936	75,731	88,146	18,059
Virginia...............	1,897,217	546,206	997,273	353,739	1,108,574	373,855	626,544	108,175
Washington............	2,362,176	727,416	1,445,661	189,100	1,382,446	444,924	851,030	86,493
West Virginia	503,147	207,721	238,348	57,078	339,636	128,861	157,881	52,894
Wisconsin	3,617,616	930,300	2,021,794	665,522	2,305,997	679,540	1,184,774	441,683
Wyoming	634,049	301,701	251,871	80,477	369,118	166,075	140,208	62,835

See footnotes at end of table.

U.S. Fish & Wildlife Service

Table 52. Expenditures for Wildlife-Related Recreation by State Where Spending Took Place: 2001—Continued

(Population 16 years old and older. Expenditures in thousands of dollars)

State where spending took place	Wildlife-watching expenditures			
	Total	Trip related	Equipment	Other
United States, total.....	**38,414,488**	**8,162,439**	**23,539,593**	**6,712,457**
Alabama...............	626,400	79,531	407,636	139,233
Alaska................	498,865	386,233	53,337	59,295
Arizona...............	820,718	304,677	484,530	31,511
Arkansas..............	243,990	20,044	204,553	19,393
California.............	2,580,875	880,805	1,239,195	460,875
Colorado..............	624,402	416,734	172,829	34,839
Connecticut............	225,964	38,010	142,817	45,137
Delaware..............	42,338	14,287	21,083	6,968
Florida	1,575,481	675,384	838,041	62,056
Georgia...............	535,771	123,264	364,702	47,805
Hawaii	131,619	69,057	52,482	10,080
Idaho.................	227,470	96,807	117,848	12,815
Illinois................	596,241	85,618	472,585	38,038
Indiana	641,239	118,525	340,081	182,633
Iowa..................	188,391	22,067	143,471	22,854
Kansas	128,663	32,175	71,949	24,539
Kentucky	601,550	49,776	328,796	222,977
Louisiana	168,420	55,424	97,339	15,657
Maine	513,566	147,530	139,786	226,251
Maryland	862,687	129,692	450,596	282,399
Massachusetts...........	469,333	162,433	252,097	54,803
Michigan..............	692,757	281,978	354,649	56,130
Minnesota.............	531,057	115,640	370,482	44,935
Mississippi	303,477	36,109	243,647	23,721
Missouri	448,756	156,986	275,687	16,083
Montana...............	350,335	207,496	115,443	27,396
Nebraska..............	129,747	18,413	103,140	8,194
Nevada................	250,145	70,164	173,445	6,537
New Hampshire..........	342,940	177,305	148,353	17,282
New Jersey.............	1,243,844	142,042	1,029,512	72,290
New Mexico............	558,290	151,015	297,857	109,417
New York..............	1,407,193	248,174	802,663	356,356
North Carolina..........	826,882	158,523	574,561	93,798
North Dakota...........	27,100	9,361	15,163	2,576
Ohio	623,051	129,788	453,354	39,909
Oklahoma..............	193,248	69,211	111,457	12,580
Oregon	769,407	304,990	340,293	124,123
Pennsylvania...........	961,799	171,658	729,868	60,274
Rhode Island	169,635	66,639	96,265	6,731
South Carolina..........	256,372	89,045	149,451	17,876
South Dakota	91,958	53,556	23,568	14,834
Tennessee	448,543	206,729	212,452	29,363
Texas.................	1,282,943	228,780	944,854	109,309
Utah	555,710	175,861	277,989	101,861
Vermont	203,715	63,243	57,660	82,811
Virginia...............	788,644	172,351	370,729	245,564
Washington............	979,730	282,492	594,631	102,607
West Virginia	163,511	78,860	80,467	4,184
Wisconsin..............	1,311,619	250,760	837,020	223,838
Wyoming	264,931	135,626	111,663	17,642

Note: U.S. totals include responses from participants residing in the District of Columbia, as described in the statistical accuracy appendix.

Table 53. Expenditures for Wildlife-Related Recreation by Participant's State of Residence: 2001

(Population 16 years old and older. Expenditures in thousands of dollars)

Participant's state of residence	Total, wildlife-associated expenditures				Fishing and hunting expenditures			
	Total	Trip related	Equipment	Other	Total	Trip related	Equipment	Other
United States, total.....	**108,390,818**	**28,070,831**	**64,493,795**	**14,826,194**	**69,976,330**	**19,908,392**	**40,954,202**	**8,113,737**
Alabama..............	2,241,999	632,522	1,264,711	344,766	1,579,426	522,596	850,551	206,279
Alaska...............	580,847	219,667	325,994	35,187	468,108	170,632	269,247	28,229
Arizona..............	1,573,354	395,623	1,054,415	123,316	802,249	221,386	546,659	34,204
Arkansas.............	1,148,365	338,882	638,801	170,683	850,043	268,071	430,642	151,331
California	5,869,216	2,351,281	2,915,644	602,291	3,266,088	1,456,534	1,671,425	138,130
Colorado.............	1,681,345	470,398	1,094,963	115,984	1,292,497	286,927	919,870	85,700
Connecticut..........	656,829	238,625	319,752	98,452	407,570	155,859	195,275	56,435
Delaware.............	172,444	64,527	77,187	30,730	113,663	48,800	50,771	14,092
Florida..............	5,585,535	2,206,710	2,986,857	391,968	4,141,515	1,698,191	2,128,045	315,278
Georgia..............	1,532,203	684,552	641,681	205,971	1,197,614	510,283	501,016	186,315
Hawaii	217,534	96,913	107,171	13,449	122,470	64,595	54,464	3,412
Idaho................	767,258	191,317	470,622	105,319	596,587	132,475	370,753	93,359
Illinois..............	2,758,847	958,928	1,573,958	225,961	2,006,777	704,229	1,134,499	168,049
Indiana	1,503,917	415,886	823,291	264,740	894,228	275,426	539,507	79,295
Iowa	873,464	289,692	514,826	68,946	634,283	212,680	374,929	46,674
Kansas	784,025	258,896	410,402	114,727	608,995	177,665	344,297	87,033
Kentucky	1,956,625	382,558	1,397,283	176,784	1,305,139	289,371	962,812	52,956
Louisiana	1,654,506	566,142	967,060	121,303	1,466,791	512,883	848,075	105,833
Maine	858,091	142,544	452,418	263,129	431,359	78,342	314,840	38,176
Maryland	1,658,126	471,869	1,046,043	140,215	925,326	283,304	572,511	69,512
Massachusetts........	1,113,321	419,913	591,045	102,363	652,078	274,149	334,015	43,915
Michigan.............	2,971,088	1,236,266	1,570,537	164,284	2,249,058	903,658	1,233,997	111,403
Minnesota............	2,868,171	1,057,136	1,524,463	286,573	2,333,131	932,949	1,155,491	244,691
Mississippi	988,335	256,105	664,521	67,709	708,690	223,302	441,544	43,843
Missouri	1,917,564	598,958	1,102,158	216,447	1,430,522	468,238	824,381	137,903
Montana	664,457	192,987	415,676	55,795	439,149	117,936	281,585	39,628
Nebraska.............	572,947	175,421	357,987	39,538	422,158	141,345	249,420	31,394
Nevada	760,873	165,748	536,234	58,891	470,055	115,586	312,710	41,758
New Hampshire	481,127	136,809	287,352	56,966	281,117	89,144	150,439	41,534
New Jersey...........	2,654,664	683,116	1,627,570	343,979	999,572	453,020	485,252	61,301
New Mexico...........	1,006,161	201,760	592,530	211,870	508,326	131,957	292,813	83,556
New York	3,833,858	1,085,249	1,941,628	806,981	2,122,592	613,956	917,408	591,228
North Carolina	2,288,942	682,895	1,398,956	207,091	1,562,312	561,165	834,974	166,173
North Dakota	364,153	106,434	234,563	23,156	337,084	99,488	216,917	20,679
Ohio	2,621,858	920,546	1,387,996	313,316	1,741,975	653,697	918,817	169,462
Oklahoma.............	1,105,577	411,959	605,009	88,609	925,637	369,547	481,013	75,077
Oregon	1,945,277	532,728	1,208,816	203,733	1,357,667	357,050	876,744	123,872
Pennsylvania..........	3,365,514	1,202,976	1,808,119	354,419	2,137,973	757,051	1,107,883	273,039
Rhode Island	180,508	59,601	107,000	13,907	141,573	49,725	84,084	7,764
South Carolina	1,252,568	448,775	736,969	66,825	995,031	369,517	576,822	48,692
South Dakota	321,540	119,516	166,334	35,690	271,311	105,322	145,181	20,809
Tennessee	1,617,118	553,401	907,851	155,866	1,279,254	438,723	715,042	125,488
Texas................	5,882,685	2,302,391	2,774,612	805,682	4,130,415	1,612,662	1,825,624	692,129
Utah	1,304,724	354,688	795,255	154,782	846,041	260,760	515,116	70,166
Vermont	271,364	71,464	164,719	35,180	161,685	41,080	105,550	15,055
Virginia..............	2,378,089	651,078	1,125,943	601,068	1,279,475	425,832	744,166	109,477
Washington...........	2,707,062	970,799	1,478,680	257,583	1,465,566	536,848	823,994	104,724
West Virginia	540,223	175,396	298,748	66,078	389,811	113,112	215,761	60,938
Wisconsin	3,123,047	808,102	1,805,091	509,854	1,905,965	539,191	1,055,855	310,919
Wyoming	344,345	108,236	222,083	14,026	251,700	81,086	159,503	11,110

See footnotes at end of table.

Table 53. **Expenditures for Wildlife-Related Recreation by Participant's State of Residence: 2001**—Continued

(Population 16 years old and older. Expenditures in thousands of dollars)

Participant's state of residence	Wildlife-watching expenditures			
	Total	Trip related	Equipment	Other
United States, total	**38,414,488**	**8,162,439**	**23,539,593**	**6,712,457**
Alabama	662,574	109,926	414,160	138,488
Alaska	112,739	49,035	56,746	6,958
Arizona	771,105	174,237	507,756	89,112
Arkansas	298,322	70,811	208,159	19,352
California	2,603,127	894,746	1,244,219	464,162
Colorado	388,848	183,470	175,093	30,284
Connecticut	249,260	82,766	124,477	42,016
Delaware	58,781	15,727	26,417	16,637
Florida	1,444,021	508,519	858,811	76,690
Georgia	334,589	174,269	140,665	19,656
Hawaii	95,063	32,319	52,708	10,037
Idaho	170,671	58,842	99,869	11,960
Illinois	752,069	254,698	439,459	57,912
Indiana	609,689	140,460	283,784	185,445
Iowa	239,181	77,012	139,897	22,272
Kansas	175,030	81,231	66,104	27,694
Kentucky	651,485	93,187	434,471	123,828
Louisiana	187,715	53,259	118,985	15,471
Maine	426,733	64,202	137,578	224,953
Maryland	732,800	188,565	473,532	70,703
Massachusetts	461,242	145,764	257,030	58,448
Michigan	722,030	332,609	336,540	52,881
Minnesota	535,040	124,187	368,972	41,881
Mississippi	279,646	32,803	222,977	23,866
Missouri	487,041	130,720	277,777	78,544
Montana	225,308	75,050	134,090	16,167
Nebraska	150,789	34,077	108,568	8,144
Nevada	290,819	50,162	223,523	17,133
New Hampshire	200,010	47,666	136,913	15,431
New Jersey	1,655,092	230,096	1,142,318	282,678
New Mexico	497,835	69,803	299,718	128,314
New York	1,711,265	471,293	1,024,219	215,753
North Carolina	726,630	121,730	563,982	40,918
North Dakota	27,068	6,946	17,646	2,477
Ohio	879,882	266,849	469,179	143,854
Oklahoma	179,940	42,413	123,995	13,532
Oregon	587,610	175,678	332,072	79,861
Pennsylvania	1,227,541	445,924	700,236	81,380
Rhode Island	38,935	9,876	22,916	6,143
South Carolina	257,537	79,258	160,147	18,133
South Dakota	50,229	14,195	21,153	14,881
Tennessee	337,864	114,678	192,809	30,377
Texas	1,752,269	689,729	948,988	113,553
Utah	458,683	93,928	280,139	84,616
Vermont	109,678	30,384	59,169	20,125
Virginia	1,098,614	225,247	381,777	491,591
Washington	1,241,496	433,951	654,686	152,859
West Virginia	150,412	62,283	82,987	5,141
Wisconsin	1,217,081	268,911	749,235	198,935
Wyoming	92,645	27,150	62,579	*2,916

*Estimate based on a small sample size.

Note: U.S. totals include responses from participants residing in the District of Columbia, as described in the statistical accuracy appendix.

Table 54. **Anglers and Hunters by Sportsperson's State of Residence: 2001**

(Population 16 years old and older. Numbers in thousands)

Sportsperson's state of residence	Population	Fished or hunted		Fished only		Hunted only		Fished and hunted	
		Number	Percent of population	Number	Percent of population	Number	Percent of population	Number	Percent of population
United States, total.....	**212,298**	**37,805**	**18**	**24,771**	**12**	**3,734**	**2**	**9,300**	**4**
Alabama...............	3,427	726	21	410	12	91	3	224	7
Alaska................	454	205	45	130	29	20	4	55	12
Arizona...............	3,700	437	12	313	8	*43	*1	81	2
Arkansas..............	1,999	621	31	312	16	*70	*4	238	12
California.............	25,982	2,486	10	2,209	9	*97	*(Z)	*180	*1
Colorado..............	3,215	679	21	511	16	*53	*2	115	4
Connecticut............	2,536	331	13	285	11	...	...	38	1
Delaware..............	599	94	16	78	13	*5	*1	11	2
Florida	12,171	2,158	18	1,888	16	...	...	221	2
Georgia...............	6,096	1,136	19	759	12	92	2	284	5
Hawaii	916	114	12	96	11	...	...	17	2
Idaho.................	972	306	31	155	16	45	5	106	11
Illinois...............	9,244	1,507	16	1,167	13	*92	*1	248	3
Indiana	4,558	914	20	630	14	*81	*2	203	4
Iowa.................	2,201	580	26	377	17	56	3	147	7
Kansas	2,017	491	24	289	14	60	3	142	7
Kentucky	3,121	703	23	432	14	73	2	198	6
Louisiana	3,306	829	25	515	16	71	2	243	7
Maine	1,005	256	26	133	13	41	4	82	8
Maryland	4,078	571	14	447	11	*40	*1	84	2
Massachusetts..........	4,837	521	11	443	9	*21	*(Z)	58	1
Michigan..............	7,587	1,325	17	600	8	285	4	439	6
Minnesota.............	3,688	1,437	39	855	23	*91	*2	490	13
Mississippi............	2,111	533	25	276	13	58	3	199	9
Missouri..............	4,206	1,076	26	663	16	94	2	318	8
Montana	699	279	40	108	15	57	8	113	16
Nebraska..............	1,266	308	24	180	14	43	3	85	7
Nevada...............	1,454	194	13	146	10	*14	*1	34	2
New Hampshire..........	954	175	18	122	13	*12	*1	42	4
New Jersey.............	6,300	669	11	544	9	*30	*(Z)	95	2
New Mexico............	1,337	256	19	142	11	40	3	74	6
New York	14,201	1,493	11	851	6	*152	*1	490	3
North Carolina	5,918	982	17	668	11	*88	*1	226	4
North Dakota	483	170	35	78	16	28	6	65	13
Ohio	8,645	1,513	17	1,031	12	122	1	359	4
Oklahoma.............	2,587	730	28	489	19	*44	*2	197	8
Oregon	2,630	611	23	376	14	60	2	176	7
Pennsylvania...........	9,303	1,648	18	781	8	378	4	489	5
Rhode Island	765	96	13	86	11	...	...	*10	*1
South Carolina	3,080	674	22	442	14	71	2	162	5
South Dakota	559	176	31	86	15	30	5	59	11
Tennessee	4,317	903	21	583	14	100	2	220	5
Texas................	15,445	2,745	18	1,619	10	364	2	762	5
Utah	1,554	468	30	290	19	44	3	134	9
Vermont	479	125	26	50	10	21	4	54	11
Virginia...............	5,471	970	18	661	12	*82	*1	226	4
Washington............	4,516	932	21	701	16	59	1	172	4
West Virginia	1,447	353	24	118	8	80	6	155	11
Wisconsin.............	4,059	1,141	28	550	14	160	4	431	11
Wyoming	377	138	37	73	19	*16	*4	49	13

* Estimate based on a small sample size.   ... Sample size too small to report data reliably.   (Z) Less than 0.5 percent.

Note: U.S. totals include responses from participants residing in the District of Columbia, as described in the statistical accuracy appendix.

U.S. Fish & Wildlife Service

Table 55. Anglers and Hunters by State Where Fishing or Hunting Took Place: 2001

(Population 16 years old and older. Numbers in thousands)

State where fishing or hunting took place	Anglers						Hunters					
	Total anglers, residents and nonresidents		Residents		Nonresidents		Total hunters, residents and nonresidents		Residents		Nonresidents	
	Number	Percent	Number	Percent	Number	Percent	Number	Percent	Number	Percent	Number	Percent
United States, total.....	34,071	100	31,218	92	7,880	23	13,034	100	12,375	95	2,029	16
Alabama..............	851	100	610	72	241	28	423	100	307	73	116	27
Alaska...............	421	100	183	43	239	57	93	100	72	77	*21	*23
Arizona..............	419	100	351	84	68	16	148	100	119	81	*28	*19
Arkansas.............	782	100	543	69	239	31	431	100	303	70	128	30
California............	2,444	100	2,288	94	156	6	274	100	261	95	*12	*5
Colorado.............	917	100	560	61	357	39	281	100	159	57	121	43
Connecticut...........	346	100	271	78	75	22	45	100	*35	*77	...	...
Delaware.............	148	100	71	47	*78	*53	16	100	13	81	...	...
Florida	3,104	100	2,057	66	1,047	34	226	100	191	84	*35	*16
Georgia..............	1,086	100	947	87	139	13	417	100	355	85	*62	*15
Hawaii	150	100	109	73	*41	*27	17	100	17	100	...	...
Idaho................	416	100	251	60	165	40	197	100	150	76	47	24
Illinois..............	1,237	100	1,157	94	80	6	310	100	246	79	*64	*21
Indiana..............	874	100	784	90	90	10	290	100	269	93	...	...
Iowa	542	100	471	87	70	13	243	100	195	80	*48	*20
Kansas	404	100	357	88	*47	*12	291	100	189	65	103	35
Kentucky	780	100	590	76	190	24	323	100	269	83	*54	*17
Louisiana	970	100	753	78	217	22	333	100	293	88	*40	*12
Maine	376	100	212	56	165	44	164	100	123	75	41	25
Maryland	701	100	457	65	243	35	145	100	115	80	*30	*20
Massachusetts..........	615	100	425	69	191	31	66	100	64	97	...	...
Michigan.............	1,354	100	1,002	74	352	26	754	100	705	94	*48	*6
Minnesota............	1,624	100	1,293	80	331	20	597	100	568	95	*29	*5
Mississippi	586	100	450	77	136	23	357	100	245	69	111	31
Missouri	1,215	100	942	78	272	22	489	100	405	83	84	17
Montana.............	349	100	212	61	138	39	229	100	170	74	59	26
Nebraska.............	296	100	241	81	55	19	173	100	124	72	*49	*28
Nevada	172	100	119	69	*53	*31	47	100	42	90	...	...
New Hampshire	267	100	147	55	119	45	78	100	52	67	*26	*33
New Jersey	806	100	531	66	275	34	135	100	108	80	...	...
New Mexico...........	314	100	197	63	*116	*37	130	100	105	80	*26	*20
New York............	1,550	100	1,243	80	307	20	714	100	635	89	79	11
North Carolina.........	1,287	100	831	65	456	35	295	100	272	92	*23	*8
North Dakota	179	100	119	67	*59	*33	139	100	87	63	*52	*37
Ohio	1,371	100	1,225	89	146	11	490	100	452	92	*38	*8
Oklahoma.............	774	100	648	84	126	16	261	100	241	92	*20	*8
Oregon	687	100	513	75	174	25	248	100	234	94	*15	*6
Pennsylvania...........	1,266	100	1,032	82	234	18	1,000	100	858	86	142	14
Rhode Island	179	100	86	48	93	52	*9	*100	*7	*83	...	...
South Carolina.........	812	100	571	70	241	30	265	100	221	83	*44	*17
South Dakota	214	100	140	65	75	35	209	100	90	43	119	57
Tennessee.............	903	100	709	79	194	21	359	100	288	80	71	20
Texas................	2,372	100	2,151	91	221	9	1,201	100	1,101	92	100	8
Utah	517	100	388	75	129	25	198	100	177	89	*22	*11
Vermont	171	100	96	56	75	44	100	100	74	74	*26	*26
Virginia..............	1,010	100	761	75	248	25	355	100	279	79	*75	*21
Washington............	938	100	808	86	130	14	227	100	210	92	...	...
West Virginia	318	100	250	79	*67	*21	284	100	229	81	*55	*19
Wisconsin.............	1,412	100	941	67	471	33	660	100	588	89	*72	*11
Wyoming	293	100	117	40	176	60	133	100	65	49	68	51

* Estimate based on a small sample size.   ... Sample size too small to report data reliably.

Note: For the U.S. row, detail does not add to total because of multiple responses. U.S. totals include responses from participants residing in the District of Columbia, as described in the statistical accuracy appendix.

Table 56. Hunters by Type of Hunting and State Where Hunting Took Place: 2001

(Population 16 years old and older. Numbers in thousands)

State where hunting took place	Total, all hunting		Big game		Small game		Migratory bird		Other animals	
	Number	Percent	Number	Percent	Number	Percent	Number	Percent	Number	Percent
United States, total.....	13,034	100	10,911	84	5,434	41	2,956	23	1,047	8
Alabama..............	423	100	392	93	109	26	95	23	*21	*5
Alaska...............	93	100	84	90	18	19	*14	*15	...	...
Arizona..............	148	100	81	55	72	49	62	42	...	...
Arkansas.............	431	100	322	75	145	34	171	40	*23	*5
California	274	100	*129	*47	*109	*40	*115	*42	...	...
Colorado.............	281	100	235	84	74	26	*55	*19	...	...
Connecticut..........	45	100	*33	*73	*22	*49	...	...	...	...
Delaware.............	16	100	11	67	*4	*28	*8	50	...	...
Florida..............	226	100	188	83	*78	*34	*64	*28	...	...
Georgia..............	417	100	342	82	135	32	*86	*21	*45	*11
Hawaii	17	100	*15	*91	*7	*44	...	...	...	...
Idaho................	197	100	156	79	74	38	*38	*19	...	...
Illinois..............	310	100	245	79	*101	*32	*60	*19	...	...
Indiana	290	100	215	74	159	55	*30	*10	...	...
Iowa	243	100	139	57	151	62	*56	*23	*29	*12
Kansas	291	100	159	55	209	72	79	27	*35	*12
Kentucky	323	100	264	82	152	47	*57	*18	*20	*6
Louisiana	333	100	212	64	139	42	147	44	...	...
Maine	164	100	156	95	63	39	...	...	...	...
Maryland	145	100	126	87	*44	*30	*47	*32	...	...
Massachusetts..........	66	100	58	88	*28	*42	*19	*28	...	...
Michigan.............	754	100	680	90	222	29	*55	*7	...	...
Minnesota............	597	100	493	83	249	42	184	31	*43	*7
Mississippi	357	100	295	83	172	48	78	22	*24	*7
Missouri	489	100	423	87	165	34	*69	*14	...	...
Montana	229	100	206	90	52	23	*23	*10	...	...
Nebraska.............	173	100	89	51	114	66	48	28	24	14
Nevada	47	100	*25	*52	*23	*49	29	61	...	...
New Hampshire	78	100	71	91	22	28	*6	*8	...	...
New Jersey...........	135	100	111	83	*61	*45	...	...	...	...
New Mexico...........	130	100	112	86	37	29	*34	*26	...	...
New York............	714	100	664	93	274	38	*101	*14	*76	*11
North Carolina	295	100	224	76	124	42	102	35	...	...
North Dakota	139	100	74	53	69	49	61	44	20	14
Ohio	490	100	422	86	313	64	*70	*14	*73	*15
Oklahoma.............	261	100	212	81	131	50	81	31	*36	*14
Oregon	248	100	226	91	60	24	*42	*17	...	...
Pennsylvania...........	1,000	100	956	96	370	37	*85	*9	*130	*13
Rhode Island	*9	*100	*6	*68	*5	*60	...	...	...	...
South Carolina	265	100	217	82	101	38	71	27	...	...
South Dakota	209	100	75	36	160	77	51	24	*14	*7
Tennessee	359	100	262	73	157	44	100	28	*44	*12
Texas................	1,201	100	888	74	371	31	500	42	*59	*5
Utah	198	100	171	86	69	35	52	26	*22	*11
Vermont	100	100	94	94	29	29	...	...	*10	*10
Virginia..............	355	100	322	91	128	36	*44	*12	...	...
Washington............	227	100	187	82	74	32	*50	*22	...	...
West Virginia	284	100	269	95	123	43	...	...	*39	*14
Wisconsin.............	660	100	606	92	230	35	*55	*8	...	...
Wyoming.............	133	100	110	82	33	25	*9	*7	*15	*11

* Estimate based on a small sample size.   ... Sample size too small to report data reliably.

Note: Detail does not add to total because of multiple responses. U.S. totals include responses from participants residing in the District of Columbia, as described in the statistical accuracy appendix.

Table 57. Days of Hunting by State Where Hunting Took Place and Hunter's State of Residence: 2001

(Population 16 years old and older. Numbers in thousands)

State	Days of hunting in state						Days of hunting by state residents					
	Total days, residents and nonresidents		Days by state residents		Days by nonresidents		Total days, in state of residence and other states		Days in state of residence		Days in other states	
	Number	Percent	Number	Percent	Number	Percent	Number	Percent	Number	Percent	Number	Percent
United States, total.....	228,368	100	209,880	92	20,891	9	228,368	100	209,880	92	20,891	9
Alabama...............	7,616	100	6,613	87	1,003	13	7,262	100	6,613	91	650	9
Alaska................	1,146	100	953	83	*193	*17	982	100	953	97	*29	*3
Arizona...............	1,694	100	1,546	91	*148	*9	1,649	100	1,546	94	...	...
Arkansas..............	8,411	100	6,970	83	1,441	17	7,249	100	6,970	96	*279	*4
California.............	3,426	100	3,378	99	...	...	3,695	100	3,378	91	...	...
Colorado..............	2,610	100	1,680	64	930	36	1,982	100	1,680	85	*303	*15
Connecticut............	766	100	*691	*90	...	...	824	100	*691	*84	*132	*16
Delaware..............	226	100	220	98	...	...	279	100	220	79	*59	*21
Florida	4,693	100	4,504	96	*190	*4	5,865	100	4,504	77	*1,362	*23
Georgia...............	7,973	100	7,339	92	*633	*8	7,882	100	7,339	93	*542	*7
Hawaii	316	100	*316	*100	...	...	322	100	*316	*98	...	...
Idaho................	2,100	100	1,737	83	363	17	1,784	100	1,737	97	...	...
Illinois...............	4,522	100	4,159	92	*363	*8	5,842	100	4,159	71	*1,683	*29
Indiana	5,000	100	4,830	97	...	...	5,016	100	4,830	96	*186	*4
Iowa.................	3,989	100	3,819	96	*170	*4	4,086	100	3,819	93	*267	*7
Kansas	3,647	100	3,067	84	579	16	3,424	100	3,067	90	357	10
Kentucky	4,664	100	4,422	95	*242	*5	4,538	100	4,422	97	*116	*3
Louisiana	6,442	100	6,109	95	*333	*5	7,152	100	6,109	85	1,043	15
Maine	2,469	100	2,131	86	338	14	2,169	100	2,131	98	...	...
Maryland	1,799	100	1,645	91	*154	*9	1,992	100	1,645	83	*347	*17
Massachusetts..........	1,158	100	1,144	99	...	...	1,727	100	1,144	66	*583	*34
Michigan..............	8,994	100	8,477	94	*517	*6	8,784	100	8,477	96	...	...
Minnesota.............	8,437	100	7,499	89	*938	*11	8,619	100	7,499	87	*1,120	*13
Mississippi	8,481	100	6,589	78	1,892	22	6,977	100	6,589	94	*388	*6
Missouri..............	6,606	100	6,225	94	381	6	6,715	100	6,225	93	*490	*7
Montana..............	2,442	100	2,052	84	390	16	2,112	100	2,052	97	...	...
Nebraska..............	2,204	100	1,834	83	*370	*17	1,963	100	1,834	93	*129	*7
Nevada	490	100	467	95	...	...	558	100	467	84	*91	*16
New Hampshire	1,459	100	1,138	78	*321	*22	1,300	100	1,138	88	*162	*12
New Jersey	3,120	100	2,500	80	...	...	3,000	100	2,500	83	*500	*17
New Mexico............	1,667	100	1,521	91	*146	*9	1,594	100	1,521	95	*73	*5
New York	13,187	100	12,797	97	390	3	13,124	100	12,797	98	*327	*2
North Carolina..........	7,526	100	7,338	98	*188	*2	8,372	100	7,338	88	*1,034	*12
North Dakota	1,635	100	1,364	83	*271	*17	1,417	100	1,364	96	*53	*4
Ohio	10,233	100	9,952	97	*282	*3	11,077	100	9,952	90	*1,125	*10
Oklahoma.............	5,642	100	5,546	98	*96	*2	5,965	100	5,546	93	*419	*7
Oregon	2,947	100	2,812	95	*135	*5	2,917	100	2,812	96	...	...
Pennsylvania...........	13,955	100	12,963	93	993	7	14,051	100	12,963	92	*1,088	*8
Rhode Island	104	100	*103	*99	...	...	193	100	*103	*53	*90	*47
South Carolina..........	4,744	100	4,437	94	*307	*6	4,657	100	4,437	95	*220	*5
South Dakota	2,425	100	1,173	48	1,252	52	1,347	100	1,173	87	*174	*13
Tennessee	6,651	100	6,069	91	582	9	6,962	100	6,069	87	893	13
Texas................	14,081	100	13,437	95	644	5	15,062	100	13,437	89	*1,625	*11
Utah	2,455	100	2,332	95	*123	*5	2,512	100	2,332	93	*180	*7
Vermont	1,510	100	1,319	87	*190	*13	1,460	100	1,319	90	*141	*10
Virginia..............	5,818	100	5,375	92	*443	*8	5,819	100	5,375	92	*444	*8
Washington............	2,951	100	2,836	96	...	...	3,311	100	2,836	86	*475	*14
West Virginia	5,166	100	4,652	90	*514	*10	4,791	100	4,652	97	*139	*3
Wisconsin.............	9,653	100	8,998	93	*655	*7	9,305	100	8,998	97	*307	*3
Wyoming	1,304	100	806	62	498	38	870	100	806	93	*64	*7

* Estimate based on a small sample size.   ... Sample size too small to report data reliably.

Note: U.S. totals include responses from participants residing in the District of Columbia, as described in the statistical accuracy appendix.

Table 58. Days of Hunting by Type of Hunting and State Where Hunting Took Place: 2001

(Population 16 years old and older. Numbers in thousands)

State where hunting took place	Total, all hunting		Big game		Small game		Migratory bird		Other animals	
	Number	Percent	Number	Percent	Number	Percent	Number	Percent	Number	Percent
United States, total.....	**228,368**	**100**	**153,191**	**67**	**60,142**	**26**	**29,310**	**13**	**19,207**	**8**
Alabama...............	7,616	100	6,658	87	898	12	481	6	*310	*4
Alaska................	1,146	100	944	82	138	12	*123	*11	...	...
Arizona...............	1,694	100	860	51	645	38	335	20	...	...
Arkansas..............	8,411	100	5,740	68	1,491	18	1,860	22	...	...
California.............	3,426	100	*1,285	*38	*693	*20	*1,782	*52	...	...
Colorado..............	2,610	100	1,634	63	483	19	*539	*21	...	...
Connecticut...........	766	100	*522	*68	*260	*34	...	...	...	...
Delaware..............	226	100	158	70	*36	*16	*50	*22	...	...
Florida...............	4,693	100	3,493	74	*555	*12	*1,052	*22	...	...
Georgia...............	7,973	100	6,131	77	1,476	19	*474	*6	*861	*11
Hawaii	*316	*100	*285	*90	*86	*27	...	...	...	...
Idaho................	2,100	100	1,384	66	551	26	*308	*15	...	...
Illinois...............	4,522	100	3,274	72	*602	*13	*862	*19	...	...
Indiana	5,000	100	2,696	54	2,293	46	...	...	...	...
Iowa	3,989	100	1,449	36	1,913	48	*584	*15	*378	*9
Kansas	3,647	100	1,570	43	1,604	44	590	16	*487	*13
Kentucky	4,664	100	2,828	61	1,634	35	*386	*8	*567	*12
Louisiana	6,442	100	4,365	68	1,106	17	1,218	19	...	...
Maine	2,469	100	2,021	82	693	28	...	...	...	...
Maryland	1,799	100	1,350	75	*292	*16	*299	*17	...	...
Massachusetts..........	1,158	100	683	59	*457	*39	*102	*9	...	...
Michigan.............	8,994	100	6,532	73	2,622	29	*573	*6	...	...
Minnesota............	8,437	100	4,869	58	2,047	24	1,661	20	*615	*7
Mississippi	8,481	100	7,196	85	2,087	25	394	5	*371	*4
Missouri	6,606	100	4,591	70	1,559	24	*841	*13	...	...
Montana..............	2,442	100	1,797	74	598	24	*222	*9	...	...
Nebraska.............	2,204	100	763	35	921	42	398	18	372	17
Nevada...............	490	100	*169	*35	*177	*36	236	48	...	...
New Hampshire	1,459	100	1,127	77	303	21	*84	*6	...	...
New Jersey	3,120	100	2,813	90	*572	*18	...	...	...	...
New Mexico...........	1,667	100	711	43	286	17	*262	*16	...	...
New York.............	13,187	100	10,864	82	2,700	20	*1,225	*9	*1,152	*9
North Carolina..........	7,526	100	5,117	68	1,648	22	1,245	17	...	...
North Dakota..........	1,635	100	574	35	654	40	409	25	216	13
Ohio.................	10,233	100	4,290	42	4,480	44	*606	*6	*2,599	*25
Oklahoma.............	5,642	100	3,465	61	2,218	39	1,073	19	*556	*10
Oregon	2,947	100	2,500	85	394	13	*341	*12	...	...
Pennsylvania...........	13,955	100	8,816	63	3,135	22	*575	*4	*2,547	*18
Rhode Island..........	*104	*100	*65	*62	*36	*34	...	...	...	...
South Carolina.........	4,744	100	3,757	79	922	19	366	8	...	...
South Dakota	2,425	100	534	22	1,547	64	526	22	*115	*5
Tennessee	6,651	100	4,112	62	2,267	34	797	12	*1,167	*18
Texas................	14,081	100	8,868	63	3,665	26	4,179	30	*467	*3
Utah	2,455	100	1,252	51	453	18	510	21	*480	*20
Vermont	1,510	100	1,218	81	347	23	...	...	*94	*6
Virginia..............	5,818	100	4,305	74	1,130	19	*194	*3	...	...
Washington............	2,951	100	1,841	62	642	22	*522	*18	...	...
West Virginia	5,166	100	3,167	61	1,954	38	...	...	*658	*13
Wisconsin.............	9,653	100	7,505	78	2,495	26	*379	*4	...	...
Wyoming	1,304	100	1,001	77	199	15	*64	*5	*188	*14

* Estimate based on a small sample size.   ... Sample size too small to report data reliably.

Note: Detail does not add to total because of multiple responses. U.S. totals include responses from participants residing in the District of Columbia, as described in the statistical accuracy appendix.

Table 59. Expenditures for Hunting by State Where Spending Took Place: 2001

(Population 16 years old and older. Expenditures in thousands of dollars)

State where spending took place	Total expenditures	Trip-related expenditures				Expenditures for equipment				Expenditures for other items[1]
		Total trip related	Food and lodging	Trans-portation	Other trip costs	Total equipment	Hunting equipment	Auxiliary equipment	Special equipment	
United States, total.....	**20,611,025**	**5,252,391**	**2,449,942**	**1,789,320**	**1,013,129**	**10,361,495**	**4,561,709**	**1,202,845**	**4,596,942**	**4,997,138**
Alabama...............	663,576	195,870	94,275	55,233	46,361	308,730	164,671	37,311	*106,749	158,976
Alaska................	216,972	160,516	26,836	39,957	93,723	38,203	20,207	8,325	...	18,252
Arizona...............	211,506	65,151	33,646	21,487	10,018	125,478	61,309	15,357	...	20,876
Arkansas..............	517,160	207,415	78,352	89,742	39,320	156,813	104,348	16,122	...	152,933
California............	315,207	159,105	62,261	42,093	54,751	131,869	110,919	*20,950	...	24,233
Colorado..............	382,599	185,738	70,048	57,139	58,552	109,543	81,581	13,241	...	87,318
Connecticut...........	43,381	6,976	*3,111	2,086	*1,779	20,561	17,193	*3,013	...	15,844
Delaware..............	14,662	3,378	1,145	836	*1,396	9,492	2,939	*830	...	1,793
Florida	394,229	119,945	51,172	38,434	30,339	226,968	89,576	*20,365	...	47,315
Georgia...............	503,677	191,531	92,546	45,212	53,773	200,191	146,286	30,853	...	111,955
Hawaii	15,076	8,102	2,816	5,028	*258	6,512	5,322	*1,189	...	463
Idaho.................	230,841	83,091	28,083	44,618	10,390	97,964	40,152	17,305	...	49,786
Illinois..............	450,865	104,426	38,710	25,766	39,950	270,255	144,069	*47,035	...	76,183
Indiana	265,152	45,399	26,378	15,407	*3,613	189,852	114,621	26,620	...	29,902
Iowa	167,359	60,335	27,378	30,687	*2,270	79,023	58,925	19,198	...	28,000
Kansas	235,549	96,364	47,461	36,296	12,607	113,359	84,582	13,143	...	25,825
Kentucky	373,185	62,853	35,701	23,598	3,554	276,488	117,752	20,987	*137,750	33,844
Louisiana	446,204	120,668	62,739	36,522	21,406	273,295	102,305	18,962	*152,028	52,240
Maine	162,397	53,779	26,340	16,679	10,760	71,690	29,047	9,665	...	36,927
Maryland	127,318	32,450	14,289	11,416	6,745	58,371	43,103	10,692	...	36,496
Massachusetts.........	58,527	10,042	5,916	3,572	...	43,030	28,649	*6,888	...	5,455
Michigan..............	490,254	163,205	103,628	50,876	8,701	264,076	194,117	66,591	...	62,973
Minnesota.............	482,614	179,291	101,287	67,552	10,451	241,510	170,832	41,979	...	61,813
Mississippi	360,293	132,141	73,063	45,432	13,646	166,185	91,328	15,343	*59,514	61,967
Missouri	424,750	106,882	62,818	36,965	7,099	236,236	118,683	38,360	...	81,632
Montana...............	237,605	107,072	42,077	36,656	28,340	98,667	33,479	22,800	...	31,866
Nebraska..............	198,120	74,819	22,074	24,846	27,899	106,119	76,746	25,268	...	17,183
Nevada................	134,102	21,494	10,892	7,354	3,248	100,976	23,861	36,715	...	11,631
New Hampshire	71,386	15,499	8,137	5,879	*1,483	47,212	36,399	7,323	...	8,675
New Jersey............	150,884	67,411	21,745	17,844	*27,822	43,515	32,010	11,505	...	39,957
New Mexico............	153,386	59,969	25,697	18,916	15,356	73,932	39,963	13,388	...	19,485
New York..............	822,215	179,227	82,419	42,942	53,866	367,360	162,342	53,142	...	275,628
North Carolina........	438,059	91,739	47,428	27,555	16,756	313,480	120,890	24,449	...	32,839
North Dakota	103,353	53,723	26,440	25,784	1,499	33,559	26,260	6,736	...	16,071
Ohio	636,492	112,660	53,435	51,107	*8,118	424,969	231,838	40,707	...	98,863
Oklahoma..............	284,071	96,942	44,939	43,654	8,349	130,198	97,178	22,768	...	56,931
Oregon................	364,859	108,604	46,205	42,251	20,148	232,503	115,873	32,440	...	23,752
Pennsylvania..........	941,036	189,881	104,014	73,084	12,782	417,181	234,438	79,119	...	333,975
Rhode Island	5,059	871	*360	*279	...	3,877	3,002	*862	...	311
South Carolina........	305,272	95,643	35,530	41,709	18,404	157,655	107,590	19,847	...	51,974
South Dakota	223,195	112,817	57,003	38,397	17,417	81,069	49,960	30,743	...	29,309
Tennessee	588,691	118,267	63,694	38,223	16,351	384,266	137,839	24,319	*222,108	86,158
Texas.................	1,513,881	555,833	285,218	167,543	103,072	591,751	314,203	65,094	...	366,297
Utah	292,108	88,324	38,842	30,271	19,211	166,701	54,793	30,232	*81,677	37,083
Vermont	52,627	16,469	10,413	5,758	*298	24,041	18,994	5,047	...	12,116
Virginia..............	320,851	96,371	40,102	33,550	22,719	140,768	108,034	20,756	...	83,712
Washington............	349,771	102,554	48,783	46,801	6,970	207,860	94,405	20,025	...	39,357
West Virginia	222,899	64,187	38,341	22,934	2,912	111,434	67,697	7,847	...	47,278
Wisconsin	800,998	167,193	88,888	60,268	18,037	321,074	200,183	59,710	*61,181	312,731
Wyoming	123,296	70,897	29,098	26,607	15,193	35,478	23,264	8,624	...	16,921

* Estimate based on a small sample size.　　... Sample size too small to report data reliably.

[1] Includes expenditures for magazine subscriptions, membership dues and contributions, land leasing and ownership, and licenses, stamps, tags, and permits.

Note: U.S. totals include responses from participants residing in the District of Columbia, as described in the statistical accuracy appendix.

Table 60. Freshwater (Except Great Lakes) Anglers and Days of Fishing by State Where Fishing Took Place: 2001

(Population 16 years old and older. Numbers in thousands)

State where fishing took place	Anglers						Days of fishing					
	Total anglers, residents and nonresidents		Residents		Nonresidents		Total days, residents and nonresidents		Days by state residents		Days by nonresidents	
	Number	Percent	Number	Percent	Number	Percent	Number	Percent	Number	Percent	Number	Percent
United States, total.....	27,913	100	25,832	93	5,555	20	443,247	100	403,656	91	39,591	9
Alabama..............	732	100	557	76	175	24	9,877	100	8,984	91	894	9
Alaska................	266	100	141	53	125	47	2,110	100	1,553	74	556	26
Arizona...............	419	100	351	84	68	16	4,246	100	3,842	91	403	9
Arkansas..............	782	100	543	69	239	31	13,006	100	11,508	88	1,498	12
California.............	1,865	100	1,776	95	89	5	19,385	100	18,788	97	597	3
Colorado..............	915	100	560	61	355	39	9,267	100	6,478	70	2,789	30
Connecticut...........	254	100	203	80	*52	*20	3,516	100	3,177	90	*339	*10
Delaware.............	73	100	35	48	*38	*52	609	100	396	65	*213	*35
Florida	1,316	100	1,079	82	237	18	20,840	100	19,221	92	1,618	8
Georgia..............	1,017	100	892	88	125	12	13,076	100	12,555	96	521	4
Hawaii	*12	*100	*12	*100	...	...	*194	*100	*194	*100	...	...
Idaho................	416	100	251	60	165	40	4,070	100	2,942	72	1,128	28
Illinois...............	1,060	100	995	94	*65	*6	14,246	100	13,881	97	*365	*3
Indiana	745	100	669	90	*77	*10	12,756	100	12,477	98	*279	*2
Iowa.................	542	100	471	87	70	13	7,485	100	7,048	94	436	6
Kansas	404	100	357	88	*47	*12	5,662	100	5,504	97	*158	*3
Kentucky	780	100	590	76	190	24	12,394	100	11,143	90	1,251	10
Louisiana	659	100	532	81	127	19	8,419	100	7,766	92	653	8
Maine	272	100	178	66	93	34	3,422	100	2,858	84	564	16
Maryland	367	100	278	76	89	24	4,269	100	3,236	76	1,033	24
Massachusetts.........	325	100	278	86	47	14	4,560	100	4,346	95	213	5
Michigan.............	979	100	749	76	231	24	12,817	100	11,719	91	1,098	9
Minnesota............	1,560	100	1,262	81	298	19	28,159	100	25,892	92	2,267	8
Mississippi	494	100	389	79	105	21	8,466	100	7,500	89	966	11
Missouri	1,215	100	942	78	272	22	13,279	100	11,309	85	1,970	15
Montana	349	100	212	61	138	39	4,068	100	3,515	86	554	14
Nebraska.............	296	100	241	81	55	19	3,204	100	2,916	91	288	9
Nevada	172	100	119	69	*53	*31	1,575	100	1,422	90	...	...
New Hampshire	221	100	125	57	96	43	2,871	100	2,380	83	491	17
New Jersey...........	331	100	271	82	*60	*18	5,553	100	5,139	93	*413	*7
New Mexico...........	314	100	197	63	*116	*37	2,485	100	2,091	84	*394	*16
New York............	901	100	720	80	180	20	13,022	100	11,369	87	1,653	13
North Carolina.........	848	100	675	80	173	20	12,073	100	11,398	94	675	6
North Dakota..........	179	100	119	67	*59	*33	2,186	100	1,969	90	*217	*10
Ohio	1,081	100	972	90	109	10	15,212	100	14,412	95	800	5
Oklahoma............	774	100	648	84	126	16	12,741	100	12,395	97	345	3
Oregon	611	100	461	75	150	25	7,895	100	7,346	93	549	7
Pennsylvania..........	1,163	100	947	81	216	19	17,201	100	16,028	93	1,173	7
Rhode Island	51	100	39	76	...	...	649	100	547	84	...	...
South Carolina.........	591	100	488	82	*104	*18	8,713	100	8,347	96	*366	*4
South Dakota..........	214	100	140	65	75	35	2,984	100	2,238	75	746	25
Tennessee	903	100	709	79	194	21	15,035	100	13,409	89	1,627	11
Texas................	1,842	100	1,685	91	157	9	25,650	100	24,830	97	820	3
Utah	517	100	388	75	129	25	5,238	100	4,701	90	537	10
Vermont	171	100	96	56	75	44	2,321	100	1,684	73	637	27
Virginia..............	721	100	601	83	120	17	10,849	100	10,332	95	516	5
Washington...........	659	100	611	93	*48	*7	9,800	100	9,465	97	*335	*3
West Virginia	318	100	250	79	*67	*21	4,152	100	3,880	93	*272	*7
Wisconsin	1,306	100	906	69	401	31	19,139	100	15,736	82	3,404	18
Wyoming	293	100	117	40	176	60	2,497	100	1,782	71	715	29

* Estimate based on a small sample size.   ... Sample size too small to report data reliably.

Note: For the U.S. row, detail does not add to total because of multiple responses. U.S. totals include responses from participants residing in the District of Columbia, as described in the statistical accuracy appendix.

Table 61. Great Lakes Anglers and Days of Great Lakes Fishing by State Where Fishing Took Place: 2001

(Population 16 years old and older. Numbers in thousands)

State where fishing took place	Anglers						Days of fishing					
	Total anglers, residents and nonresidents		Residents		Nonresidents		Total days, residents and nonresidents		Days by state residents		Days by nonresidents	
	Number	Percent	Number	Percent	Number	Percent	Number	Percent	Number	Percent	Number	Percent
United States, total.....	**1,847**	**100**	**1,610**	**87**	**348**	**19**	**23,138**	**100**	**21,048**	**91**	**2,090**	**9**
Illinois................	*120	*100	*114	*95	...	...	*756	*100	*729	*96	...	...
Indiana	*45	*100	*42	*93	...	...	*721	*100	*702	*97	...	...
Michigan...............	680	100	522	77	158	23	7,002	100	6,303	90	699	10
Minnesota.............	*60	*100	...	...	*20	*33	*603	*100	...	...	*255	*42
New York	368	100	304	83	64	17	6,324	100	5,875	93	449	7
Ohio	430	100	390	91	*39	*9	4,241	100	4,100	97	*142	*3
Pennsylvania...........	*80	*100	*60	*75	...	...	*1,406	*100	*1,247	*89	...	...
Wisconsin.............	198	100	137	69	*61	*31	2,085	100	1,743	84	*341	*16

* Estimate based on a small sample size.   ... Sample size too small to report data reliably.

Note: For the U.S. row, detail does not add to total because of multiple responses.

Table 62. Saltwater Anglers and Days of Saltwater Fishing by State Where Fishing Took Place: 2001

(Population 16 years old and older. Numbers in thousands)

State where fishing took place	Anglers						Days of fishing					
	Total anglers, residents and nonresidents		Residents		Nonresidents		Total days, residents and nonresidents		Days by state residents		Days by nonresidents	
	Number	Percent	Number	Percent	Number	Percent	Number	Percent	Number	Percent	Number	Percent
United States, total.....	**9,051**	**100**	**6,914**	**76**	**2,661**	**29**	**90,838**	**100**	**75,670**	**83**	**15,168**	**17**
Alabama...............	167	100	109	65	*59	*35	1,340	100	1,194	89	*145	*11
Alaska................	271	100	102	38	169	62	1,531	100	942	62	589	38
California..............	932	100	875	94	57	6	8,345	100	8,118	97	227	3
Connecticut............	161	100	139	87	*22	*13	1,398	100	1,337	96	*60	*4
Delaware..............	88	100	44	50	*44	*50	698	100	385	55	*314	*45
Florida	2,437	100	1,591	65	846	35	30,123	100	25,712	85	4,410	15
Georgia................	*98	*100	*71	*73	...	...	*467	*100	*388	*83	...	...
Hawaii	144	100	105	73	*40	*27	2,567	100	2,494	97	*73	*3
Louisiana	504	100	386	77	118	23	4,673	100	4,113	88	560	12
Maine	150	100	71	47	79	53	727	100	447	61	280	39
Maryland	370	100	243	66	126	34	3,169	100	2,543	80	626	20
Massachusetts...........	376	100	231	61	145	39	3,304	100	2,718	82	587	18
Mississippi	106	100	90	85	...	...	988	100	940	95	...	...
New Hampshire..........	70	100	42	60	*28	*40	320	100	193	60	*127	*40
New Jersey	572	100	338	59	234	41	5,114	100	3,106	61	2,007	39
New York	406	100	344	85	62	15	4,430	100	3,649	82	782	18
North Carolina..........	657	100	335	51	321	49	3,402	100	2,032	60	1,370	40
Oregon	183	100	130	71	*53	*29	953	100	873	92	*81	*8
Rhode Island	149	100	67	45	82	55	1,508	100	928	62	580	38
South Carolina..........	348	100	197	56	152	44	2,013	100	1,471	73	541	27
Texas.................	860	100	791	92	*69	*8	7,538	100	6,553	87	*985	*13
Virginia...............	385	100	276	72	109	28	3,279	100	2,789	85	491	15
Washington.............	386	100	329	85	*56	*15	2,941	100	2,737	93	*204	*7

* Estimate based on a small sample size.   ... Sample size too small to report data reliably.

Note: For the U.S. row, detail does not add to total because of multiple responses. U.S. totals include responses from participants residing in the District of Columbia, as described in the statistical accuracy appendix.

Table 63. Days of Fishing by State Where Fishing Took Place and Angler's State of Residence: 2001

(Population 16 years old and older. Numbers in thousands)

State	Days of fishing in state						Days of fishing by state residents					
	Total days, residents and nonresidents		Days by state residents		Days by nonresidents		Total days, in state of residence and other states		Days in state of residence		Days in other states	
	Number	Percent	Number	Percent	Number	Percent	Number	Percent	Number	Percent	Number	Percent
United States, total.....	557,394	100	501,321	90	56,965	10	557,394	100	501,321	90	56,965	10
Alabama.............	11,275	100	10,173	90	1,102	10	10,841	100	10,173	94	668	6
Alaska..............	3,408	100	2,395	70	1,013	30	2,445	100	2,395	98	*50	*2
Arizona.............	4,246	100	3,842	91	403	9	4,327	100	3,842	89	485	11
Arkansas............	13,006	100	11,508	88	1,498	12	11,954	100	11,508	96	*445	*4
California.............	27,663	100	26,802	97	861	3	27,878	100	26,802	96	1,076	4
Colorado............	9,269	100	6,478	70	2,791	30	7,639	100	6,478	85	1,161	15
Connecticut..........	4,768	100	4,363	91	405	9	5,482	100	4,363	80	1,120	20
Delaware............	1,355	100	824	61	*531	*39	1,341	100	824	61	517	39
Florida	48,417	100	42,416	88	6,002	12	43,439	100	42,416	98	1,023	2
Georgia.............	13,757	100	13,145	96	613	4	15,559	100	13,145	84	2,414	16
Hawaii	2,633	100	2,561	97	*73	*3	2,662	100	2,561	96	*101	*4
Idaho...............	4,070	100	2,942	72	1,128	28	3,097	100	2,942	95	155	5
Illinois..............	16,133	100	15,699	97	434	3	21,603	100	15,699	73	5,904	27
Indiana	14,192	100	13,889	98	*302	*2	15,537	100	13,889	89	1,647	11
Iowa................	7,485	100	7,048	94	436	6	8,534	100	7,048	83	1,486	17
Kansas	5,662	100	5,504	97	*158	*3	6,426	100	5,504	86	922	14
Kentucky	12,394	100	11,143	90	1,251	10	12,135	100	11,143	92	992	8
Louisiana	12,637	100	11,518	91	1,119	9	11,952	100	11,518	96	434	4
Maine	4,234	100	3,392	80	842	20	3,449	100	3,392	98	*58	*2
Maryland	7,471	100	5,818	78	1,653	22	7,112	100	5,818	82	1,294	18
Massachusetts...........	7,685	100	6,853	89	832	11	8,387	100	6,853	82	1,534	18
Michigan............	19,320	100	17,613	91	1,707	9	18,869	100	17,613	93	*1,256	*7
Minnesota...........	30,083	100	27,482	91	2,601	9	29,344	100	27,482	94	1,862	6
Mississippi	9,461	100	8,406	89	1,056	11	9,325	100	8,406	90	920	10
Missouri	13,279	100	11,309	85	1,970	15	12,396	100	11,309	91	1,087	9
Montana	4,068	100	3,515	86	554	14	3,656	100	3,515	96	141	4
Nebraska............	3,204	100	2,916	91	288	9	3,378	100	2,916	86	462	14
Nevada	1,575	100	1,422	90	...	...	2,230	100	1,422	64	809	36
New Hampshire........	3,203	100	2,590	81	613	19	2,974	100	2,590	87	384	13
New Jersey...........	10,857	100	8,490	78	2,367	22	10,973	100	8,490	77	2,483	23
New Mexico...........	2,485	100	2,091	84	*394	*16	2,407	100	2,091	87	315	13
New York............	24,720	100	21,736	88	2,984	12	23,181	100	21,736	94	1,445	6
North Carolina........	15,369	100	13,493	88	1,876	12	14,615	100	13,493	92	1,122	8
North Dakota	2,186	100	1,969	90	*217	*10	2,584	100	1,969	76	615	24
Ohio	19,882	100	18,882	95	1,000	5	22,014	100	18,882	86	3,132	14
Oklahoma............	12,741	100	12,395	97	345	3	13,228	100	12,395	94	832	6
Oregon	8,698	100	8,098	93	600	7	8,720	100	8,098	93	622	7
Pennsylvania.........	18,313	100	16,964	93	1,349	7	21,417	100	16,964	79	4,453	21
Rhode Island	2,047	100	1,393	68	655	32	1,638	100	1,393	85	246	15
South Carolina........	10,679	100	9,769	91	910	9	10,321	100	9,769	95	553	5
South Dakota	2,984	100	2,238	75	746	25	2,414	100	2,238	93	176	7
Tennessee	15,035	100	13,409	89	1,627	11	15,451	100	13,409	87	2,042	13
Texas...............	32,823	100	30,768	94	2,055	6	34,148	100	30,768	90	3,380	10
Utah	5,238	100	4,701	90	537	10	5,346	100	4,701	88	644	12
Vermont	2,321	100	1,684	73	637	27	1,969	100	1,684	86	285	14
Virginia.............	14,468	100	13,402	93	1,066	7	14,774	100	13,402	91	1,373	9
Washington...........	12,841	100	12,284	96	558	4	13,520	100	12,284	91	1,236	9
West Virginia	4,152	100	3,880	93	*272	*7	4,346	100	3,880	89	466	11
Wisconsin............	22,042	100	18,323	83	3,719	17	19,360	100	18,323	95	*1,037	*5
Wyoming	2,497	100	1,782	71	715	29	1,901	100	1,782	94	119	6

* Estimate based on a small sample size.   ... Sample size too small to report data reliably.

Note: U.S. totals include responses from participants residing in the District of Columbia, as described in the statistical accuracy appendix.

Table 64. Expenditures for Fishing by State Where Spending Took Place: 2001

(Population 16 years old and older. Expenditures in thousands of dollars)

State where spending took place	Total expenditures	Trip-related expenditures				Expenditures for equipment				Expenditures for other items[1]
		Total trip related	Food and lodging	Transportation	Other trip costs	Total equipment	Fishing equipment	Auxiliary equipment	Special equipment	
United States, total.....	35,632,257	14,656,000	5,880,997	3,515,756	5,259,247	16,963,253	4,617,612	721,049	11,624,802	4,012,733
Alabama.............	723,467	358,210	114,227	68,725	175,258	286,455	104,179	9,010	173,266	78,802
Alaska..............	537,355	424,182	154,886	118,875	150,421	92,541	36,732	10,280	45,529	20,632
Arizona.............	336,293	142,209	68,764	39,871	33,574	181,524	48,655	7,283	*125,585	12,560
Arkansas............	445,778	183,719	72,392	58,224	53,102	207,957	66,560	*5,624	*135,773	54,102
California...........	2,029,581	1,129,693	445,790	232,308	451,595	807,327	459,202	52,981	295,144	92,562
Colorado............	645,891	305,716	157,182	102,845	45,689	297,232	75,412	22,147	199,673	42,943
Connecticut..........	224,139	100,561	28,724	18,252	53,585	103,914	44,722	6,187	*53,006	19,663
Delaware............	69,956	30,603	9,869	7,587	13,148	32,750	20,888	*1,767	*10,095	6,603
Florida..............	4,083,409	2,091,312	765,284	393,668	932,360	1,733,364	509,158	68,053	1,156,154	258,733
Georgia.............	543,504	246,467	105,637	70,811	70,020	261,797	105,372	16,693	*139,732	35,240
Hawaii	107,002	66,718	20,715	16,021	29,982	39,552	22,539	3,941	*13,072	732
Idaho...............	310,872	116,222	53,463	40,458	22,301	121,498	35,863	22,785	*62,850	73,152
Illinois.............	598,376	206,285	74,076	72,541	59,668	346,554	118,636	19,412	*208,505	45,538
Indiana	518,863	152,757	62,989	36,352	53,416	347,407	105,914	*7,638	*233,855	18,699
Iowa	335,878	105,275	35,622	36,607	33,047	219,005	42,520	12,200	*164,285	11,598
Kansas	192,629	80,948	32,112	25,650	23,186	101,043	29,733	4,268	*67,042	10,638
Kentucky	544,660	221,393	94,734	47,715	78,944	300,732	56,851	*3,944	*239,937	22,535
Louisiana	703,373	398,751	138,825	83,153	176,773	272,126	91,912	7,955	172,259	32,497
Maine	250,939	95,538	53,579	20,988	20,971	135,524	24,194	16,254	*95,076	19,877
Maryland	480,185	245,627	78,477	36,373	130,777	218,996	56,404	9,907	*152,685	15,562
Massachusetts........	464,991	217,395	50,211	30,404	136,780	235,942	77,522	10,728	*147,692	11,653
Michigan............	838,558	518,553	238,149	131,825	148,578	263,452	178,042	*8,860	*76,550	56,553
Minnesota...........	1,284,522	794,526	385,949	228,246	180,331	407,372	204,262	20,793	*182,317	82,625
Mississippi	210,697	118,202	44,585	28,588	45,029	82,648	52,549	4,996	*25,103	9,847
Missouri	745,514	318,072	165,923	88,755	63,394	395,549	109,632	18,254	*267,662	31,894
Montana	292,050	148,824	79,341	51,121	18,362	109,107	25,251	*3,250	*80,606	34,119
Nebraska............	146,359	60,283	26,471	18,401	15,411	76,671	49,070	10,562	*17,039	9,404
Nevada	216,721	76,535	25,257	39,679	11,599	119,707	18,059	8,795	*92,853	20,479
New Hampshire	164,634	76,055	26,179	12,749	37,128	71,688	28,333	5,841	*37,514	16,891
New Jersey...........	699,826	374,144	96,585	50,654	226,905	303,972	104,988	11,786	*187,198	21,710
New Mexico..........	176,476	90,653	35,924	29,764	24,965	77,830	32,274	6,738	*38,818	7,993
New York	1,073,019	380,766	146,930	69,049	164,786	517,027	186,364	27,120	*303,543	175,226
North Carolina........	1,118,028	452,303	233,813	85,480	133,010	567,323	102,219	7,678	*457,426	98,401
North Dakota	159,023	57,703	23,808	22,360	11,535	96,413	21,784	1,232	*73,396	4,908
Ohio	761,619	380,887	127,414	83,735	169,738	341,481	163,594	34,554	*143,332	39,252
Oklahoma............	476,019	212,235	84,111	58,409	69,716	250,218	67,598	*36,099	*146,521	13,565
Oregon	601,780	258,963	99,880	84,839	74,244	245,469	76,026	11,343	158,100	97,348
Pennsylvania..........	580,351	282,752	118,171	78,031	86,549	237,023	112,677	20,293	*104,053	60,576
Rhode Island	105,649	70,198	18,433	7,990	43,775	33,132	11,366	*668	*21,098	2,320
South Carolina........	558,731	317,966	126,983	64,041	126,942	227,616	79,262	32,885	*115,469	13,149
South Dakota	182,480	86,439	40,290	29,003	17,146	85,987	16,091	2,190	...	10,054
Tennessee	480,221	264,985	113,584	50,996	100,406	171,789	114,019	14,842	*42,928	43,447
Texas...............	1,950,902	871,368	340,768	229,359	301,241	698,590	245,128	30,870	*422,592	380,944
Utah	392,617	172,423	78,990	52,676	40,756	196,430	59,771	13,973	122,686	23,764
Vermont	92,536	59,262	26,980	22,656	9,627	26,500	17,937	*1,752	...	6,773
Virginia.............	517,802	277,484	105,317	63,412	108,756	221,944	101,601	*10,575	*109,769	18,373
Washington...........	853,761	342,369	119,783	98,846	123,741	468,641	116,991	26,329	325,321	42,751
West Virginia	102,281	64,673	29,302	18,471	16,900	30,154	23,106	*4,546	...	7,454
Wisconsin...........	1,005,149	512,347	260,820	125,247	126,279	360,919	149,368	17,988	193,563	131,883
Wyoming	211,530	95,178	43,563	33,824	17,791	71,049	10,988	*2,386	*57,676	45,303

* Estimate based on a small sample size.   ... Sample size too small to report data reliably.

[1] Includes expenditures for magazine subscriptions, membership dues and contributions, land leasing and ownership, and licenses, stamps, tags, and permits.

Note: U.S. totals include responses from participants residing in the District of Columbia, as described in the statistical accuracy appendix.

Table 65. Participants in Wildlife-Watching Activities by Participant's State of Residence: 2001

(Population 16 years old and older. Numbers in thousands)

Participant's state of residence	Population	Total participants		Nonresidential		Residential	
		Number	Percent of population	Number	Percent of population	Number	Percent of population
United States, total.....	**212,298**	**66,105**	**31**	**21,823**	**10**	**62,928**	**30**
Alabama...............	3,427	965	28	280	8	925	27
Alaska................	454	241	53	118	26	221	49
Arizona...............	3,700	1,107	30	329	9	1,063	29
Arkansas..............	1,999	778	39	190	10	762	38
California.............	25,982	5,491	21	2,191	8	4,853	19
Colorado..............	3,215	1,213	38	531	17	1,127	35
Connecticut............	2,536	883	35	248	10	859	34
Delaware..............	599	170	28	43	7	168	28
Florida...............	12,171	2,856	23	1,279	11	2,635	22
Georgia...............	6,096	1,326	22	302	5	1,305	21
Hawaii	916	126	14	50	5	120	13
Idaho.................	972	388	40	214	22	333	34
Illinois................	9,244	2,492	27	683	7	2,379	26
Indiana	4,558	1,786	39	484	11	1,727	38
Iowa	2,201	983	45	354	16	939	43
Kansas	2,017	735	36	286	14	718	36
Kentucky	3,121	1,264	40	329	11	1,234	40
Louisiana	3,306	840	25	250	8	802	24
Maine	1,005	520	52	174	17	501	50
Maryland	4,078	1,311	32	413	10	1,261	31
Massachusetts..........	4,837	1,493	31	427	9	1,443	30
Michigan..............	7,587	2,424	32	747	10	2,361	31
Minnesota.............	3,688	1,993	54	562	15	1,932	52
Mississippi	2,111	579	27	103	5	576	27
Missouri	4,206	1,612	38	581	14	1,514	36
Montana..............	699	362	52	195	28	341	49
Nebraska..............	1,266	498	39	150	12	469	37
Nevada...............	1,454	334	23	128	9	300	21
New Hampshire	954	450	47	139	15	445	47
New Jersey............	6,300	1,694	27	564	9	1,640	26
New Mexico...........	1,337	471	35	205	15	449	34
New York.............	14,201	3,524	25	1,112	8	3,442	24
North Carolina.........	5,918	1,884	32	367	6	1,815	31
North Dakota	483	135	28	48	10	125	26
Ohio	8,645	2,768	32	887	10	2,653	31
Oklahoma.............	2,587	1,042	40	340	13	997	39
Oregon	2,630	1,286	49	561	21	1,204	46
Pennsylvania..........	9,303	3,522	38	1,173	13	3,371	36
Rhode Island	765	242	32	58	8	237	31
South Carolina.........	3,080	1,079	35	282	9	1,045	34
South Dakota	559	251	45	77	14	241	43
Tennessee	4,317	1,706	40	375	9	1,655	38
Texas.................	15,445	3,088	20	1,043	7	2,930	19
Utah	1,554	572	37	323	21	515	33
Vermont	479	287	60	109	23	280	58
Virginia...............	5,471	2,168	40	581	11	2,105	38
Washington............	4,516	2,234	49	874	19	2,105	47
West Virginia..........	1,447	517	36	166	11	492	34
Wisconsin.............	4,059	2,159	53	769	19	2,076	51
Wyoming	377	172	46	95	25	154	41

Note: Detail does not add to total because of multiple responses. U.S. totals include responses from participants residing in the District of Columbia, as described in the statistical accuracy appendix.

U.S. Fish & Wildlife Service

Table 66. Participants in Wildlife-Watching Activities by State Where Activity Took Place: 2001

(Population 16 years old and older. Numbers in thousands)

State where activity took place	Total participants		Nonresidential		Residential	
	Number	Percent	Number	Percent	Number	Percent
United States, total........	66,105	100	21,823	33	62,928	95
Alabama...................	1,016	100	276	27	925	91
Alaska....................	420	100	292	69	221	53
Arizona...................	1,465	100	638	44	1,063	73
Arkansas..................	845	100	211	25	762	90
California................	5,720	100	2,270	40	4,853	85
Colorado..................	1,552	100	838	54	1,127	73
Connecticut...............	965	100	279	29	859	89
Delaware..................	232	100	96	41	168	72
Florida...................	3,240	100	1,503	46	2,635	81
Georgia...................	1,494	100	411	28	1,305	87
Hawaii	220	100	141	64	120	54
Idaho....................	643	100	451	70	333	52
Illinois...................	2,621	100	638	24	2,379	91
Indiana	1,866	100	474	25	1,727	93
Iowa	1,028	100	310	30	939	91
Kansas	807	100	297	37	718	89
Kentucky	1,362	100	385	28	1,234	91
Louisiana	931	100	314	34	802	86
Maine....................	778	100	419	54	501	64
Maryland	1,524	100	533	35	1,261	83
Massachusetts..............	1,686	100	542	32	1,443	86
Michigan..................	2,666	100	884	33	2,361	89
Minnesota.................	2,155	100	634	29	1,932	90
Mississippi	631	100	131	21	576	91
Missouri	1,826	100	738	40	1,514	83
Montana	687	100	511	74	341	50
Nebraska..................	565	100	186	33	469	83
Nevada	543	100	309	57	300	55
New Hampshire	766	100	425	56	445	58
New Jersey................	1,895	100	688	36	1,640	87
New Mexico...............	671	100	387	58	449	67
New York.................	3,887	100	1,330	34	3,442	89
North Carolina	2,168	100	588	27	1,815	84
North Dakota..............	190	100	93	49	125	66
Ohio	2,897	100	898	31	2,653	92
Oklahoma.................	1,131	100	403	36	997	88
Oregon	1,680	100	910	54	1,204	72
Pennsylvania..............	3,794	100	1,279	34	3,371	89
Rhode Island	298	100	98	33	237	80
South Carolina	1,186	100	331	28	1,045	88
South Dakota	358	100	181	51	241	67
Tennessee	2,084	100	683	33	1,655	79
Texas....................	3,240	100	1,002	31	2,930	90
Utah	806	100	530	66	515	64
Vermont	496	100	307	62	280	56
Virginia..................	2,460	100	772	31	2,105	86
Washington...............	2,496	100	1,065	43	2,105	84
West Virginia	605	100	219	36	492	81
Wisconsin.................	2,442	100	1,000	41	2,076	85
Wyoming	498	100	416	84	154	31

Note: Detail does not add to total because of multiple responses. U.S. totals include responses from participants residing in the District of Columbia, as described in the statistical accuracy appendix.

Table 67. Participants in Nonresidential Wildlife-Watching Activities by State Where Activity Took Place: 2001

(Population 16 years old and older. Numbers in thousands)

State where activity took place	Total participants		State residents		State nonresidents	
	Number	Percent	Number	Percent	Number	Percent
United States, total.....	21,823	100	18,041	83	6,570	30
Alabama..............	276	100	204	74	*72	*26
Alaska................	292	100	106	36	185	64
Arizona...............	638	100	271	42	367	58
Arkansas..............	211	100	*144	*68	*67	*32
California.............	2,270	100	1,885	83	384	17
Colorado.............	838	100	477	57	362	43
Connecticut...........	279	100	189	68	*90	*32
Delaware..............	96	100	31	33	*64	*67
Florida	1,503	100	1,013	67	490	33
Georgia..............	411	100	234	57	*178	*43
Hawaii	141	100	45	32	*96	*68
Idaho................	451	100	188	42	264	58
Illinois...............	638	100	462	72	176	28
Indiana	474	100	395	83	*80	*17
Iowa	310	100	248	80	*63	*20
Kansas	297	100	221	74	*76	*26
Kentucky	385	100	282	73	*102	*27
Louisiana	314	100	203	65	*111	*35
Maine	419	100	159	38	260	62
Maryland	533	100	299	56	234	44
Massachusetts...........	542	100	337	62	205	38
Michigan.............	884	100	634	72	250	28
Minnesota............	634	100	463	73	171	27
Mississippi	131	100	*77	*58	...	...
Missouri	738	100	519	70	219	30
Montana..............	511	100	187	36	325	64
Nebraska.............	186	100	115	62	*71	*38
Nevada...............	309	100	86	28	*222	*72
New Hampshire	425	100	105	25	320	75
New Jersey............	688	100	462	67	225	33
New Mexico............	387	100	185	48	202	52
New York.............	1,330	100	938	71	392	29
North Carolina..........	588	100	288	49	300	51
North Dakota...........	93	100	38	40		
Ohio	898	100	753	84	*145	*16
Oklahoma.............	403	100	298	74	*105	*26
Oregon	910	100	509	56	401	44
Pennsylvania...........	1,279	100	986	77	293	23
Rhode Island	98	100	40	41	*58	*59
South Carolina..........	331	100	204	61	*128	*39
South Dakota...........	181	100	71	39	110	61
Tennessee	683	100	301	44	382	56
Texas................	1,002	100	828	83	174	17
Utah	530	100	286	54	244	46
Vermont	307	100	94	30	214	70
Virginia..............	772	100	459	59	313	41
Washington............	1,065	100	779	73	286	27
West Virginia	219	100	114	52	*105	*48
Wisconsin	1,000	100	717	72	283	28
Wyoming	416	100	89	21	327	79

* Estimate based on a small sample size.   ... Sample size too small to report data reliably.

Note: Detail does not add to total because of multiple responses. U.S. totals include responses from participants residing in the District of Columbia, as described in the statistical accuracy appendix.

Table 68. Days of Nonresidential Wildlife-Watching Activity by State Where Activity Took Place and Participant's State of Residence: 2001

(Population 16 years old and older. Numbers in thousands)

State	Days of activity in state						Days of activity by state residents					
	Total days, residents and nonresidents		Days by residents		Days by nonresidents		Total days, in state of residence and other states		Days in state of residence		Days in other states	
	Number	Percent	Number	Percent	Number	Percent	Number	Percent	Number	Percent	Number	Percent
United States, total.....	372,006	100	306,170	82	65,837	18	372,006	100	306,170	82	65,837	18
Alabama...............	3,643	100	3,350	92	*294	*8	4,052	100	3,350	83	*702	*17
Alaska................	3,892	100	1,654	43	2,237	57	1,799	100	1,654	92	*144	*8
Arizona...............	4,584	100	2,464	54	2,120	46	3,693	100	2,464	67	1,229	33
Arkansas..............	1,562	100	*1,229	*79	*333	*21	1,551	100	*1,229	*79	...	...
California.............	23,807	100	21,661	91	2,145	9	26,556	100	21,661	82	4,895	18
Colorado..............	9,510	100	5,874	62	3,636	38	6,613	100	5,874	89	*739	*11
Connecticut...........	7,241	100	6,227	86	*1,014	*14	7,091	100	6,227	88	864	12
Delaware..............	722	100	417	58	*304	*42	668	100	417	62	251	38
Florida	21,388	100	17,725	83	3,663	17	21,705	100	17,725	82	*3,980	*18
Georgia...............	4,868	100	4,219	87	*648	*13	5,211	100	4,219	81	*991	*19
Hawaii	1,718	100	1,072	62	*646	*38	1,157	100	1,072	93	*85	*7
Idaho.................	3,610	100	2,063	57	1,547	43	2,686	100	2,063	77	*623	*23
Illinois...............	7,656	100	6,971	91	685	9	9,378	100	6,971	74	2,407	26
Indiana	11,999	100	11,386	95	*613	*5	12,986	100	11,386	88	*1,600	*12
Iowa.................	6,393	100	6,135	96	*258	*4	7,135	100	6,135	86	1,000	14
Kansas	2,416	100	1,667	69	*749	*31	2,783	100	1,667	60	1,116	40
Kentucky	5,689	100	5,287	93	*402	*7	7,108	100	5,287	74	*1,821	*26
Louisiana	2,432	100	2,167	89	*265	*11	2,399	100	2,167	90	...	...
Maine	4,981	100	3,251	65	1,730	35	3,452	100	3,251	94	*201	*6
Maryland	6,809	100	5,137	75	1,672	25	6,570	100	5,137	78	1,434	22
Massachusetts...........	10,198	100	9,094	89	1,103	11	10,796	100	9,094	84	1,701	16
Michigan..............	13,999	100	12,285	88	1,714	12	14,180	100	12,285	87	*1,895	*13
Minnesota.............	13,234	100	12,354	93	880	7	13,489	100	12,354	92	*1,135	*8
Mississippi	3,288	100	*3,121	*95	...	...	3,486	100	*3,121	*90	*365	*10
Missouri	12,448	100	10,937	88	1,510	12	12,611	100	10,937	87	*1,673	*13
Montana..............	4,612	100	2,812	61	1,799	39	3,074	100	2,812	91	*262	*9
Nebraska..............	2,240	100	1,538	69	*702	*31	1,968	100	1,538	78	*430	*22
Nevada	1,567	100	673	43	*894	*57	1,161	100	673	58	488	42
New Hampshire	3,178	100	1,232	39	1,946	61	1,810	100	1,232	68	578	32
New Jersey	9,873	100	8,988	91	886	9	12,560	100	8,988	72	3,572	28
New Mexico............	6,381	100	5,209	82	1,173	18	5,474	100	5,209	95	*266	*5
New York.............	21,583	100	18,836	87	2,748	13	22,099	100	18,836	85	*3,263	*15
North Carolina..........	5,947	100	4,551	77	1,396	23	5,548	100	4,551	82	*997	*18
North Dakota	523	100	396	76	...	...	469	100	396	85	*72	*15
Ohio	19,814	100	18,995	96	*819	*4	21,366	100	18,995	89	2,371	11
Oklahoma..............	4,058	100	3,680	91	*378	*9	3,912	100	3,680	94	...	...
Oregon	8,517	100	6,458	76	2,059	24	7,571	100	6,458	85	1,113	15
Pennsylvania...........	18,990	100	16,534	87	2,456	13	20,066	100	16,534	82	3,532	18
Rhode Island	1,414	100	773	55	*641	*45	1,003	100	773	77	*230	*23
South Carolina..........	4,616	100	3,828	83	*788	*17	4,557	100	3,828	84	*729	*16
South Dakota	1,923	100	1,409	73	514	27	2,015	100	1,409	70	*606	*30
Tennessee	6,144	100	3,138	51	3,007	49	3,706	100	3,138	85	*569	*15
Texas.................	7,711	100	6,345	82	1,366	18	12,561	100	6,345	51	*6,216	*49
Utah	4,414	100	3,199	72	1,215	28	4,007	100	3,199	80	808	20
Vermont	3,717	100	1,705	46	2,012	54	2,143	100	1,705	80	*439	*20
Virginia...............	8,906	100	7,541	85	1,365	15	10,212	100	7,541	74	2,671	26
Washington............	11,256	100	9,647	86	1,609	14	12,763	100	9,647	76	3,115	24
West Virginia	2,619	100	2,195	84	*424	*16	2,508	100	2,195	88	*313	*12
Wisconsin.............	16,499	100	13,573	82	2,926	18	15,028	100	13,573	90	*1,455	*10
Wyoming	3,924	100	1,724	44	2,200	56	1,791	100	1,724	96	*67	*4

* Estimate based on a small sample size.   ... Sample size too small to report data reliably.

Note: Detail does not add to total because of nonresponse. U.S. totals include responses from participants residing in the District of Columbia, as described in the statistical accuracy appendix.

Table 69. Expenditures for Wildlife-Watching Activities by State Where Spending Took Place: 2001

(Population 16 years old and older. Expenditures in thousands of dollars)

State where spending took place	Total expenditures	Trip-related expenditures				Expenditures for equipment				Expenditures for other items[1]
		Total trip related	Food and lodging	Trans-portation	Other trip costs	Total equipment	Wildlife-watching equipment	Auxiliary equipment	Special equipment	
United States, total.....	**38,414,488**	**8,162,439**	**4,818,843**	**2,595,542**	**748,054**	**23,539,593**	**7,353,977**	**716,900**	**15,468,716**	**6,712,457**
Alabama.............	626,400	79,531	32,846	36,772	*9,913	407,636	119,232	*3,216	*285,187	139,233
Alaska...............	498,865	386,233	174,348	157,007	54,878	53,337	26,563	*2,749	...	59,295
Arizona.............	820,718	304,677	193,511	98,217	12,950	484,530	128,202	20,470	*335,858	31,511
Arkansas............	243,990	20,044	9,142	9,540	*1,361	204,553	80,980	*22,709	...	19,393
California...........	2,580,875	880,805	531,229	300,502	49,074	1,239,195	561,514	51,816	...	460,875
Colorado...........	624,402	416,734	278,931	120,020	17,784	172,829	136,154	19,969	...	34,839
Connecticut.........	225,964	38,010	25,911	10,255	*1,844	142,817	113,152	*6,533	...	45,137
Delaware...........	42,338	14,287	9,381	3,191	*1,715	21,083	19,677	*1,405	...	6,968
Florida	1,575,481	675,384	399,998	171,131	104,255	838,041	275,540	*29,814	...	62,056
Georgia.............	535,771	123,264	76,011	32,963	14,290	364,702	132,760	*14,086	...	47,805
Hawaii	131,619	69,057	39,786	24,537	4,735	52,482	15,261	*1,397	...	10,080
Idaho..............	227,470	96,807	52,140	40,346	4,321	117,848	42,017	*5,499	...	12,815
Illinois.............	596,241	85,618	50,906	27,711	*7,000	472,585	243,767	*12,988	...	38,038
Indiana.............	641,239	118,525	70,951	41,991	5,582	340,081	221,295	*10,665	...	182,633
Iowa	188,391	22,067	11,104	9,740	*1,223	143,471	109,448	...	...	22,854
Kansas.............	128,663	32,175	19,827	11,388	*960	71,949	68,719	...	...	24,539
Kentucky	601,550	49,776	26,723	22,344	*710	328,796	107,864	*9,617	...	222,977
Louisiana	168,420	55,424	28,741	20,502	*6,181	97,339	70,326	*3,918	...	15,657
Maine	513,566	147,530	78,551	36,659	32,319	139,786	55,437	*7,023	...	226,251
Maryland	862,687	129,692	94,261	30,482	4,949	450,596	150,630	10,914	...	282,399
Massachusetts........	469,333	162,433	71,543	46,264	44,625	252,097	153,852	*11,025	...	54,803
Michigan............	692,757	281,978	189,425	55,156	37,397	354,649	296,279	...	...	56,130
Minnesota...........	531,057	115,640	66,717	40,070	8,853	370,482	204,449	*4,859	...	44,935
Mississippi	303,477	36,109	*20,572	*12,285	*3,252	243,647	53,082	...	...	23,721
Missouri	448,756	156,986	93,056	58,100	5,830	275,687	166,191	*8,304	...	16,083
Montana	350,335	207,496	118,394	75,571	13,531	115,443	53,823	*3,934	...	27,396
Nebraska...........	129,747	18,413	9,115	8,860	*439	103,140	42,924	*4,788	...	8,194
Nevada	250,145	70,164	31,280	36,093	2,790	173,445	36,312	*7,035	...	6,537
New Hampshire	342,940	177,305	132,641	32,523	12,140	148,353	62,514	5,660	...	17,282
New Jersey..........	1,243,844	142,042	94,534	32,274	15,234	1,029,512	180,472	*8,926	...	72,290
New Mexico..........	558,290	151,015	92,938	52,514	5,564	297,857	126,379	39,842	...	109,417
New York	1,407,193	248,174	124,398	63,911	59,865	802,663	504,293	*10,374	...	356,356
North Carolina........	826,882	158,523	107,682	45,662	*5,179	574,561	216,033	*9,487	...	93,798
North Dakota.........	27,100	9,361	6,145	2,870	*346	15,163	8,245	...	...	2,576
Ohio	623,051	129,788	79,646	41,361	*8,782	453,354	286,339	*38,204	...	39,909
Oklahoma...........	193,248	69,211	30,297	33,167	*5,747	111,457	104,186	*3,798	...	12,580
Oregon	769,407	304,990	182,183	108,457	14,350	340,293	136,998	29,672	*173,624	124,123
Pennsylvania.........	961,799	171,658	101,996	59,749	9,913	729,868	359,445	*44,851	*325,572	60,274
Rhode Island	169,635	66,639	17,518	9,908	*39,213	96,265	13,760	...	...	6,731
South Carolina........	256,372	89,045	55,833	25,075	*8,137	149,451	113,069	*6,463	...	17,876
South Dakota	91,958	53,556	28,227	19,777	5,552	23,568	15,305	*2,417	...	14,834
Tennessee	448,543	206,729	148,601	55,118	*3,009	212,452	165,441	*5,730	...	29,363
Texas..............	1,282,943	228,780	146,525	61,227	*21,028	944,854	314,319	*61,297	...	109,309
Utah	555,710	175,861	103,573	58,169	14,118	277,989	71,662	18,044	*188,282	101,861
Vermont	203,715	63,243	36,855	23,632	2,756	57,660	37,115	*2,904	...	82,811
Virginia............	788,644	172,351	106,629	58,065	7,657	370,729	267,653	23,147	...	245,564
Washington..........	979,730	282,492	158,195	102,233	22,064	594,631	277,239	62,080	*255,312	102,607
West Virginia	163,511	78,860	28,073	46,270	*4,516	80,467	63,791	*3,766	...	4,184
Wisconsin...........	1,311,619	250,760	151,554	77,512	21,694	837,020	251,856	24,380	*560,784	223,838
Wyoming	264,931	135,626	79,584	47,630	8,412	111,663	24,619	*2,383	...	17,642

* Estimate based on a small sample size.　　... Sample size too small to report data reliably.

[1] Includes expenditures for magazine subscriptions, membership dues, and contributions.

Note: U.S. totals include responses from participants residing in the District of Columbia, as described in the statistical accuracy appendix.

Appendix A

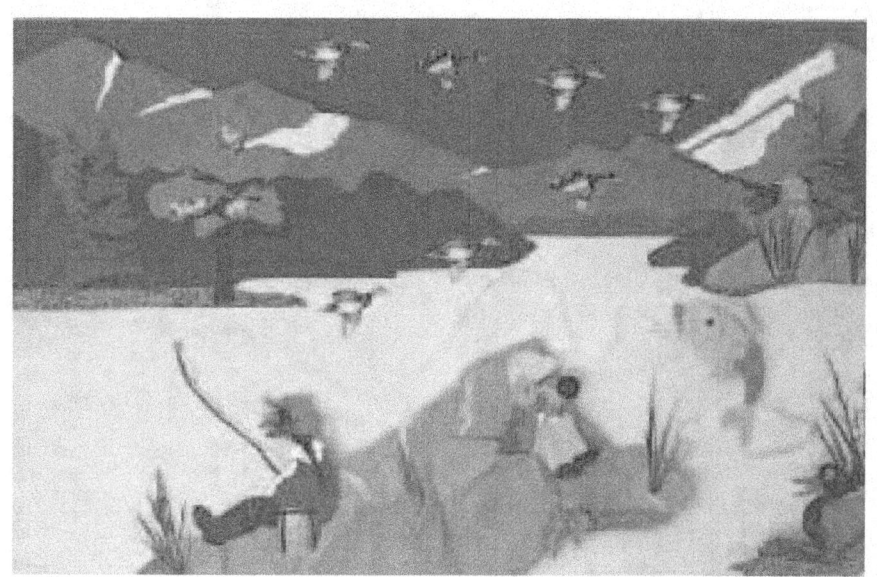

Appendix A.
Definitions

Annual household income—Total 2001 income of household members before taxes and other deductions.

Auxiliary equipment—Equipment owned primarily for wildlife-associated recreation. These include for the sportspersons section—camping bags, packs, duffel bags and tents, binoculars, field glasses, telescopes, special fishing and hunting clothing, foul weather gear, boots, waders, and processing and taxidermy costs; and for the wildlife-watching section—tents, tarps, frame packs, backpacking equipment and other camping equipment, day packs, carrying case, and special clothing.

Big game—Antelope, bear, deer, elk, moose, wild turkey, and similar large animals which are hunted.

Birding life list—A tally of bird species seen during a birder's lifetime.

Census Divisions

East North Central
Illinois
Indiana
Michigan
Ohio
Wisconsin

East South Central
Alabama
Kentucky
Mississippi
Tennessee

Middle Atlantic
New Jersey
New York
Pennsylvania

Mountain
Arizona
Colorado
Idaho
Montana
Nevada

New Mexico
Utah
Wyoming

New England
Connecticut
Maine
Massachusetts
New Hampshire
Rhode Island
Vermont

Pacific
Alaska
California
Hawaii
Oregon
Washington

South Atlantic
Delaware
District of Columbia
Florida
Georgia
Maryland
North Carolina
South Carolina
Virginia
West Virginia

West North Central
Kansas
Iowa
Minnesota
Missouri
Nebraska
North Dakota
South Dakota

West South Central
Arkansas
Louisiana
Oklahoma
Texas

Day—Any part of a day spent in a given activity. For example, if someone hunted 2 hours 1 day and 3 hours another day, it would be recorded as 2 days of hunting. If someone hunted 2 hours in the morning and 3 hours in the evening of the same day, it would be considered 1 day of hunting.

Education—The highest completed grade of school or year of college.

Expenditures—Money spent in 2001 for wildlife-related recreation trips in the United States and wildlife-related recreational equipment purchased in the United States. Expenditures include both money spent by participants for themselves and the value of gifts they received.

Federal land—Public land owned by the federal government such as National Forests and National Wildlife Refuges.

Fishing—The sport of catching or attempting to catch fish with a hook, line, bow and arrow, or spear; it also includes catching or gathering shellfish (clams, crabs, etc.); and the noncommercial seining or netting of fish, unless the fish are for use as bait. For example, seining for smelt is fishing, but seining for bait minnows is not included as fishing.

Fishing equipment—Items owned primarily for fishing. These items are listed in Table 13.

Freshwater—Reservoirs, lakes, ponds, and the nontidal portions of rivers and streams.

Great Lakes fishing—Fishing in Lakes Superior, Michigan, Huron, St. Clair, Erie, and Ontario, their connecting waters such as the St. Marys River system, Detroit River, St. Clair River, and the Niagara River, and the St. Lawrence River south of the bridge at Cornwall, New York. Great Lakes fishing includes fishing in tributaries of the Great Lakes for smelt, steelhead, and salmon.

Home—The starting point of a wildlife-related recreational trip. It may be a permanent residence or a temporary or seasonal residence such as a cabin.

Hunting—The sport of shooting or attempting to shoot wildlife with firearms or archery equipment.

Hunting equipment—Items owned primarily for hunting. These items are listed in Table 18.

Local land—Public land owned by local government such as county parks or municipal watersheds.

Maintain natural areas—To set aside one-quarter acre or more of natural environment such as wood lots or open fields for the primary purpose of benefiting wildlife.

Maintain plantings—To introduce or encourage the growth of food and cover plants for the primary purpose of benefiting wildlife.

Metropolitan statistical area (MSA)—Except in the New England States, an MSA is a county or group of contiguous counties containing at least one city of 50,000 or more inhabitants or twin cities (i.e., cities with contiguous boundaries and constituting, for general social and economic purposes, a single community) with a combined population of at least 50,000. Also included in an MSA are contiguous counties that are socially and economically integrated with the central city. In the New England States, an MSA consists of towns and cities instead of counties. Each MSA must include at least one central city.

Migratory birds—Birds that regularly migrate from one region or climate to another. The survey focuses on migratory birds which may be hunted, including bandtailed pigeons, coots, ducks, doves, gallinules, geese, rails, and woodcocks.

Multiple responses—The term used to reflect the fact that individuals or their characteristics fall into more than one reporting category. An example of a big game hunter who hunted for deer and elk demonstrates the effect of multiple responses. In this case, adding the number of deer hunters (1) and elk hunters (1) would over state the number of big game hunters (1) because deer and elk hunters are not mutually exclusive

categories. In contrast, total participants is the sum of male and female participants, because male and female are mutually exclusive categories.

Nonresidential activity (away from home)—Trips or outings at least 1 mile from home for the primary purpose of observing, photographing, or feeding wildlife. Trips to zoos, circuses, aquariums, and museums are not included.

Nonresidents—Individuals who do not live in the state being reported. For example, a person living in Texas who watches whales in California is a nonresident participant in California.

Nonresponse—Nonresponse is a term used to reflect the fact that some survey respondents provide incomplete sets of information. For example, a survey respondent may have been unable to identify the primary type of hunting for which a gun was bought. Hunting expenditures will reflect the gun purchase, but it will not appear as spending for big game or any other type of hunting. Nonresponses result in reported totals that are greater than the sum of their parts.

Observe—To take special interest in or try to identify birds, fish, or other wildlife.

Other animals—Coyotes, crows, foxes, groundhogs, prairie dogs, raccoons, and similar animals that are often regarded as varmints or pests. Other animals may be classified as unprotected or nongame animals by the state in which they are hunted.

Participants—Individuals who engaged in fishing, hunting, or a wildlife-watching activity.

Primary purpose—The principal motivation for an activity, trip, or expenditure.

Public areas—Public lands owned by local, state, or federal governments.

Public land—Land that is owned by the local, state, or federal government.

Private land—Land that is owned by a private individual, group of individuals, or nongovernmental organization.

Residential activity (around the home)—Activity within 1 mile of home with a primary purpose: (1) closely observing or trying to identify birds or other wildlife, (2) photographing wildlife, (3) feeding birds or other wildlife, (4) maintaining natural areas of at least one-quarter acre primarily for the benefit to wildlife, (5) maintaining plantings (shrubs, agricultural crops, etc.) primarily for the benefit of wildlife, or (6) visiting public parks within 1 mile of home to observe, photograph, or feed wildlife.

Residents—Individuals who lived in the state being reported. For example, persons who live in California and watch whales in California are resident participants in California.

Rural—Respondent lived in a rural nonfarm, or rural farm area, as determined by Census.

Saltwater—Oceans, tidal bays and sounds, and the tidal portions of rivers and streams.

Screening interviews—The first survey contact with a household. Screening interviews with a household representative in each household to identify respondents who are eligible for indepth interviews. Screening interviews gather data about the individuals in the households, such as their age and sex. Screening interviews are discussed in the Survey Background and Method section of this report.

Small game—Grouse, partridge, pheasants, quail, rabbits, squirrels, and similar small animals and birds for which many states have small game seasons and bag limits.

Special equipment—Items of equipment that are owned primarily for wildlife-related recreation. These include for the sportsmen section bass boat and other types of motor boat; canoe and other types of nonmotor boat; boat motor, boat trailer/hitch, and other boat accessories; pickup, camper, van, travel or tent trailer, motor home, house trailer, RV, cabin; and trail bike, dune buggy, 4x4 vehicle, four-wheeler, and snowmobile. For the wildlife-watching section these include off-the-road vehicles such as snowmobiles, four-wheeler, 4x4 vehicle, trail bike, dune buggy, travel or tent trailer, motor home, pickup, camper, van, house trailer, RV boat and boat accessories, and cabin.

Spenders—Individuals who reported an expenditure value for fishing, hunting, or wildlife-watching activities or equipment.

Sportspersons—Individuals who engaged in fishing, hunting, or both.

State land—Public land owned by a state such as state parks or state wildlife management areas.

Trip—An outing involving fishing, hunting, or wildlife-watching activities. In the context of this survey, a trip may begin from an individual's principal residence or from another place, such as a vacation home or the home of a relative. A trip may last an hour, a day, or many days.

Type of fishing—Three types of fishing are reported: fishing in (1) freshwater except Great Lakes, (2) Great Lakes, and (3) saltwater.

Type of hunting—Four types of hunting are reported: hunting for (1) big game, (2) small game, (3) migratory bird, and (4) other animals.

Urban—Respondent lived in an urban area, as determined by the U.S. Census Bureau.

Wildlife—Animals such as birds, fish, insects, mammals, amphibians, and reptiles that are living in natural or wild environments. Wildlife does not include animals living in aquariums, zoos, and other artificial surroundings or domestic animals such as farm animals or pets.

Wildlife-associated recreation—Recreational fishing, hunting, or wildlife watching.

Wildlife-watching activity—An activity engaged in primarily for the purpose of feeding, photographing, or observing fish or other wildlife. In previous years, this was termed nonconsumptive activity. (See also residential and nonresidential activities.)

Wildlife-watching equipment—Items owned primarily for observing, photographing, or feeding wildlife. These items are listed in Table 43.

Appendix B

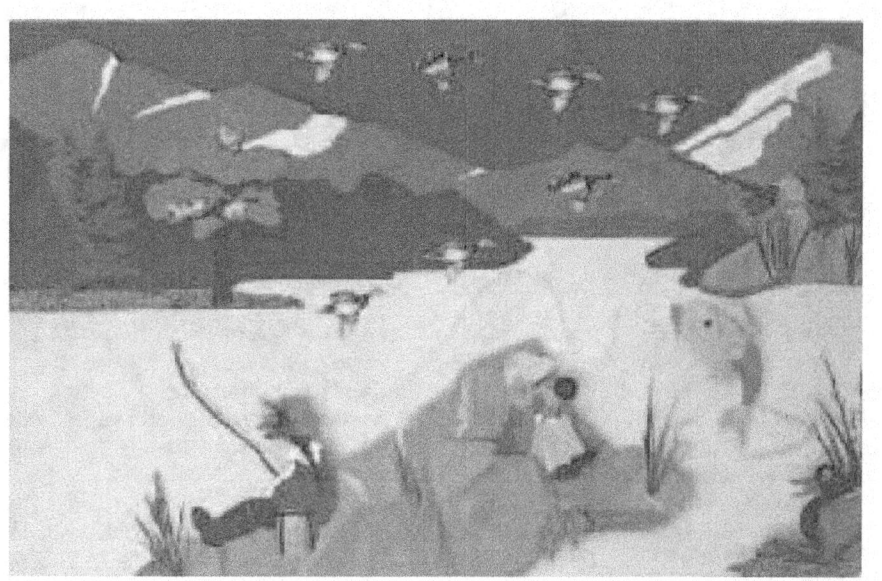

Appendix B.
Comparability With Previous Surveys

The 2001 National Survey of Fishing, Hunting, and Wildlife-Associated Recreation (FHWAR) was designed to continue the data collection of the 1955 to 1996 Surveys. While complete comparability between any two surveys cannot be achieved, this Appendix compares major findings of all the surveys and presents trends for the major categories of wildlife-related recreation where feasible. Differences among the Surveys are discussed in the following two sections under the headings of the year in which each survey was conducted.

The principal characteristics of the 1955 to 2001 Surveys are summarized in Table B-1. The table shows the scope and design of all 10 surveys.

This Appendix provides trend information in two sections (1991 to 2001 and 1955 to 1985). Beginning with 1991, a significant change was made in the recall period used in the detailed phase of the FHWAR Surveys. The recall period in 1991 was shortened from 12 months to 4 months to improve the accuracy of the data collected. As a result of that change in methodology, the surveys conducted since 1991 cannot be compared with those conducted earlier.

The 1955 to 1985 Surveys required respondents to recall their recreation activities for the survey year at the beginning of the following year. The 1991 Survey went back to the respondents three times during the survey year to get their activity information. This change in the recall period was due to a study of the effect of the respondent recall length on survey estimates. The recall study found significant differences in FHWAR survey results using annual recall periods and shorter recall periods. Longer recall periods lead to higher estimates. Even when everything else was held constant, such as questionnaire content and sample

design, increasing the respondent's recall period resulted in significantly higher estimates for the same phenomenon.

The recall study also found that the extent of recall bias varied for different types of fishing and hunting participation and expenditures. For example, annual recall respondents gave an estimate of average annual days of saltwater fishing that was 46 percent higher than the trimester recall estimate, while the annual recall estimate of average annual saltwater fishing trips was 30 percent higher than the trimester recall estimate. This is evidence against a single "correction factor" for all survey estimates when calculating trends from surveys using different recall periods. Applying a correction factor to estimates of FHWAR surveys with different recall periods is not feasible.

Reliable trends analysis needs to use data compiled from surveys in which the important elements, such as the sample design and recall period, are not significantly different.

Section I. Trends for 1991 to 2001

This trends section covers the period from 1991 to 2001. The 1991, 1996, and 2001 Surveys used similar methodologies, therefore all published information for the three surveys is directly comparable.

The most significant design differences in the three surveys are as follows:

1. The 1991 Survey data was collected by interviewers filling out paper questionnaires. The data entries were keyed in a separate operation after the interview. The 1996 and 2001 survey data were collected by the use of computer-assisted interviews. The questionnaires were programmed into computers, and the interviewer keyed in the responses at the time of the interview.

2. The 1991 Survey screening phase was conducted in January and February of 1991, when the sample households were contacted and a household respondent was interviewed on behalf of the entire household. The 1991 screening interview consisted primarily of sociodemographic questions and wildlife-related recreation questions concerning activity in the year 1990 and intentions for the year 1991. The screening interviews for the 1996 and 2001 Surveys were conducted April through June of their survey years in conjunction with the first wave of the detailed interviews. The screening interviews consisted primarily of sociodemographic questions and wildlife-related recreation questions concerning activity in the previous year (1995 or 2000) and intentions for the survey year (1996 or 2001).

3. In the 1991 Survey, an attempt was made to contact every sample person in all three detailed interview waves. In 1996 and 2001, respondents who were interviewed in the first detailed interview wave were not contacted again until the third wave. Also, all interviews in the second wave were conducted by telephone. In-person interviews were only conducted in the first and third wave.

Important instrument differences in the 1991, 1996, and 2001 Surveys

1. The 1991 Survey collected information on all wildlife-related recreation purchases made by participants without reference to where the purchase was made. The 1996 and 2001 Surveys asked in which state the purchase was made.

2. In 1991, respondents were asked what kind of fishing they did, i.e., Great Lakes, other freshwater, or

Table B-1. Major Characteristics of Surveys: 1955 to 2001

Characteristic	1955	1960	1965	1970	1975	1980	1985	1991	1996	2001
Survey design:										
Screening interview mode and population of interest	Combined with detailed phase	Personal interview, 12 years old and older	Personal interview, 9 years old and older	Mail question-naire, 9 years old and older	Telephone interview, 6 years old and older	Telephone/ personal interview, 6 years old and older	Telephone/ personal interview, 6 years old and older	Telephone/ personal interview, 6 years old and older	Telephone/ personal interview, 6 years old and older	Telephone/ personal interview, 6 years old and older
Detailed interview mode and population of interest	Personal interview, 12 years old and older	Personal interview, 12 years old and older. Substantial partici-pants[1]	Personal interview, 12 years old and older. Substantial partici pants[1]	Personal interview, 12 years old and older. Substantial partici-pants[2]	Mail question-naire, 9 years old and older	Personal interview, 16 years old and older	Personal interview, 16 years old and older	Telephone/ personal interview, 16 years old and older.	Telephone/ personal interview, 16 years old and older	Telephone/ personal interview, 16 years old and older
Respondent's recall period.	1 year	1 year	1 year	1 year	1 year	1 year	1 year	4 months	4-8 months	4-8 months
Sample sizes:										
Screening phase (households)	20,000	18,000	16,000	24,000	106,294	116,025	102,694	102,804	44,000	52,508
Detailed phase (individuals):										
Fishing and hunting . . .	9,328	10,300	6,400	8,700	20,211	30,291	28,011	23,179	13,222	25,070
Wildlife watching[3]	(X)	(X)	(X)	(X)	(X)	5,997	26,671	22,723	9,802	15,303
Response rates:										
Screening phase	(NA)	(NA)	(NA)	(NA)	95 percent	95 percent	93 percent	95 percent	71 percent	75 percent
Detailed phase:										
Fishing and hunting . . .	(NA)	93 percent	(NA)	(NA)	37 percent	90 percent	92 percent	95 percent	80 percent	88 percent
Wildlife watching[3]	(X)	(X)	(X)	(X)	(X)	95 percent	94 percent	95 percent	82 percent	90 percent
Level of reporting	National	National	National	National	State and National	State and National	State and National	State and National	State and National	State and National
Data collection agent	Private contractor	U.S. Census Bureau	U.S. Census Bureau	U.S. Census Bureau	Private contractor	U.S. Census Bureau	U.S. Census Bureau	U.S. Census Bureau	U.S. Census Bureau	U.S. Census Bureau

(NA) Not available.   (X) Not applicable; wildlife-watching (nonconsumptive) interviews were not conducted prior to 1980.

[1] Spent $5.00 or more or participated 3 days or more during the year.
[2] Spent $7.50 or more or participated 3 days or more during the year.
[3] Termed "nonconsumptive" in 1980, 1985, and 1991 surveys.

saltwater, and then were asked in what states they fished. In 1996 and 2001, respondents were asked in which states they fished and then were asked the pertinent kind of fishing questions. This method had the advantage of not asking about, for example, saltwater fishing when they only fished in a noncoastal state.

3. In 1991, respondents were asked how many days they "actually" hunted or fished for a particular type of game or fish and then how many days they "chiefly" hunted or fished for the same type of game or fish rather than another type of game or fish. To get total days of hunting or fishing for a particular type of game or fish, the "actually" day response was used, while to get the sum of all days of hunting or fishing, the "chiefly" days were summed. In 1996 and 2001, respondents were asked their total days of hunting or fishing in the country and each state, then how many days they hunted or fished for a particular type of game or fish.

4. Trip-related and equipment expenditure categories were not the same for all Surveys. "Guide fee" and "Pack trip or package fee" were two separate trip-related expenditure items in 1991, while they were combined into one category in the 1996 and 2001 Surveys. "Boating costs" was added to the 1996 and 2001 hunting and wildlife- watching trip-related expenditure sections. "Heating and cooking fuel" was added to all of the trip-related expenditure sections. "Spearfishing equipment" was moved from a separate category to the "Other" list. "Rods" and "Reels" were two separate categories in 1991 but were combined in 1996 and 2001. "Lines, hooks, sinkers, etc." was one category in 1991 but split into "Lines" and "Hooks, sinkers, etc." in 1996 and 2001. "Food used to feed other wildlife" was added to the wildlife-watching equipment section, "Boats" and "Cabins" were added to the wildlife-watching special equipment section, and "Land leasing and ownership" was added to the wildlife-watching expenditures section.

5. Questions asking sportspersons if they participated as much as they wanted were added in 1996 and 2001. If the sportspersons said no, they were asked why not.

6. The 1991 Survey included questions about participation in organized fishing competitions; anglers using bows and arrows, nets or seines, or spearfishing; hunters using pistols or handguns and target shooting in preparation for hunting. These questions were not asked in 1996 and 2001.

7. The 1996 Survey included questions about catch and release fishing and persons with disabilities participating in wildlife-related recreation. These questions were not part of the 1991 Survey. The 2001 Survey included questions about persons with disabilities participating in wildlife-related recreation but not about catch and release fishing.

8. The 1991 Survey included questions about average distance traveled to recreation sites. These questions were not included in the 1996 and 2001 Surveys.

9. The 1996 Survey included questions about the last trip the respondent took. Included were questions about the type of trip, where the activity took place, and the distance and direction to the site visited. These questions were not asked in 2001.

10. The 1991 Survey collected data on hunting, fishing, and wildlife watching by U.S. residents in Canada. The 1996 and 2001 Surveys collected data on fishing and wildlife- watching by U.S. residents in Canada.

Important instrument changes in the 2001 Survey

1. The 1991 and 1996 single race category "Asian or Pacific Islander" was changed to two categories "Asian" and "Native Hawaiian or Other Pacific Islander." In 1991 and 1996, the respondent was required to pick only one category, while in 2001 the respondent could pick any combination of categories. The next question stipulated that the

respondent could only be identified with one category and then asked what that category was.

2. The 1991 and 1996 land leasing and ownership sections asked the respondent to combine the two types of land use into one and give total acreage and expenditures. In 2001, the two types of land use were explored separately.

3. The 1991 and 1996 wildlife-watching sections included questions on birdwatching for residential users only. The 2001 Survey added a question on birdwatching for nonresidential users. Also, questions on the use of birding life lists and how many species the respondent can identify were added in 2001.

4. "Recreational vehicles" was added to the sportspersons and wildlife-watchers special equipment section in 2001. "House trailer" was added to the sportspersons special equipment section.

5. Total personal income was asked in the detailed phase of the 1996 Survey. This was changed to total household income in the 2001 Survey.

6. A question was added to the trip-related expenditures section in the 2001 Survey to ascertain how much of the total was spent in the respondents state of residence when the respondent participated in hunting, fishing, or wildlife watching out-of-state.

7. Boating questions were added to the 2001 Surveys fishing section. The respondent was asked about the extent of boat usage for the three types of fishing.

8. The 1996 Survey included questions about the months residential wildlife watchers fed birds. These questions were not repeated in the 2001 Survey.

9. The contingent valuation sections of the three types of wildlife-related recreation were altered, using an open-ended question format instead of 1996's dichotomous choice format.

Table B-2. Anglers and Hunters by Census Division: 1991, 1996, and 2001

(U.S. population 16 years old and older. Numbers in thousands)

Sportspersons	1991 Number	1991 Percent	1996 Number	1996 Percent	2001 Number	2001 Percent
UNITED STATES						
Total population............................	189,964	100	201,472	100	212,298	100
Sportspersons.............................	39,979	21	39,694	20	37,805	18
Anglers..................................	35,578	19	35,246	17	34,067	16
Hunters..................................	14,063	7	13,975	7	13,034	6
New England						
Total population............................	10,180	100	10,306	100	10,575	100
Sportspersons.............................	1,658	16	1,673	16	1,504	14
Anglers..................................	1,545	15	1,520	15	1,402	13
Hunters..................................	444	4	465	5	386	4
Middle Atlantic						
Total population............................	29,216	100	29,371	100	29,806	100
Sportspersons.............................	4,508	15	4,192	14	3,810	13
Anglers..................................	3,871	13	3,627	12	3,250	11
Hunters..................................	1,746	6	1,453	5	1,633	5
East North Central						
Total population............................	32,188	100	33,121	100	34,082	100
Sportspersons.............................	7,202	22	6,912	21	6,400	19
Anglers..................................	6,264	19	6,006	18	5,655	17
Hunters..................................	2,789	9	2,712	8	2,421	7
West North Central						
Total population............................	13,504	100	13,875	100	14,430	100
Sportspersons.............................	4,143	31	3,977	29	4,239	29
Anglers..................................	3,647	27	3,416	25	3,836	27
Hunters..................................	1,709	13	1,917	14	1,710	12
South Atlantic						
Total population............................	33,682	100	36,776	100	39,286	100
Sportspersons.............................	6,996	21	7,282	20	6,957	18
Anglers..................................	6,441	19	6,636	18	6,451	16
Hunters..................................	2,083	6	2,050	6	1,875	5
East South Central						
Total population............................	11,667	100	12,459	100	12,976	100
Sportspersons.............................	2,984	26	2,907	23	2,865	22
Anglers..................................	2,635	23	2,514	20	2,543	20
Hunters..................................	1,279	11	1,301	10	1,164	9
West South Central						
Total population............................	19,926	100	21,811	100	23,337	100
Sportspersons.............................	5,125	26	5,093	23	4,924	21
Anglers..................................	4,592	23	4,616	21	4,375	19
Hunters..................................	1,843	9	1,812	8	1,988	9
Mountain						
Total population............................	10,092	100	11,966	100	13,308	100
Sportspersons.............................	2,488	25	2,761	23	2,757	21
Anglers..................................	2,079	21	2,411	20	2,443	18
Hunters..................................	1,069	11	1,061	9	1,020	8
Pacific						
Total population............................	29,508	100	31,787	100	34,498	100
Sportspersons.............................	4,875	17	4,897	15	4,349	13
Anglers..................................	4,505	15	4,501	14	4,111	12
Hunters..................................	1,101	4	1,203	4	837	2

Table B-3. Wildlife-Watching Participants by Census Division: 1991, 1996, and 2001

(U.S. population 16 years old and older. Numbers in thousands)

Sportspersons	1991 Number	1991 Percent	1996 Number	1996 Percent	2001 Number	2001 Percent
UNITED STATES						
Total population	189,964	100	201,472	100	212,298	100
Wildlife watching, total	76,111	40	62,868	31	66,105	31
Nonresidential	29,999	16	23,652	12	21,823	10
Residential	73,904	39	60,751	30	62,928	30
New England						
Total population	10,180	100	10,306	100	10,575	100
Wildlife watching, total	4,598	45	3,710	36	3,875	37
Nonresidential	1,856	18	1,443	14	1,155	11
Residential	4,544	45	3,586	35	3,765	36
Middle Atlantic						
Total population	29,216	100	29,371	100	29,806	100
Wildlife watching, total	10,556	36	8,185	28	8,740	29
Nonresidential	4,166	14	2,960	10	2,849	10
Residential	10,282	35	8,023	27	8,452	28
East North Central						
Total population	32,188	100	33,121	100	34,082	100
Wildlife Watching, total	14,511	45	11,731	35	11,631	34
Nonresidential	5,572	17	4,501	14	3,571	10
Residential	14,175	44	11,297	34	11,196	33
West North Central						
Total population	13,504	100	13,875	100	14,430	100
Wildlife watching, total	6,924	51	5,089	37	6,206	43
Nonresidential	2,654	20	1,927	14	2,059	14
Residential	6,722	50	4,900	35	5,938	41
South Atlantic						
Total population	33,682	100	36,776	100	39,286	100
Wildlife watching, total	13,047	39	11,252	31	11,395	29
Nonresidential	4,450	13	3,992	11	3,469	9
Residential	12,813	38	10,964	30	10,911	28
East South Central						
Total population	11,667	100	12,459	100	12,976	100
Wildlife watching, total	4,864	42	3,904	31	4,514	35
Nonresidential	1,592	14	1,118	9	1,086	8
Residential	4,765	41	3,795	30	4,390	34
West South Central						
Total population	19,926	100	21,811	100	23,337	100
Wildlife watching, total	7,035	35	5,933	27	5,747	25
Nonresidential	2,459	12	2,096	10	1,822	8
Residential	6,817	34	5,773	26	5,490	24
Mountain						
Total population	10,092	100	11,966	100	13,308	100
Wildlife watching, total	4,437	44	4,099	34	4,619	35
Nonresidential	2,215	22	1,967	16	2,019	15
Residential	4,145	41	3,855	32	4,282	32
Pacific						
Total population	29,508	100	31,787	100	34,498	100
Wildlife watching, total	10,139	34	8,966	28	9,377	27
Nonresidential	5,035	17	3,648	11	3,793	11
Residential	9,641	33	8,558	27	8,504	25

Section II. Trends from 1955 to 1985

1955 to 1970 Surveys

The 1955 to 1970 Surveys included only substantial participants. Substantial participants were defined as people who participated at least 3 days and/or spent at least $5 (the 1955-1965 Surveys) or $7.50 (the 1970 Survey) during the surveyed year. Under most circumstances, the surveys may be compared for totals, but the effects of differences should be considered when comparing the details of the surveys.

The 1960, 1965, and 1970 Surveys differed from the 1955 National Survey in classification of expenditures as outlined below.

1. Alaska and Hawaii were not included in the 1955 Survey.

2. Expenditure categories were more detailed in 1970 than in earlier surveys.

3. The 1960 to 1970 classification of some expenditures differs from the 1955 Survey in the following respects:

   a. "Boats and boat motors" shown under "auxiliary equipment" were included in "equipment, other" in 1955.

   b. "Entrance and other privilege fees" shown separately were included in "trip expenditures, other" in 1955.

   c. "Snacks and refreshments" not included with "food" expenditures in the 1960 to 1970 reports were under "trip expenditures, other" in 1955.

   d. Expenditures on equipment, magazines, club dues, licenses, and similar items were classified by the one sport activity for which expenditures were chiefly made. In 1955, these expenditures were evenly divided among all the activities in which the sportsman took part.

   e. Compared with 1955, the 1960 to 1970 Surveys reported fewer expenditures within the "other" category because selected items were transferred to more appropriate categories.

   f. Expenditures on alcoholic beverages were reported separately in the 1970 Survey.

   g. In 1970, definition of a "substantial participant" was changed from one who spent at least $5.00 during the year or spent 3 days fishing or hunting to one who spent $7.50 for the year or spent 3 days fishing or hunting.

4. The number of waterfowl hunters in the 1970 Survey is not comparable with those reported in the 1960 and 1965 Surveys. In 1960 and 1965, respondent sportsmen were not included in the waterfowl hunter total if they reported that they went waterfowl hunting but did not take the trip chiefly to hunt waterfowl. In 1970, all respondents who reported that they had hunted waterfowl during 1970, regardless of trip purpose, were included in the total. The number of hunters who did not take trips chiefly to hunt waterfowl in 1970 was 1,054,000.

1975 Survey

In contrast to previous surveys which covered substantial participants 12 years old and older, the 1975 Survey based all the estimates on responses from individuals 9 years of age and older and did not select respondents based upon substantial participation as defined above. As a result, individuals who participated fewer than 3 days or spent less than $7.50 on hunting or fishing were included in the estimates of participants, days of activity, and expenditures.

Categories of hunting and fishing expenditures differed from the previous four surveys in that only major categories were reported. For example, hunting equipment expenditures were not further delineated by subcategory. Similarly, no detail was provided within the category of fishing equipment expenditures. Expenses for "other" items such as daily entrance fees, magazines, club dues, and dogs were categorized as "other" in the 1975 report.

In addition to the above differences, the 1975 Survey gathered data on species sought for the favorite hunting and fishing activity. This data replaced the "chiefly" category where hunting or fishing was the primary purpose of the trip or day of activity. Data omitted in the 1975 Survey that were included in previous surveys include the respondents population density of residence, occupation, and level of education.

1980 to 1985 Surveys

The 1980 and 1985 Surveys were similar. Each measured participants, rather than substantial participants. Questions were incorporated into the 1980 and 1985 Survey questionnaires to facilitate the construction of categories of data for comparisons with earlier surveys. The use of "chiefly" to delimit primary purpose appeared in the 1970 and prior surveys, and its use was continued in the 1980 and 1985 Surveys. The expenditure categories in 1980 and 1985 are similar to the 1970 categories with the addition of fish finders, motor homes, and camper trucks as separate categories. The definition of fishing included the use of nets or seines and spearfishing.

As in the 1970 and 1975 Surveys, the 1980 and 1985 Surveys used a two-phase process to gather information from households and individuals. In the first phase, household respondents were asked to identify each participant 6 years of age and older who resided in their household. In comparison, the 1975 and 1970 Surveys screened households for participants who were 9 years of age and older. In the second phase, the detailed interview phase, interviews were conducted in person for the 1985, 1980, and 1970 Surveys and were conducted by mail for the 1975 Survey. Participants were included in the detailed phase of the Survey if they were at least 12 years old in 1970, 9 years old in 1975, and 16 years old in 1980 and 1985. As a result, the population of hunters and anglers was more narrowly defined in 1980 and 1985 to include individuals 16 years old and older. However, estimates of sportsmen 6 years old and older, 9 years old and older, and 12 years old and older are available for comparison with past surveys.

Table B-4. Comparison of Major Findings of the National Surveys: 1955 to 1985

(U.S. population 12 years old and older. Numbers in thousands)

Sportspersons	1955	1960	1965	1970	1975	1980	1985
Total sportspersons	**24,917**	**30,435**	**32,881**	**36,277**	**45,773**	**46,966**	**49,827**
Anglers	20,813	25,323	28,348	33,158	41,299	41,873	45,345
Freshwater	18,420	21,677	23,962	29,363	36,599	35,782	39,122
Saltwater	4,557	6,292	8,305	9,460	13,738	11,972	12,893
Hunters	11,784	14,637	13,583	14,336	17,094	16,758	16,340
Small game	9,822	12,105	10,576	11,671	14,182	12,496	11,130
Big game	4,414	6,277	6,566	7,774	11,037	11,047	12,576
Waterfowl	1,986	1,955	1,650	2,894	4,284	3,177	3,201
Expenditures[1]	**11,401,464**	**13,948,974**	**14,991,502**	**19,618,548**	**33,398,677**	**34,517,421**	**42,058,860**
Anglers	7,655,522	9,743,971	9,952,411	13,699,311	23,498,506	23,387,469	28,585,686
Freshwater	5,700,187	7,476,454	7,231,851	10,315,966	17,333,212	16,663,239	18,942,060
Saltwater	1,955,336	2,267,512	2,720,574	3,383,345	6,165,294	5,581,976	7,191,387
Hunters	3,745,942	4,204,997	3,814,303	5,919,236	9,900,171	10,812,058	10,256,668
Small game	1,975,707	2,629,360	2,093,137	2,612,390	4,525,942	3,335,852	2,342,860
Big game	1,295,357	1,251,800	1,424,711	2,631,532	4,238,341	5,638,395	5,345,606
Waterfowl	474,878	323,840	296,452	675,315	1,135,889	766,033	783,315
Days	**566,870**	**658,308**	**708,578**	**909,876**	**1,459,551**	**1,300,983**	**1,415,379**
Fishing	397,447	465,769	522,759	706,187	1,058,075	952,420	1,064,986
Freshwater	338,826	385,167	426,922	592,494	890,576	788,392	895,027
Saltwater	58,621	80,602	95,837	113,694	167,499	164,040	171,055
Hunting	169,423	192,539	185,819	203,689	401,476	348,543	350,393
Small game	118,630	138,192	128,448	124,041	269,653	225,793	214,544
Big game	30,834	39,190	43,845	54,536	100,600	117,406	135,447
Waterfowl	19,959	15,158	13,526	25,113	31,223	26,179	25,933

[1] In 1985 dollars.

Note: Methodological differences described in the text make the estimates in this table not comparable with the estimates in Tables B-2 and B-3.

Table B-5. Anglers and Hunters by Census Division: 1955 to 1985

(U.S. population 12 years old and older. Numbers in thousands)

Year	Population		Sportspersons, fished or hunted		Anglers		Hunters	
	Number	Percent	Number	Percent	Number	Percent	Number	Percent
UNITED STATES								
1955	118,366	100	24,917	21.1	20,813	17.6	11,784	10.0
1960	131,226	100	30,435	23.2	25,323	19.3	14,637	11.2
1965	141,928	100	32,881	23.2	28,348	20.0	13,585	9.6
1970	155,230	100	36,277	23.4	33,158	21.4	14,336	9.2
1975	171,860	100	45,773	26.6	41,299	24.0	17,094	9.9
1980	184,691	100	46,966	25.4	41,873	22.7	16,758	9.1
1985	195,659	100	49,827	25.5	45,345	23.2	16,340	8.4
New England								
1955	7,919	100	1,224	15.4	1,002	12.7	589	7.4
1960	8,349	100	1,368	16.4	1,205	14.4	517	6.2
1965	9,256	100	1,650	17.8	1,488	16.0	583	6.3
1970	8,652	100	1,579	18.3	1,430	16.5	582	6.7
1975	9,910	100	2,004	20.2	1,861	18.8	566	5.7
1980	10,205	100	1,974	19.3	1,788	17.5	572	5.6
1985	10,554	100	2,058	19.5	1,914	18.1	552	5.2
Middle Atlantic								
1955	24,869	100	3,539	14.2	2,811	11.3	1,608	6.5
1960	26,493	100	3,432	13.0	2,569	9.7	1,723	6.5
1965	27,346	100	3,602	13.2	2,760	10.1	1,631	6.0
1970	28,244	100	4,539	16.1	4,504	14.4	1,731	6.1
1975	30,449	100	5,919	19.4	5,097	16.7	2,096	6.9
1980	30,256	100	5,181	17.1	4,332	14.3	2,001	6.6
1985	31,099	100	5,565	17.9	4,820	15.5	1,972	6.3
East North Central								
1955	25,733	100	5,489	21.3	4,583	17.8	2,538	9.9
1960	26,833	100	6,316	32.5	5,317	19.8	2,985	11.1
1965	28,124	100	6,214	22.1	5,336	19.0	2,563	9.1
1970	31,550	100	7,284	23.1	6,699	21.2	2,812	8.9
1975	32,796	100	9,049	27.6	8,181	24.9	3,392	10.3
1980	33,526	100	8,725	26.0	7,891	23.5	2,955	8.8
1985	33,747	100	8,973	26.6	8,270	24.5	2,814	8.3
West North Central								
1955	9,201	100	2,913	31.7	2,346	25.5	1,534	16.7
1960	10,149	100	3,383	33.3	2,855	28.1	1,709	16.8
1965	11,681	100	3,678	31.5	3,226	27.6	1,620	13.9
1970	12,904	100	4,000	31.0	3,579	27.7	1,783	13.8
1975	13,564	100	4,524	33.3	4,089	30.1	1,863	13.7
1980	13,826	100	4,770	34.5	4,220	30.5	1,965	14.2
1985	14,137	100	5,140	36.4	4,681	33.1	1,971	13.9
South Atlantic								
1955	14,336	100	3,223	22.5	2,805	19.6	1,449	10.1
1960	17,798	100	4,423	24.9	3,695	20.8	2,045	11.5
1965	20,593	100	5,626	27.3	5,054	24.5	1,900	9.2
1970	23,539	100	5,461	23.2	5,129	21.8	1,904	8.1
1975	27,127	100	7,110	26.2	6,479	23.9	2,494	9.2
1980	30,512	100	7,769	25.5	7,086	23.2	2,444	8.0
1985	33,636	100	8,721	25.9	8,056	24.0	2,467	7.3
East South Central								
1955	7,959	100	1,963	24.7	1,665	20.9	989	12.4
1960	9,277	100	2,778	29.9	2,207	23.8	1,510	16.3
1965	9,652	100	2,587	26.8	2,201	22.8	1,294	13.4
1970	9,862	100	2,660	27.0	2,464	25.0	1,162	11.8
1975	10,798	100	3,007	27.8	2,689	24.9	1,355	12.5
1980	11,771	100	3,614	30.7	3,173	27.0	1,567	13.3
1985	12,364	100	3,671	29.7	3,308	26.8	1,441	11.7

(U.S. population 12 years old and older. Numbers in thousands)

Year	Population		Sportspersons, fished or hunted		Anglers		Hunters	
	Number	Percent	Number	Percent	Number	Percent	Number	Percent
West South Central								
1955	10,250	100	2,560	25.0	2,237	21.8	1,165	11.4
1960	11,837	100	3,666	31.0	3,133	26.5	1,750	14.8
1965	12,724	100	3,713	29.2	3,278	25.8	1,571	12.3
1970	14,624	100	4,380	30.0	4,006	27.4	1,918	13.1
1975	16,628	100	5,781	34.8	5,267	31.7	2,563	15.4
1980	19,136	100	5,862	30.6	5,136	26.8	2,456	12.8
1985	21,184	100	6,418	30.3	5,704	26.9	2,572	12.1
Mountain								
1955	4,529	100	1,369	30.2	1,112	24.6	796	17.6
1960	5,222	100	1,646	31.5	1,372	26.3	1,120	21.4
1965	5,029	100	1,565	31.1	1,261	25.1	988	19.6
1970	5,656	100	2,044	36.1	1,769	31.3	980	17.3
1975	7,576	100	2,570	33.9	2,252	29.7	1,159	15.3
1980	9,160	100	2,903	31.7	2,500	27.3	1,268	13.8
1985	10,215	100	3,128	30.6	2,765	27.1	1,241	12.1
Pacific								
1955	13,570	100	2,637	19.4	2,252	16.6	1,116	8.2
1960	15,268	100	3,422	22.4	2,971	19.5	1,279	8.4
1965	17,523	100	4,246	24.2	3,744	21.4	1,433	8.2
1970	20,199	100	4,332	21.4	4,030	20.0	1,466	7.3
1975	23,012	100	5,811	25.2	5,386	23.4	1,607	7.0
1980	26,299	100	6,168	23.5	5,747	21.9	1,531	5.0
1985	38,725	100	6,154	21.4	5,829	20.3	1,310	4.6

Note: Methodological differences described in the text make the estimates in this table not comparable with the estimates in Tables B-2 and B-3.

Appendix C

Appendix C.
Selected Data From Screening Interviews

The *2001 National Survey of Fishing, Hunting, and Wildlife-Associated Recreation* was carried out in two phases. The first (or screening) phase began in April 2001. The main purpose of this phase was to collect information about persons 16 years old and older in order to develop a sample of potential sportspersons and wildlife watchers for the second (or detailed) phase. Also, information was collected on the number of persons 6 to 15 years old who participated in wildlife-related recreation activities in 2000. This data is included here to report the recreation activity of 6- to 15-year-olds.

It is important to emphasize that the information reported from the 2001 screen relates to activity only up to and including 2000. Also, this data is based on long-term recall (at least a 12-month recall) and is reported in most cases by one household respondent speaking for all household members rather than the actual participant, as in the case of the 2001 detailed phase.

Tables C-1 thru C-4 report data on first-time participation and the most recent year of hunting and fishing for participants 6 years of age and older. The remainder of the Tables, C-5 thru C-11, reports data specifically on 6- to 15-year-old participants in 2000. Detailed expenditures and recreational activity data were not gathered for the 6- to 15-year-old participants.

Because of differences in methodologies of the screening phase and the detailed phase of the 2001 Survey, their data are not comparable. Only participants 16 years old and older were eligible for the detailed phase. The detailed phase was a series of three interviews conducted at 4-month intervals. The screening interviews were 1-year recall. The shorter recall period of the detailed phase had better data accuracy. Survey research has found that in many cases longer recall periods result in over-estimating participation in and expenditures on wildlife-related recreation.

Table C-1. Anglers and Hunters Participating for the First Time in 2000 by Age Group

(Population 6 years old and older. Numbers in thousands)

Age group	Total anglers in 2000	Fishing for first time		Total hunters in 2000	Hunting for first time	
		Number	Percent of anglers in age group		Number	Percent of hunters in age group
Total, all ages	55,430	4,149	7	15,175	1,239	8
6 to 8 years	3,325	927	28	128	63	49
9 to 11 years.............	4,458	731	16	474	205	43
12 to 15 years	5,363	560	10	1,139	399	35
16 to 17 years	2,032	151	7	630	83	13
18 to 24 years	4,626	301	7	1,653	157	9
25 to 34 years	8,180	463	6	2,504	110	4
35 to 44 years	10,765	514	5	3,387	128	4
45 to 54 years	8,252	292	4	2,764	*50	*2
55 to 64 years	4,624	128	3	1,427	*36	*3
65 years or older	3,805	83	2	1,068	...	...

* Estimate based on a small sample size.   ... Sample size too small to report data reliably.

Note: Data reported on this table are from screening interviews in which one adult household member responded for all household members. The screening interview required the respondent to recall 12 months worth of activity.

Table C-2. Anglers and Hunters Participating in 1999 But Not in 2000 by Age Group

(Population 6 years old and older. Numbers in thousands)

Age group	Anglers		Hunters	
	Number	Percent	Number	Percent
Total, all ages	9,754	100	2,994	100
6 to 8 years	396	4	...	...
9 to 11 years.....................	556	6	*60	*2
12 to 15 years	760	8	158	5
16 to 17 years	335	3	98	3
18 to 24 years	1,011	10	411	14
25 to 34 years	1,503	15	628	21
35 to 44 years	2,067	21	659	22
45 to 54 years	1,582	16	505	17
55 to 64 years	805	8	266	9
65 years or older	741	8	197	7

* Estimate based on a small sample size.   ... Sample size too small to report data reliably.

Note: Data reported on this table are from screening interviews in which one adult household member responded for all household members. The screening interview required the respondent to recall 12 months worth of activity. Includes persons who fished or hunted only in other countries.

Table C-3. Most Recent Year of Hunting by Age Group

(Population 6 years old and older. Numbers in thousands)

Age group	Total, all persons who hunted in 2000 or earlier year		2000		1999		1998	
	Number	Percent	Number	Percent	Number	Percent	Number	Percent
Total, all ages	**43,745**	**100**	**15,148**	**35**	**2,988**	**7**	**1,761**	**4**
6 to 11 years..............	747	100	602	80	72	10	...	...
12 to 15 years	1,488	100	1,139	77	158	11	*52	*3
16 to 17 years	919	100	630	69	98	11	*44	*5
18 to 24 years	3,237	100	1,638	51	411	13	286	9
25 to 34 years	5,968	100	2,504	42	623	10	336	6
35 to 44 years	8,466	100	3,377	40	658	8	388	5
45 to 54 years	9,094	100	2,763	30	505	6	296	3
55 to 64 years	6,047	100	1,426	24	266	4	176	3
65 years or older	7,779	100	1,068	14	197	3	161	2

Most recent year of hunting

Age group	1997		1996		1995		Before 1995	
	Number	Percent	Number	Percent	Number	Percent	Number	Percent
Total, all ages	**1,193**	**3**	**1,231**	**3**	**927**	**2**	**20,062**	**46**
6 to 11 years	...	...	...	...	...	...	...	...
12 to 15 years	*48	*3	...	...	...	...	*46	*3
16 to 17 years	*32	*4	...	...	...	...	*54	*6
18 to 24 years	175	5	134	4	121	4	424	13
25 to 34 years	231	4	238	4	176	3	1,793	30
35 to 44 years	283	3	227	3	169	2	3,258	38
45 to 54 years	211	2	252	3	216	2	4,787	53
55 to 64 years	104	2	183	3	96	2	3,777	62
65 years or older	105	1	165	2	140	2	5,913	76

* Estimate based on a small sample size.　　... Sample size too small to report data reliably.

Note: Data reported on this table are from screening interviews in which one adult household member responded for all household members. The screening interview required the respondent to recall 12 months worth of activity.

Table C-4. Most Recent Year of Fishing by Age Group

(Population 6 years old and older. Numbers in thousands)

Age group	Total, all persons who fished in 2000 or earlier year		Most recent year of fishing					
			2000		1999		1998	
	Number	Percent	Number	Percent	Number	Percent	Number	Percent
Total, all ages	**111,066**	**100**	**55,263**	**50**	**9,689**	**9**	**5,847**	**5**
6 to 11 years..............	9,774	100	7,783	80	952	10	412	4
12 to 15 years	7,587	100	5,360	71	753	10	441	6
16 to 17 years	3,372	100	2,032	60	335	10	318	9
18 to 24 years	9,116	100	4,575	50	1,001	11	682	7
25 to 34 years	15,381	100	8,098	53	1,475	10	915	6
35 to 44 years	20,351	100	10,747	53	2,059	10	1,020	5
45 to 54 years	18,982	100	8,248	43	1,575	8	1,035	5
55 to 64 years	11,695	100	4,620	40	799	7	477	4
65 years or older	14,808	100	3,800	26	741	5	547	4

Age group	Most recent year of fishing							
	1997		1996		1995		Before 1995	
	Number	Percent	Number	Percent	Number	Percent	Number	Percent
Total, all ages..............	**3,678**	**3**	**3,317**	**3**	**2,218**	**2**	**29,935**	**27**
6 to 11 years	203	2	113	1	*80	*1	137	1
12 to 15 years	264	3	201	3	120	2	400	5
16 to 17 years	155	5	102	3	53	2	326	10
18 to 24 years	414	5	372	4	267	3	1,594	17
25 to 34 years	593	4	484	3	341	2	3,245	21
35 to 44 years	713	4	561	3	420	2	4,636	23
45 to 54 years	665	4	661	3	424	2	6,217	33
55 to 64 years	340	3	489	4	211	2	4,709	40
65 years or older	331	2	333	2	304	2	8,671	59

* Estimate based on a small sample size.

Note: Data reported on this table are from screening interviews in which one adult household member responded for all household members. The screening interview required the respondent to recall 12 months worth of activity.

Table C-5. Anglers and Hunters 6 to 15 Years Old: 2000

(Population 6 to 15 years old. Numbers in thousands)

Sportspersons	Total, 6 to 15 years old		12 to 15 years old		9 to 11 years old		6 to 8 years old	
	Number	Percent	Number	Percent	Number	Percent	Number	Percent
Total sportspersons, fished or hunted ...	**13,369**	**100**	**5,524**	**100**	**4,504**	**100**	**3,342**	**100**
Total anglers	**13,145**	**98**	**5,363**	**97**	**4,458**	**99**	**3,325**	**99**
Fished only......................	11,628	87	4,385	79	4,030	89	3,213	96
Fished and hunted	1,517	11	978	18	428	9	112	3
Total hunters....................	**1,741**	**13**	**1,139**	**21**	**474**	**11**	**128**	**4**
Hunted only	224	2	161	3	*46	*1	*17	*1
Hunted and fished	1,517	11	978	18	428	9	112	3

* Estimate based on a small sample size.

Note: Detail does not add to total because of multiple responses. Data reported on this table are from screening interviews in which one adult household member responded for all household members 6 to 15 years old. The screening interview required the respondent to recall 12 months worth of activity. Includes persons who fished or hunted only in other countries.

Table C-6. Wildlife-Watching Participants 6 to 15 Years Old by Wildlife-Watching Activity: 2000

(Population 6 to 15 years old. Numbers in thousands)

Activity	Total, 6 to 15 years old			12 to 15 years old			9 to 11 years old			6 to 8 years old		
	Number	Percent of participants	Percent of population	Number	Percent of participants	Percent of population	Number	Percent of participants	Percent of population	Number	Percent of participants	Percent of population
Total participants	**15,066**	**100**	**37**	**5,564**	**100**	**34**	**5,192**	**100**	**41**	**4,311**	**100**	**36**
Nonresidential (away from home)................	6,091	40	15	2,265	41	14	2,043	39	16	1,783	41	15
Residential (around the home).................	13,542	90	33	4,895	88	30	4,718	91	37	3,929	91	33
Observe wildlife	10,659	71	26	3,761	68	23	3,774	73	29	3,124	72	26
Photograph wildlife......	1,756	12	4	732	13	4	682	13	5	341	8	3
Feed wild birds or other wildlife	8,062	54	20	2,836	51	17	2,825	54	22	2,400	56	20
Maintain plantings or natural areas	2,111	14	5	795	14	5	743	14	6	572	13	5

Note: Detail does not add to total because of multiple responses. Columns showing percent of participants are based on the first row of each column. Columns showing percent of population in age group are based on the U.S. population in each age category, including those who did not participate in wildlife-watching activities. Data reported on this table are from screening interviews in which one adult household member responded for household members 6 to 15 years old. The screening interview required the respondent to recall 12 months worth of activity. Includes persons who participated only in other countries.

Table C-7. Selected Characteristics of Anglers and Hunters 6 to 15 Years Old: 2000

(Population 6 to 15 years old. Numbers in thousands)

Characteristic	U.S. population Number	U.S. population Percent	Sportspersons, fished or hunted Number	Sportspersons, fished or hunted Percent who participated	Sportspersons, fished or hunted Percent	Fished only Number	Fished only Percent who participated	Fished only Percent
Total persons......................	**40,949**	**100**	**13,369**	**33**	**100**	**11,628**	**28**	**100**
Population Density of Residence								
Urban...........................	29,935	73	8,583	29	64	7,875	26	68
Rural...........................	11,014	27	4,787	43	36	3,753	34	32
Population Size of Residence								
Metropolitan statistical areas (MSA)...	33,020	81	9,888	30	74	8,925	27	77
1,000,000 or more	21,513	53	5,827	27	44	5,371	25	46
250,000 to 999,999..............	8,161	20	2,799	34	21	2,517	31	22
50,000 to 249,999..............	3,346	8	1,263	38	9	1,037	31	9
Outside MSA	7,929	19	3,481	44	26	2,703	34	23
Census Geographic Division								
New England	1,905	5	613	32	5	566	30	5
Middle Atlantic..................	5,445	13	1,466	27	11	1,291	24	11
East North Central	6,620	16	2,396	36	18	2,119	32	18
West North Central..............	2,797	7	1,413	51	11	1,156	41	10
South Atlantic...................	7,288	18	2,276	31	17	2,005	28	17
East South Central	2,404	6	921	38	7	731	30	6
West South Central..............	4,825	12	1,510	31	11	1,215	25	10
Mountain.......................	2,809	7	1,043	37	8	909	32	8
Pacific.........................	6,856	17	1,731	25	13	1,636	24	14
Age								
6 to 8 years.....................	11,848	29	3,342	28	25	3,213	27	28
9 to 11 years....................	12,795	31	4,504	35	34	4,030	31	35
12 to 15 years...................	16,305	40	5,524	34	41	4,385	27	38
Sex								
Male, total.....................	21,172	52	8,572	40	64	7,105	34	61
6 to 8 years....................	6,044	15	1,963	32	15	1,866	31	16
9 to 11 years...................	6,707	16	2,917	43	22	2,516	38	22
12 to 15 years..................	8,421	21	3,693	44	28	2,724	32	23
Female, total...................	19,777	48	4,797	24	36	4,523	23	39
6 to 8 years....................	5,804	14	1,379	24	10	1,347	23	12
9 to 11 years...................	6,089	15	1,587	26	12	1,515	25	13
12 to 15 years..................	7,884	19	1,831	23	14	1,661	21	14
Ethnicity								
Hispanic	6,343	15	1,092	17	8	1,045	16	9
Non-Hispanic	34,606	85	12,277	35	92	10,583	31	91
Race								
White..........................	33,378	82	12,337	37	92	10,655	32	92
Black..........................	5,519	13	602	11	5	577	10	5
Asian..........................	1,320	3	208	16	2	204	15	2
All others	731	2	222	30	2	191	26	2
Annual Household Income								
Under $10,000	1,849	5	310	17	2	259	14	2
$10,000 to $19,999..............	3,012	7	662	22	5	593	20	5
$20,000 to $24,999..............	2,223	5	592	27	4	534	24	5
$25,000 to $29,999..............	2,344	6	674	29	5	574	24	5
$30,000 to $34,999..............	2,492	6	778	31	6	678	27	6
$35,000 to $39,999..............	2,009	5	736	37	6	630	31	5
$40,000 to $49,999..............	3,956	10	1,454	37	11	1,219	31	10
$50,000 to $74,999..............	7,239	18	3,137	43	23	2,684	37	23
$75,000 to $99,999.............	4,168	10	1,847	44	14	1,620	39	14
$100,000 or more................	4,036	10	1,652	41	12	1,504	37	13
Not reported	7,621	19	1,526	20	11	1,333	17	11

See footnotes at end of table.

(Population 6 to 15 years old. Numbers in thousands)

Characteristic	Hunted only			Fished and hunted		
	Number	Percent who participated	Percent	Number	Percent who participated	Percent
Total persons......................	**224**	**1**	**100**	**1,517**	**4**	**100**
Population Density of Residence						
Urban............................	87	(Z)	39	621	2	41
Rural............................	137	1	61	896	8	59
Population Size of Residence						
Metropolitan statistical areas (MSA)...	115	(Z)	51	847	3	56
1,000,000 or more	*71	*(Z)	*32	384	2	25
250,000 to 999,999.............	...	...	...	259	3	17
50,000 to 249,999...............	*21	*1	*10	204	6	13
Outside MSA	109	1	49	670	8	44
Census Geographic Division						
New England	...	...	...	41	2	3
Middle Atlantic..................	...	...	...	156	3	10
East North Central	...	...	...	240	4	16
West North Central..............	*31	*1	*14	227	8	15
South Atlantic...................	*33	*(Z)	*15	238	3	16
East South Central	*28	*1	*12	162	7	11
West South Central..............	*44	*1	*20	251	5	17
Mountain........................	*19	*1	*8	116	4	8
Pacific..........................	*9	*(Z)	*4	86	1	6
Age						
6 to 8 years.....................	*17	*(Z)	*8	112	1	7
9 to 11 years....................	*46	*(Z)	*20	428	3	28
12 to 15 years..................	161	1	72	978	6	64
Sex						
Male, total......................	170	1	76	1,298	6	86
6 to 8 years...................	...	...	...	85	1	6
9 to 11 years..................	*39	*1	*17	362	5	24
12 to 15 years.................	119	1	53	851	10	56
Female, total....................	54	(Z)	24	220	1	14
6 to 8 years...................	...	...	...	*27	*(Z)	*2
9 to 11 years..................	...	...	...	66	1	4
12 to 15 years.................	*43	*1	*19	127	2	8
Ethnicity						
Hispanic	...	...	...	*33	*1	*2
Non-Hispanic	210	1	94	1,484	4	98
Race						
White...........................	207	1	92	1,475	4	97
Black...........................	...	...	...	...	...	...
Asian...........................	...	...	...	...	...	...
All others	*14	*2	*6	*16	*2	*1
Annual Household Income						
Under $10,000	...	...	...	*37	*2	*2
$10,000 to $19,999.............	...	...	...	59	2	4
$20,000 to $24,999.............	...	...	...	*47	*2	*3
$25,000 to $29,999.............	...	...	...	86	4	6
$30,000 to $34,999.............	...	...	...	95	4	6
$35,000 to $39,999.............	*16	*1	*7	90	4	6
$40,000 to $49,999.............	...	...	...	218	6	14
$50,000 to $74,999.............	59	1	26	393	5	26
$75,000 to $99,999.............	*41	*1	*18	186	4	12
$100,000 or more................	...	...	...	139	3	9
Not reported	*27	*(Z)	*12	166	2	11

* Estimate based on a small sample size.   ...Sample size too small to report data reliably.   (Z) Less than 0.5 percent.

Note: Percent who participated columns show the percent of each row's population who participated in the activity named by the column (the percent of those living in urban areas who fished only, etc.). Percent columns show the percent of each column's participants who are described by the row heading (the percent of those who fished only who lived in urban areas, etc.). Data reported on this table are from screening interviews in which one adult household member responded for all household members. The screening interview required the respondent to recall 12 months worth of activity.

Table C-8. Selected Characteristics of Wildlife-Watching Participants 6 to 15 Years Old: 2000

(Population 6 to 15 years old. Numbers in thousands)

Characteristic	U.S. population Number	U.S. population Percent	Total Number	Total Percent who participated	Total Percent	Nonresidential (away from home) Number	Nonresidential (away from home) Percent who participated	Nonresidential (away from home) Percent	Residential (around the home) Number	Residential (around the home) Percent who participated	Residential (around the home) Percent
Total persons	40,949	100	15,066	37	100	6,091	15	100	13,542	33	100
Population Density of Residence											
Urban.........................	29,935	73	10,126	34	67	4,291	14	70	9,030	30	67
Rural.........................	11,014	27	4,941	45	33	1,800	16	30	4,513	41	33
Population Size of Residence											
Metropolitan statistical areas (MSA) ..	33,020	81	11,790	36	78	4,837	15	79	10,586	32	78
1,000,000 or more	21,513	53	7,360	34	49	3,119	14	51	6,582	31	49
250,000 to 999,999	8,161	20	3,061	38	20	1,131	14	19	2,805	34	21
50,000 to 249,999	3,346	8	1,369	41	9	587	18	10	1,199	36	9
Outside MSA..................	7,929	19	3,277	41	22	1,254	16	21	2,957	37	22
Census Geographic Division											
New England..................	1,905	5	714	37	5	244	13	4	664	35	5
Middle Atlantic	5,445	13	2,015	37	13	781	14	13	1,875	34	14
East North Central.............	6,620	16	2,689	41	18	1,074	16	18	2,485	38	18
West North Central	2,797	7	1,292	46	9	568	20	9	1,159	41	9
South Atlantic	7,288	18	2,493	34	17	869	12	14	2,277	31	17
East South Central.............	2,404	6	873	36	6	307	13	5	811	34	6
West South Central	4,825	12	1,502	31	10	569	12	9	1,337	28	10
Mountain.....................	2,809	7	1,121	40	7	554	20	9	938	33	7
Pacific.......................	6,856	17	2,367	35	16	1,125	16	18	1,998	29	15
Age											
6 to 8 years	11,848	29	4,311	36	29	1,783	15	29	3,929	33	29
9 to 11 years	12,795	31	5,192	41	34	2,043	16	34	4,718	37	35
12 to 15 years	16,305	40	5,564	34	37	2,265	14	37	4,895	30	36
Sex											
Male, total	21,172	52	7,951	38	53	3,243	15	53	7,154	34	53
6 to 8 years	6,044	15	2,145	35	14	870	14	14	1,952	32	14
9 to 11 years	6,707	16	2,827	42	19	1,171	17	19	2,566	38	19
12 to 15 years	8,421	21	2,978	35	20	1,202	14	20	2,636	31	19
Female, total	19,777	48	7,116	36	47	2,848	14	47	6,388	32	47
6 to 8 years	5,804	14	2,165	37	14	913	16	15	1,977	34	15
9 to 11 years	6,089	15	2,365	39	16	872	14	14	2,152	35	16
12 to 15 years	7,884	19	2,586	33	17	1,063	13	17	2,259	29	17
Ethnicity											
Hispanic......................	6,343	15	1,483	23	10	597	9	10	1,294	20	10
Non-Hispanic..................	34,606	85	13,584	39	90	5,494	16	90	12,248	35	90
Race											
White.........................	33,378	82	13,435	40	89	5,548	17	91	12,085	36	89
Black.........................	5,519	13	1,029	19	7	336	6	6	926	17	7
Asian.........................	1,320	3	276	21	2	106	8	2	231	17	2
All others.....................	731	2	326	45	2	101	14	2	301	41	2
Annual Household Income											
Under $10,000.................	1,849	5	456	25	3	115	6	2	438	24	3
$10,000 to $19,999	3,012	7	757	25	5	276	9	5	668	22	5
$20,000 to $24,999	2,223	5	659	30	4	225	10	4	608	27	4
$25,000 to $29,999	2,344	6	818	35	5	328	14	5	707	30	5
$30,000 to $34,999	2,492	6	883	35	6	365	15	6	799	32	6
$35,000 to $39,999	2,009	5	787	39	5	290	14	5	716	36	5
$40,000 to $49,999	3,956	10	1,637	41	11	707	18	12	1,471	37	11
$50,000 to $74,999	7,239	18	3,205	44	21	1,301	18	21	2,936	41	22
$75,000 to $99,999	4,168	10	2,085	50	14	975	23	16	1,831	44	14
$100,000 or more..............	4,036	10	2,002	50	13	941	23	15	1,751	43	13
Not reported..................	7,621	19	1,779	23	12	567	7	9	1,619	21	12

Note: Detail does not add to total because of multiple responses. Percent who participated columns show the percent of each row's population who participated in the activity named by the column (the percent of those living in urban areas who were residential participants, etc.). Percent columns show the percent of each column's participants who are described by the row heading (the percent of those who were residential participants who lived in urban areas, etc.). Data reported on this table are from screening interviews in which one adult household member responded for all household members 6 to 15 years old. The screening interview required the respondent to recall 12 months worth of activity. Includes persons who participated in wildlife-watching activities only in other countries.

Table C-9. Participants in Wildlife-Related Recreation 6 to 15 Years Old by Participant's State of Residence: 2000

(Population 6 to 15 years old. Numbers in thousands)

Participant's state of residence	Population	Total participants		Sportspersons		Wildlife-watching participants	
		Number	Percent of population	Number	Percent of population	Number	Percent of population
United States, total........	**40,949**	**20,245**	**49**	**13,369**	**33**	**15,066**	**37**
Alabama...................	618	297	48	247	40	178	29
Alaska....................	112	83	74	60	54	64	57
Arizona...................	806	349	43	211	26	249	31
Arkansas..................	373	213	57	154	41	145	39
California.................	5,239	2,040	39	1,145	22	1,589	30
Colorado..................	623	388	62	234	38	289	46
Connecticut................	478	225	47	132	28	173	36
Delaware..................	193	136	71	35	18	122	64
Florida	2,159	800	37	586	27	537	25
Georgia...................	1,224	501	41	406	33	325	27
Hawaii	160	69	43	47	29	46	29
Idaho.....................	206	139	67	110	54	93	45
Illinois....................	1,833	955	52	609	33	694	38
Indiana	874	500	57	363	41	368	42
Iowa.....................	413	265	64	205	50	172	42
Kansas	392	260	66	208	53	180	46
Kentucky	557	333	60	238	43	261	47
Louisiana	677	306	45	174	26	235	35
Maine	170	125	73	83	49	106	62
Maryland	778	404	52	222	29	343	44
Massachusetts..............	848	358	42	234	28	255	30
Michigan..................	1,498	811	54	489	33	625	42
Minnesota.................	733	577	79	456	62	434	59
Mississippi	438	211	48	171	39	144	33
Missouri	809	443	55	334	41	320	40
Montana..................	132	82	62	69	52	55	42
Nebraska..................	248	145	58	105	43	103	42
Nevada	302	126	42	80	27	99	33
New Hampshire.............	182	112	62	79	43	85	47
New Jersey.................	1,192	545	46	316	27	443	37
New Mexico................	285	150	53	102	36	105	37
New York..................	2,597	1,062	41	555	21	872	34
North Carolina.............	1,171	561	48	400	34	397	34
North Dakota	89	56	63	47	53	34	38
Ohio	1,637	800	49	595	36	577	35
Oklahoma.................	498	288	58	206	41	207	41
Oregon	476	308	65	167	35	254	53
Pennsylvania...............	1,656	897	54	594	36	700	42
Rhode Island	144	69	48	44	30	49	34
South Carolina.............	553	275	50	176	32	213	39
South Dakota	112	74	66	58	51	48	43
Tennessee	790	404	51	265	34	290	37
Texas.....................	3,276	1,389	42	976	30	916	28
Utah	384	253	66	195	51	188	49
Vermont	83	54	65	41	50	46	56
Virginia...................	977	575	59	342	35	443	45
Washington................	869	518	60	312	36	414	48
West Virginia	233	155	66	110	47	113	49
Wisconsin.................	778	501	64	340	44	426	55
Wyoming	71	55	77	41	58	43	61

Note: Detail does not add to total because of multiple responses. U.S. totals include responses from participants residing in the District of Columbia, as described in the statistical accuracy appendix. Data reported on this table are from screening interviews in which one adult household member responded for household members 6 to 15 years old. The screening interview required the respondent to recall 12 months worth of activity. Includes persons who participated only in other countries.

Table C-10. Anglers and Hunters 6 to 15 Years Old by Sportsperson's State of Residence: 2000

(Population 6 to 15 years old. Numbers in thousands)

Sportsperson's state of residence	Population	Fished or hunted		Fished only		Hunted only		Fished and hunted	
		Number	Percent of population	Number	Percent of population	Number	Percent of population	Number	Percent of population
United States, total........	**40,949**	**13,369**	**33**	**11,628**	**28**	**224**	**1**	**1,517**	**4**
Alabama.................	618	247	40	191	31	...	...	45	7
Alaska....................	112	60	54	49	44	*6	*5	*5	*5
Arizona.................	806	211	26	183	23	...	...	*22	*3
Arkansas................	373	154	41	112	30	...	...	*38	*10
California................	5,239	1,145	22	1,099	21	...	...	...	...
Colorado................	623	234	38	211	34	...	...	*23	*4
Connecticut..............	478	132	28	128	27	...	...	...	...
Delaware................	193	35	18	32	17	...	...	...	...
Florida	2,159	586	27	543	25	...	...	...	...
Georgia.................	1,224	406	33	348	28	...	...	*49	*4
Hawaii	160	47	29	45	28	...	...	...	...
Idaho....................	206	110	54	97	47	...	...	*12	*6
Illinois..................	1,833	609	33	549	30	...	...	...	...
Indiana	874	363	41	312	36	...	...	*50	*6
Iowa	413	205	50	172	42	...	...	*31	*8
Kansas	392	208	53	180	46	...	...	*26	*7
Kentucky	557	238	43	206	37	...	...	*29	*5
Louisiana	677	174	26	147	22	...	...	*22	*3
Maine	170	83	49	71	42	...	...	*10	*6
Maryland	778	222	29	201	26	...	...	...	...
Massachusetts.............	848	234	28	227	27	...	...	...	...
Michigan................	1,498	489	33	452	30	...	...	...	...
Minnesota...............	733	456	62	388	53	...	...	*61	*8
Mississippi	438	171	39	117	27	...	...	46	11
Missouri	809	334	41	242	30	...	...	*79	*10
Montana.................	132	69	52	51	39	...	...	*15	*11
Nebraska................	248	105	43	90	36	...	...	*11	*5
Nevada.................	302	80	27	77	25	...	...	...	...
New Hampshire	182	79	43	68	37	...	...	*8	*5
New Jersey...............	1,192	316	27	303	25	...	...	...	...
New Mexico.............	285	102	36	87	30	...	...	*10	*4
New York...............	2,597	555	21	490	19	...	...	*66	*3
North Carolina	1,171	400	34	353	30	...	...	*43	*4
North Dakota.............	89	47	53	38	42	...	...	*8	*9
Ohio	1,637	595	36	526	32	...	...	*62	*4
Oklahoma................	498	206	41	155	31	...	...	*47	*9
Oregon	476	167	35	152	32	...	...	...	...
Pennsylvania.............	1,656	594	36	498	30	...	...	*80	*5
Rhode Island	144	44	30	42	29	...	...	...	...
South Carolina	553	176	32	150	27	...	...	*23	*4
South Dakota	112	58	51	45	40	...	...	*10	*9
Tennessee	790	265	34	217	27	...	...	*41	*5
Texas...................	3,276	976	30	801	24	...	...	*143	*4
Utah	384	195	51	169	44	...	...	*23	*6
Vermont	83	41	50	31	37	...	...	*10	*13
Virginia.................	977	342	35	304	31	...	...	...	...
Washington..............	869	312	36	292	34	...	...	*20	*2
West Virginia	233	110	47	73	31	...	...	*31	*13
Wisconsin................	778	340	44	280	36	...	...	*48	*6
Wyoming	71	41	58	33	47	...	...	*7	*10

* Estimate based on a small sample size.   ... Sample size too small to report data reliably.

Note: U.S. totals include responses from participants residing in the District of Columbia, as described in the statistical accuracy appendix. Data reported on this table are from screening interviews in which one adult household member responded for household members 6 to 15 years old. The screening interviews required the respondent to recall 12 months worth of activity. Includes persons who participated only in other countries.

Table C-11. Participants in Wildlife-Watching Activities 6 to 15 Years Old by Participant's State of Residence: 2000

(Population 6 to 15 years old. Numbers in thousands)

Participant's state of residence	Population	Participants					
		Total		Nonresidential		Residential	
		Number	Percent of population	Number	Percent of population	Number	Percent of population
United States, total........	**40,949**	**15,066**	**37**	**6,091**	**15**	**13,542**	**33**
Alabama..................	618	178	29	52	8	161	26
Alaska....................	112	64	57	28	25	54	48
Arizona...................	806	249	31	95	12	215	27
Arkansas.................	373	145	39	*44	*12	138	37
California................	5,239	1,589	30	742	14	1,339	26
Colorado.................	623	289	46	143	23	236	38
Connecticut..............	478	173	36	43	9	166	35
Delaware.................	193	122	64	57	30	119	62
Florida	2,159	537	25	*168	*8	492	23
Georgia..................	1,224	325	27	136	11	286	23
Hawaii	160	46	29	24	15	38	24
Idaho....................	206	93	45	51	25	82	40
Illinois...................	1,833	694	38	210	11	658	36
Indiana	874	368	42	137	16	350	40
Iowa	413	172	42	75	18	153	37
Kansas	392	180	46	72	18	160	41
Kentucky	557	261	47	113	20	238	43
Louisiana	677	235	35	78	12	203	30
Maine	170	106	62	40	23	102	60
Maryland	778	343	44	145	19	319	41
Massachusetts.............	848	255	30	80	9	238	28
Michigan.................	1,498	625	42	288	19	579	39
Minnesota................	733	434	59	152	21	403	55
Mississippi	438	144	33	*38	*9	137	31
Missouri	809	320	40	188	23	283	35
Montana	132	55	42	39	29	45	34
Nebraska.................	248	103	42	45	18	88	36
Nevada	302	99	33	44	15	79	26
New Hampshire	182	85	47	47	26	71	39
New Jersey	1,192	443	37	184	15	397	33
New Mexico...............	285	105	37	50	17	89	31
New York.................	2,597	872	34	323	12	806	31
North Carolina............	1,171	397	34	117	10	366	31
North Dakota	89	34	38	17	20	30	34
Ohio	1,637	577	35	207	13	525	32
Oklahoma.................	498	207	41	98	20	178	36
Oregon	476	254	53	128	27	212	44
Pennsylvania..............	1,656	700	42	274	17	671	41
Rhode Island	144	49	34	15	10	44	31
South Carolina............	553	213	39	73	13	195	35
South Dakota.............	112	48	43	18	16	41	36
Tennessee	790	290	37	104	13	274	35
Texas....................	3,276	916	28	350	11	818	25
Utah	384	188	49	108	28	159	41
Vermont	83	46	56	19	23	43	52
Virginia..................	977	443	45	149	15	393	40
Washington...............	869	414	48	203	23	356	41
West Virginia	233	113	49	*24	*10	106	46
Wisconsin................	778	426	55	233	30	372	48
Wyoming	71	43	61	25	34	35	48

* Estimate based on a small sample size.

Note: Detail does not add to total because of multiple responses. U.S. totals include responses from participants residing in the District of Columbia, as described in the statistical accuracy appendix. Data reported on this table are from screening interviews in which one adult household member responded for all household members 6 to 15 years old. The screening interview required the respondent to recall 12 months worth of activity. Includes persons who participated only in other countries.

Appendix D

Appendix D.
Sample Design and Statistical Accuracy

This Appendix is presented in two parts. The first part is the U.S. Census Bureau Source and Accuracy Statement. This statement describes the sampling design for the 2001 Survey and highlights the steps taken to produce estimates from the completed questionnaires. The statement explains the use of standard errors and confidence intervals. It also provides comprehensive information about errors characteristic of surveys, and formulas and parameters to calculate an approximate standard error or confidence interval for each number published in this report. The second part, Tables D-1 to D-4, reports approximate standard errors and 95-percent confidence intervals for selected measures of participation and expenditures for wildlife-related recreation.

Source and Accuracy Statement for the 2001 National Survey of Fishing, Hunting, and Wildlife-Associated Recreation

Source of Data

The estimates in this report are based on data collected in the *2001 National Survey of Fishing, Hunting, and Wildlife-Associated Recreation* (FHWAR).

The 2001 FHWAR Survey was designed to provide state-level estimates of the number of participants in recreational hunting and fishing, and in wildlife-watching activities (e.g., wildlife observation). Information was collected on the number of participants, where and how often they participated, the type of wildlife encountered, and the amounts of money spent on wildlife-related recreation.

The survey was conducted in two stages: an initial screening of households to identify likely sportspersons and wildlife-watching participants, and a series of follow-up interviews of selected persons

to collect detailed data about their wildlife-related recreation during 2001.

The 2001 FHWAR sample was selected from expired samples of the Current Population Survey (CPS).

Sample Design

A. CPS - Current Population Survey

The expired CPS samples used for the 2001 FHWAR had been selected initially from 1990 decennial census files with coverage in all 50 states and the District of Columbia. The samples, while active, had been continually updated to reflect new construction. The sample addresses were located in 754 geographic areas consisting of a county or several contiguous counties.

B. The FHWAR Screening Sample

The total screening sample consisted of 80,000 households identified from the expired CPS samples. About 3,300 households were removed from sample because they did not have accurate or consistent address or contact information. Of the remaining households, roughly 8.8 percent were found to be vacant or otherwise not to be enumerated. About 23.1 percent could not be enumerated because the occupants were not found at home, refused to participate in the survey, or were unavailable.

Overall, about 52,508 completed household interviews were obtained for a national response rate of approximately 74.8 percent. Local field representatives conducted interviews by telephone when possible, otherwise through a personal visit. The field representatives asked screening questions for all household members

6 years old and older. Interviewing for the screen was conducted during April, May, and June of 2001.

Data for the FHWAR sportspersons sample and wildlife-watchers sample were collected in three waves. The first wave started in April 2001, the second in September 2001, and the third in January 2002. In the sportspersons sample, all persons who hunted or fished in 2001 by the time of the screening interview were interviewed in the first wave. The remaining sportspersons sample were interviewed in the second wave. All sample persons (from both the first and second waves) were interviewed in the third wave.

The reference period was the preceding 4 months for waves 1 and 2. In wave 3, the reference period was either 4 or 8 months depending on when the sample person was first interviewed.

C. The Detailed Samples

Two independent detailed samples were chosen from the FHWAR screening sample. One consisted of sportspersons (people who hunt or fish) and the other of wildlife watchers (people who observed, photographed, or fed wildlife).

1. Sportspersons

The Census Bureau selected the detailed samples based on information reported during the screening phase. Every person 16 years old and older in the FHWAR screening sample was assigned to a sportspersons stratum based on time devoted to hunting/fishing in the past and time expected to be devoted to hunting/fishing in the future. The sportspersons categories were:

Active - a person who had already participated in hunting/fishing in 2001 at the time of the screener interview.

Likely - a person who had not participated in 2001 at the time of the screener but had participated in 2000 OR said they were likely to participate in 2001.

Inactive - a person who had not participated in 2000 or 2001 AND said they were somewhat unlikely to participate in 2001.

Nonparticipant - a person who had not participated in 2000 or 2001 AND said they were very unlikely to participate in 2001.

Persons were selected for the detailed phase based on these groupings.

Active sportspersons were given the detailed interview twice—at the same time of the screening interview (April-June 2001) and again in January/February 2002. Likely sportspersons and a subsample of the inactive sportspersons were also interviewed twice—first in September/October 2001, then in January/February 2002. If Census field representatives were not able to obtain the first interview, they attempted to interview the person in the final interviewing period with the reference period being the entire year. Persons in the nonparticipant group were not eligible for a detailed interview.

About 28,700 persons were designated for interviews. The detailed sportspersons sample sizes varied by state to get reliable state level estimates. During each interview period, about 12 percent of the designated people were not found at home or were unavailable. Overall, about 25,100 detailed sportspersons interviews were completed for a national response rate of 88 percent.

2. Wildlife Watchers

The wildlife-watching detailed sample also was selected based on information reported during the screening phase. Every person 16 years of age and older was assigned to a category based on time devoted to wildlife-watching activities in previous years, participation in 2001 by the time of the screening interview, and intentions to participate in activities during the remainder of 2001.

Each person was placed into one of the following groups based on their past participation:

Active - a person who had already participated in 2001 at the time of the screening interview.

Avid - a person who had not yet participated in 2001 but in 2000 had taken trips to participate in wildlife-watching activities for 21 or more days or had spent $300 or more.

Average - a person who had not yet participated in 2001 but in 2000 had taken trips to wildlife-watch for less than 21 days and had spent less than $300 OR had not participated in wildlife-watching activities but said they were very likely to in the remainder of 2001.

Infrequent - a person who had not participated in 2000 or 2001 but said they were somewhat likely or somewhat unlikely to participate in the remainder of 2001.

Nonparticipant - a person who had not participated in 2000 or 2001 and said they were very unlikely to participate during the remainder of 2001.

Persons were selected for the detailed phase based on these groupings. Persons in the nonparticipant group were not eligible for a detailed interview. A subsample of each of the other groups was selected to receive a detailed interview with the chance of being selected

diminishing as the likelihood of participation diminished.

Wildlife-watching participants were given the detailed interview twice. Some received their first detailed interview at the same time as the screening interview (April-June 2001). The rest received their first detailed interview in September/October 2001. All wildlife-watching participants received their second interview in January/February 2002. If Census field representatives were not able to obtain the first interview, they attempted to interview the person in the final interviewing period with the reference period being the entire year.

About 17,100 persons were designated for interviews. The detailed wildlife-watching sample sizes varied by state to get reliable state-level estimates. During each interview period, 11 percent of the designated people were not found at home or were unavailable. Overall, about 15,300 detailed wildlife-watcher interviews were completed for a national response rate of 90 percent.

Estimation Procedure

Several stages of adjustments were used to derive the final 2001 FHWAR person weights. A brief description of the major components of the weights is given below.

All statistics for the population 6 to 15 years of age were derived from the screening interview. Statistics for the population 16 and over came from both the screening and detailed interviews. Estimates which came from the screening sample are presented in Appendix C.

A. Screening Sample

Every interviewed person in the screening sample received a weight that was the product of the following factors:

1. *Base Weight.* The base weight is the inverse of the household's probability of selection.

2. *Household Noninterview Adjustment.* The noninterview adjustment inflated the weight assigned to interviewed households to account for households eligible for interview but for which no interview was obtained.

3. *First-Stage Adjustment.* The 754 areas designated for our samples were selected from over 2,000 such areas of the United States. Some sample areas represent only themselves and are referred to as self-representing. The remaining areas represent other areas similar in selected characteristics and are thus designated nonself-representing. The first-stage factor reduces the component of variation arising from sampling the nonself-representing areas.

4. *Second-Stage Adjustment.* This adjustment brings the estimates of the total population in each state into agreement with census-based estimates of the civilian noninstitutional and nonbarrack military populations for each state.

B. Sportspersons Sample

Every interviewed person in the sportspersons detailed sample received a weight that was the product of the following factors:

1. *Screening Weight.* This is the individual's final weight from the screening sample.

2. *Sportspersons Stratum Adjustment.* This factor inflated the weights of persons selected for the detailed sample to account for the subsampling done within each sportsperson's stratum.

3. *Sportspersons Noninterview Adjustment.* This factor adjusts the weights of the interviewed sportspersons to account for sportspersons selected for the detailed sample for whom no interview was obtained. A person was considered a noninterview if he/she were not interviewed in the third wave of interviewing.

4. *Sportspersons Ratio Adjustment Factor.* This is a ratio adjustment of the detailed sample to the screening sample within sportspersons sampling stratum. This adjustment brings the population estimates of persons age 16 years old or older from the detailed sample into agreement with the same estimates from the screening sample, which was a much larger sample.

C. Wildlife-Watchers Sample

Every interviewed person in the wildlife-watchers detailed sample received a weight that was the product of the following factors:

1. *Screening Weight.* This is the individual's final weight from the screening sample.

2. *Wildlife-Watchers Stratum Adjustment.* This factor inflated the weights of persons selected for the detailed sample to account for the subsampling done within each wildlife-watcher stratum.

3. *Wildlife-Watchers Noninterview Adjustment.* This factor adjusts the weights of the interviewed wildlife-watching participants to account for wildlife watchers selected for the detailed sample for which no interview was obtained. A person was considered a noninterview if he/she were not interviewed in the third wave of interviewing.

4. *Wildlife-Watchers Ratio Adjustment Factor.* This is a ratio adjustment of the detailed sample to the screening sample within wildlife-watchers sampling strata. This adjustment brings the population estimates of persons age 16 years old or older from the detailed sample into agreement with the same estimates from the screening sample, which was a much larger sample.

Accuracy of the Estimates

Since the 2001 estimates came from a sample, they may differ from figures from a complete census using the same questionnaires, instructions, and enumerators. A sample survey estimate has two possible types of error—sampling and nonsampling. The accuracy of an estimate depends on both types of error, but the full extent of the nonsampling error is unknown. Consequently, one should be particularly careful when interpreting results based on a relatively small number of cases or on small differences between estimates. The standard errors for the 2001 FHWAR estimates primarily indicate the magnitude of sampling error. They also partially measure the effect of some nonsampling errors in responses and enumeration, but do not measure systematic biases in the data. (Bias is the average over all possible samples of the differences between the sample estimate and the actual value.)

Nonsampling Variability

Let us suppose that a comparable complete enumeration was conducted, that is, an interview is attempted for every person 16 years old and over in the United States. Chances are we will not correctly estimate every parameter under consideration (for example, the proportion of people who fished). In this instance, the difference is due solely to nonsampling errors. Nonsampling errors also occur in sample surveys and can be attributed to several sources including the following:

- The inability to obtain information about all cases in the sample.

- Definitional difficulties.

- Differences in the interpretation of questions.

- Respondents' inability or unwillingness to provide correct information.

- Respondents' inability to recall information.

- Errors made in data collection such as in recording or coding the data.

- Errors made in the processing of data.

- Errors made in estimating values for missing data.

- Failure to represent all units with the sample (undercoverage).

Overall CPS undercoverage is estimated to be about 8 percent. Generally, undercoverage is larger for males than for females and larger for Blacks and other races combined than for Whites. Ratio estimation to independent population controls, as described previously, partially corrects for the bias due to survey undercoverage. However, biases exist in the estimates to the extent that missed persons in missed households or missed persons in interviewed households have different characteristics from those of interviewed persons in the same age group.

Comparability of Data. Data obtained from the 2001 FHWAR and other sources are not entirely comparable. This results from differences in field interviewer training and experience and in differing survey processes. This is an example of nonsampling variability not reflected in the standard errors. Use caution when comparing results from different sources (See Appendix B).

Note When Using Small Estimates. Because of the large standard errors involved, summary measures (such as medians and percentage distributions) would probably not reveal useful information when computed on a base smaller than 100,000. Take care in the interpretation of small differences. For instance, even a small amount of nonsampling error can cause a borderline difference to appear significant or not, thus distorting a seemingly valid hypothesis test.

Sampling Variability

The particular sample used for the 2001 FHWAR Survey is one of a large number of all possible samples of the same size that could have been selected using the same sample design. Estimates derived from the different samples would differ from each other. This sample-to-sample variability is referred to as sampling variability and is generally measured by the standard error. The exact sampling error is unknown. However, guides to the potential size of the sampling error are provided by the standard error of the estimate.

Since the standard error of a survey estimate attempts to provide a measure of the variation among the estimates from the possible samples, it is a measure of the precision with which an estimate from a particular sample approximates the average result of all possible samples. Standard errors, as calculated by methods described next in "Standard Errors and Their Use," are primarily measures of sampling variability, although they may include some nonsampling error.

The sample estimate and its standard error enable one to construct a confidence interval, a range that would include the average result of all possible samples with a known probability. For example, if all possible samples were surveyed under essentially the same general conditions and using the same sample design, and if an estimate and its standard error were calculated from each sample, then approximately 95 percent of the intervals from 1.96 standard errors below the estimate to 1.96 standard errors above the estimate would include the average result of all possible samples.

A particular confidence interval may or may not contain the average estimate derived from all possible samples. However, one can say with specified confidence that the interval includes the average estimate calculated from all possible samples.

Standard errors may also be used to perform hypothesis testing—a procedure for distinguishing between population parameters using sample estimates. One common type of hypothesis is that the population parameters are different. An example would be comparing the proportion of anglers to the proportion of hunters.

Tests may be performed at various levels of significance where a significance level is the probability of concluding that the characteristics are different when, in fact, they are the same. To conclude that two characteristics are different at the 0.05 level of significance, the absolute value of the estimated difference between characteristics must be greater than or equal to 1.96 times the standard error of the difference.

This report uses 95-percent confidence intervals and 0.05 levels of significance to determine statistical validity. Consult standard statistical textbooks for alternative criteria.

Standard Errors and Their Use. A number of approximations are required to derive, at a moderate cost, standard errors applicable to all the estimates in this report. Instead of providing an individual standard error for each estimate, parameters are provided to calculate standard errors for each type of characteristic. These parameters are listed in tables D-5 to D-10. Methods for using the parameters to calculate standard errors of various estimates are given in the next sections.

Standard Errors of Estimated Numbers. The approximate standard error, s_x, of an estimated number shown in this report can be obtained using the following formulas. Formula (1) is used to calculate the standard errors of levels of sportspersons, anglers, and wildlife watchers.

$$s_x = \sqrt{ax^2 + bx} \tag{1}$$

Here, x is the size of the estimate and a and b are the parameters in the tables associated with the particular characteristic.

Formula (2) is used for standard errors of aggregates, i.e., trips, days, and expenditures.

$$s_x = \sqrt{ax^2 + bx + \frac{cx^2}{y}} \tag{2}$$

Here, x is again the size of the estimate; y is the base of the estimate; and a, b, and c are the parameters in the tables associated with the particular characteristic.

Illustration of the Computation of the Standard Error of an Estimated Number

Table 1 in this report shows that 37,805,000 persons 16+ either fished or hunted in the United States in 2001. Using formula (1) with the parameters a= -0.000020 and b= 4,289 from table D-6, the approximate standard error of the estimates number of 37,805,000 sportspersons 16+ is

$$s_x = \sqrt{(-0.000020)(37,805,000)^2 + (4,289)(37,805,000)} = 365,500$$

The 95-percent confidence interval for the estimated number of sportspersons 16+ is from 37,088,600 to 38,521,400, ie., 37,805,000 ± 1.96 x 365,500. Therefore, a conclusion that the average estimate derived from all possible samples lies within a range computed in this way would be correct for roughly 95 percent of all possible samples.

Table 1 shows that 13,034,300 hunters 16+ engaged in 228,367,800 days of participation in 2001. Using formula (2) with the parameters a = 0.000168, b = -11,904, and c = 12,496 from table D-8, the approximate standard error on 228,367,800 estimated days on an estimated base of 13,034,300 hunters is

$$s_x = \sqrt{0.000168 \times 228,367,800^2 + (-11,904) \times 228,367,800 + \frac{12,496 \times 228,367,800^2}{13,034,300}} = 7,486,100$$

The 95-percent confidence interval on the estimate of 228,367,800 days is from 213,695,000 to 243,040,600, ie., 228,367,800 ± 1.96 x 7,486,100. Again, a conclusion that the average estimate derived from all possible samples lies within a range computed in this way would be correct for roughly 95 percent of all possible samples.

Standard Errors of Estimated Percentages. The reliability of an estimated percentage, computed using sample data for both numerator and denominator, depends on the size of the percentage and its base. Estimated percentages are relatively more reliable than the corresponding estimates of the numerators of the percentages, particularly if the percentages are 50 percent or more. When the numerator and the denominator of the percentage are in different categories, use the parameter in the tables indicated by the numerator.

The approximate standard error, $s_{x,p}$, can be obtained by use of the formula

$$s_{x,p} = \sqrt{\frac{bp(100-p)}{x}} \tag{3}$$

Here, x is the total number of sportspersons, hunters, etc., which is the base of the percentage; p is the percentage ($0 \leq p \leq 100$); and b is the parameter in the tables associated with the characteristic in the numerator of the percentage.

Illustration of the Computation of the Standard Error of an Estimated Percentage

Table 1 shows that of the 13,034,300 hunters 16+, 22.7 percent hunted migratory birds. From table D-6, the appropriate b parameter is 3,793. Using formula (3), the approximate standard error on the estimate of 22.7 percent is

$$s_{x,p} = \sqrt{\frac{3,793 \times 22.7 \times (100-22.7)}{13,034,300}} = 0.71$$

Consequently, the 95-percent confidence interval for the estimate percentage of migratory bird hunters 16+ is from 21.3 percent to 24.1 percent, ie. 22.7 ± 1.96 x 0.71.

Standard Error of a Difference. The standard error of the difference between two sample estimates is approximately equal to

$$s_{x-y} = \sqrt{s_x^2 + s_y^2}$$

(4)

where s_x and s_y are the standard errors of the estimates x and y. The estimates can be numbers, percentages, ratios, etc. This will represent the actual standard error quite accurately for the difference between estimates of the same characteristic in two different areas, or for the difference between separate and uncorrelated characteristics in the same area. However, if there is a high positive (negative) correlation between the two characteristics, the formula will overestimate (underestimate) the true standard error.

Illustration of the Computation of the Standard Error of a Difference

Table 24 shows that of the 13,034,300 hunters, 10,688,000 were licensed hunters, and 1,689,300 were exempt from a hunting license. The corresponding percentages are 82.0 percent and 13.0 percent, respectively. The apparent difference between the percent of licensed hunters and hunters who are exempt from a license is 69.0 percent. Using formula (3) and the appropriate b parameter from table D-6, the approximate standard errors of 82.0 percent and 13.0 percent are 0.66 and 0.57, respectively. Using formula (4), the approximate standard error of the estimated difference of 69.0 percent is

$$s_{x-y} = \sqrt{0.66^2 + 0.57^2} = 0.87$$

The 95-percent confidence interval on the difference between licensed hunters and those who were exempt from a hunting license is from 67.3 to 70.7 percent, i.e., 69.0 ± 1.96 x 0.87. Since the interval does not contain zero, we can conclude with 95 percent confidence that the percentage of licensed hunters is greater than the percentage of hunters who are exempt from a hunting license.

Standard Errors of Estimated Averages. Certain mean values for sportspersons, anglers, etc., shown in the report were calculated as the ratio of two numbers. For example, average days per angler is calculated as:

$$\frac{x}{y} = \frac{\text{total days}}{\text{total anglers}}$$

Standard errors for these averages may be approximated by the use of formula (5) below.

$$s_{x/y} = \frac{x}{y} \sqrt{\left[\frac{s_x}{x}\right]^2 + \left[\frac{s_y}{y}\right]^2 - 2r\frac{s_x s_y}{xy}}$$

(5)

In formula (5), r represents the correlation coefficient between the numerator and the denominator of the estimate. In the above formula, use 0.7 as an estimate of r.

Illustration of the Computation of the Standard Error of an Estimated Average

Table 2 shows that the average days per angler 16 years old or older for all fishing was 16.4 days. Using formulas (1) and (2) above, we compute the standard error on total days, 557,393,900, and total anglers, 34,071,100, to be 8,726,000 and 350,600, respectively. The approximate standard error on the estimated average of 16.4 days is

$$s_{x/y} = \frac{557{,}393{,}900}{34{,}071{,}100} \sqrt{\left[\frac{8{,}726{,}000}{557{,}393{,}900}\right]^2 + \left[\frac{350{,}600}{34{,}071{,}100}\right]^2 - 2\times0.7\frac{8{,}726{,}000\times350{,}600}{557{,}393{,}900\times34{,}071{,}100}} = 0.18$$

therefore, the 95-percent confidence interval on the estimated average of 16.4 days is from 16.0 to 16.8, i.e., 16.4 ± 1.96 x 0.18.

Table D-1. Approximate Standard Errors and 95-Percent Confidence Intervals for Selected Fishing Estimates: 2001

Anglers, days, and expenditures	Estimate	Standard error	Lower 95 percent	Upper 95 percent
ANGLERS (thousands)				
Total	**34,071**	**351**	**33,384**	**34,758**
Freshwater...	28,439	325	27,801	29,077
Freshwater except Great Lakes........................	27,913	323	27,281	28,545
Great Lakes..	1,847	89	1,673	2,021
Saltwater...	9,051	193	8,673	9,429
DAYS OF FISHING (thousands)				
Total	**557,394**	**8,726**	**540,291**	**574,497**
Freshwater...	466,984	8,919	449,502	484,466
Freshwater except Great Lakes........................	443,247	8,614	426,364	460,130
Great Lakes..	23,138	2,391	18,451	27,825
Saltwater...	90,838	3,929	83,137	98,539
Average Days per Angler				
Total	**16.4**	**0.18**	**16.0**	**16.8**
Freshwater...	16.4	0.23	16.0	16.8
Freshwater except Great Lakes........................	15.9	0.22	15.5	16.3
Great Lakes..	12.5	0.97	10.6	14.4
Saltwater...	10.0	0.32	9.4	10.6
FISHING EXPENDITURES (thousands)				
Total	**$35,632,257**	**$945,263**	**$33,779,541**	**$37,484,973**
Freshwater...	$21,348,370	$604,067	$20,164,398	$22,532,342
Freshwater except Great Lakes........................	$19,972,014	$568,976	$18,856,821	$21,087,207
Great Lakes..	$1,274,435	$122,992	$1,033,371	$1,515,499
Saltwater...	$8,388,962	$381,702	$7,640,826	$9,137,098
Average Expenditure per Spender				
Total	**$1,115**	**$22**	**$1,073**	**$1,157**
Freshwater...	$817	$16	$785	$849
Freshwater except Great Lakes........................	$782	$16	$751	$813
Great Lakes..	$750	$49	$653	$847
Saltwater...	$1,034	$32	$972	$1,096

Table D-2. Approximate Standard Errors and 95-Percent Confidence Intervals for Selected Hunting Estimates: 2001

Hunters, days, and expenditures	Estimate	Standard error	Lower 95 percent	Upper 95 percent
HUNTERS (thousands)				
Total	**13,034**	**215**	**12,612**	**13,456**
Big game	10,911	198	10,523	11,299
Small game	5,434	142	5,156	5,712
Migratory bird	2,956	105	2,750	3,162
Other animals	1,047	63	924	1,170
DAYS OF HUNTING (thousands)				
Total	**228,368**	**7,486**	**213,695**	**243,041**
Big game	153,191	5,385	142,637	163,745
Small game	60,142	2,865	54,526	65,758
Migratory bird	29,310	1,851	25,682	32,938
Other animals	19,207	2,058	15,173	23,241
Average Days per Hunter				
Total	**17.5**	**0.64**	**16.2**	**18.8**
Big game	14.0	0.56	12.9	15.1
Small game	11.1	0.60	9.9	12.3
Migratory bird	9.9	0.72	8.5	11.3
Other animals	18.3	2.25	13.9	22.7
HUNTING EXPENDITURES (thousands)				
Total	**$20,611,025**	**$941,534**	**$18,765,618**	**$22,456,432**
Big game	$10,087,930	$485,235	$9,136,869	$11,038,991
Small game	$1,816,199	$110,041	$1,600,519	$2,031,879
Migratory bird	$1,388,581	$108,766	$1,175,400	$1,601,762
Other animals	$243,760	$29,928	$185,101	$302,419
Average Expenditures per Spender				
Total	**$1,638**	**$77**	**$1,487**	**$1,789**
Big game	$1,013	$48	$920	$1,106
Small game	$399	$22	$356	$442
Migratory bird	$548	$40	$469	$627
Other animals	$376	$32	$314	$438

Table D-3. Approximate Standard Errors and 95-Percent Confidence Intervals for Selected Fishing and Hunting Expenditure Estimates: 2001

(Numbers in thousands)

Expenditures	Estimate	Standard error	Lower 95 percent	Upper 95 percent
FISHING AND HUNTING EXPENDITURES				
Total..	**$69,976,330**	**$1,791,976**	**$66,464,058**	**$73,488,602**
Trip-related..............................	$19,908,392	$508,674	$18,911,390	$20,905,394
Food and Lodging	$8,330,938	$211,927	$7,915,561	$8,746,315
Transportation..........................	$5,305,077	$134,367	$5,041,717	$5,568,437
Other trip costs............................	$6,272,377	$159,162	$5,960,420	$6,584,334
Equipment	$40,954,202	$1,048,104	$38,899,918	$43,008,486
Fishing/hunting..........................	$9,507,114	$242,075	$9,032,648	$9,981,580
Auxiliary..................................	$2,627,686	$65,733	$2,498,850	$2,756,522
Special	$28,819,402	$737,075	$27,374,736	$30,264,068
Other..	$9,113,737	$231,992	$8,659,033	$9,568,441
Magazine subscriptions	$307,981	$6,089	$296,046	$319,916
Membership dues and contributions...........	$515,282	$11,498	$492,745	$537,819
Land leasing and ownership	$7,128,486	$181,106	$6,773,518	$7,483,454
Licenses, stamps, tags, and permits	$1,161,988	$28,139	$1,106,835	$1,217,141
Fishing Expenditures				
Total..	**$35,632,257**	**$945,263**	**$33,779,541**	**$37,484,973**
Trip-related..............................	$14,656,000	$387,889	$13,895,738	$15,416,262
Food and Lodging	$5,880,997	$154,718	$5,577,750	$6,184,244
Transportation..........................	$3,515,756	$91,865	$3,335,702	$3,695,810
Other trip costs............................	$5,259,247	$138,196	$4,988,382	$5,530,112
Equipment	$16,963,523	$449,204	$16,083,084	$17,843,962
Fishing	$4,617,612	$121,146	$4,380,166	$4,855,058
Auxiliary..................................	$721,049	$17,550	$686,651	$755,447
Special	$11,624,862	$307,346	$11,022,465	$12,227,259
Other..	$4,012,733	$105,072	$3,806,793	$4,218,673
Land leasing and ownership	$3,152,594	$82,213	$2,991,456	$3,313,732
Licenses, stamps, tags, and permits	$639,876	$15,384	$609,724	$670,028
Hunting Expenditures				
Total..	**$20,611,025**	**$941,534**	**$18,765,618**	**$22,456,432**
Trip-related..............................	$5,252,391	$237,159	$4,787,560	$5,717,222
Food and Lodging	$2,449,942	$108,603	$2,237,080	$2,662,804
Transportation..........................	$1,789,320	$78,283	$1,635,886	$1,942,754
Other trip costs............................	$1,013,129	$42,614	$929,606	$1,096,652
Equipment	$10,361,496	$471,479	$9,437,397	$11,285,595
Hunting..................................	$4,561,709	$205,479	$4,158,969	$4,964,449
Auxiliary..................................	$1,202,845	$51,341	$1,102,216	$1,303,474
Special	$4,596,942	$207,095	$4,191,035	$5,002,849
Other..	$4,997,138	$225,451	$4,555,253	$5,439,023
Land leasing and ownership	$3,975,892	$178,609	$3,625,819	$4,325,965
Licenses, stamps, tags, and permits	$693,038	$27,850	$638,452	$747,624

Table D-4. Approximate Standard Errors and 95-Percent Confidence Intervals for Selected Wildlife-Watching Estimates: 2001

Participants and expenditures	Estimate	Standard error	Lower 95 percent	Upper 95 percent
WILDLIFE-WATCHING PARTICIPANTS (thousands)				
Total participants	**66,105**	**625**	**64,880**	**67,330**
Nonresidential (away from home)	21,823	559	20,727	22,919
Observe wildlife	20,080	395	19,307	20,853
Photograph wildlife...................................	9,427	278	8,883	9,971
Feed wildlife..	7,077	242	6,603	7,551
Residential (around the home)	62,928	616	61,720	64,136
Observe wildlife	42,111	538	41,057	43,165
Photograph wildlife...................................	13,937	334	13,283	14,591
Feed wildlife.......................................	53,988	588	52,836	55,140
Maintain natural areas or plantings	13,072	324	12,437	13,707
Visit public parks	10,981	299	10,396	11,566
DAYS OF PARTICIPATION IN NONRESIDENTIAL ACTIVITIES (thousands)				
Total	**372,006**	**16,700**	**339,274**	**404,738**
Observe wildlife	295,345	14,584	266,761	323,929
Photograph wildlife....................................	76,324	6,969	62,665	89,983
Feed wildlife...	103,307	8,558	86,534	120,080
Average Days of Participation in Nonresidential Activities				
Total	**17.0**	**0.56**	**16.0**	**18.1**
Observe wildlife	14.7	0.56	13.6	15.8
Photograph wildlife....................................	8.1	0.60	6.9	9.3
Feed wildlife	14.6	0.93	12.8	16.4
EXPENDITURES (thousands)				
Total	**$38,414,488**	**$644,659**	**$37,150,955**	**$39,678,021**
Trip-related	$8,162,439	$135,441	$7,896,974	$8,427,904
Food and lodging	$4,818,843	$79,151	$4,663,706	$4,973,980
Transportation	$2,595,542	$41,707	$2,513,796	$2,677,288
Other trip costs	$748,054	$10,478	$727,518	$768,590
Equipment and other expenses..........................	$30,252,049	$507,267	$29,257,805	$31,246,293
Wildlife watching	$7,353,977	$121,832	$7,115,187	$7,592,767
Auxiliary	$716,900	$9,944	$697,410	$736,390
Special...	$15,468,716	$258,428	$14,962,197	$15,975,235
Magazines	$331,955	$3,095	$325,888	$338,022
Membership dues and contributions....................	$920,183	$13,413	$893,893	$946,473

Table D-5. Parameters a and b for Calculating Approximate Standard Errors of Sportspersons, Anglers, Hunters, and Wildlife-Watching Participants

(These parameters are to be used only to calculate estimates of standard errors for characteristics developed from the screening sample)

State	6 years old and over		6-15 year olds only	
	a	b	a	b
United States..........................	**−0.000017**	**4,191**	**−0.000103**	**4,052**
Alabama...............................	−0.000380	1,493	−0.002270	1,417
Alaska.................................	−0.000948	512	−0.004485	489
Arizona...............................	−0.000399	1,559	−0.001931	1,303
Arkansas..............................	−0.001069	2,456	−0.006381	2,444
California.............................	−0.000221	6,329	−0.001083	5,240
Colorado..............................	−0.000521	1,819	−0.002707	1,551
Connecticut...........................	−0.000336	996	−0.002227	1,007
Delaware..............................	−0.000428	283	−0.002753	284
Florida................................	−0.000427	5,619	−0.002768	5,390
Georgia...............................	−0.000506	3,361	−0.002856	3,156
Hawaii................................	−0.000659	705	−0.003146	538
Idaho.................................	−0.001285	1,393	−0.006911	1,424
Illinois................................	−0.000427	4,572	−0.002310	4,043
Indiana................................	−0.000578	3,064	−0.003388	2,867
Iowa..................................	−0.000803	2,084	−0.004015	1,702
Kansas................................	−0.000659	1,528	−0.004453	1,804
Kentucky..............................	−0.000493	1,760	−0.002857	1,623
Louisiana..............................	−0.000874	3,461	−0.004231	3,101
Maine.................................	−0.000903	1,035	−0.005933	1,086
Maryland..............................	−0.000463	2,151	−0.002684	1,973
Massachusetts.........................	−0.000193	1,065	−0.001155	928
Michigan..............................	−0.000606	5,281	−0.003588	5,206
Minnesota.............................	−0.001004	4,226	−0.006232	4,574
Mississippi............................	−0.000955	2,368	−0.005090	2,275
Missouri..............................	−0.000681	3,305	−0.004295	3,440
Montana..............................	−0.001327	1,085	−0.008909	1,292
Nebraska..............................	−0.000479	714	−0.002742	713
Nevada................................	−0.000588	845	−0.003740	838
New Hampshire........................	−0.000455	482	−0.002565	446
New Jersey............................	−0.000220	1,591	−0.001309	1,434
New Mexico...........................	−0.000887	1,389	−0.004190	1,228
New York.............................	−0.000298	4,907	−0.001768	4,458
North Carolina........................	−0.000506	3,353	−0.004040	4,161
North Dakota..........................	−0.000994	581	−0.007996	816
Ohio..................................	−0.000402	4,091	−0.002543	4,199
Oklahoma.............................	−0.000774	2,323	−0.003822	2,007
Oregon................................	−0.000429	1,261	−0.002347	1,105
Pennsylvania..........................	−0.000563	6,176	−0.004018	6,755
Rhode Island..........................	−0.000327	291	−0.002062	276
South Carolina........................	−0.000542	1,838	−0.002857	1,566
South Dakota..........................	−0.000788	522	−0.005465	667
Tennessee.............................	−0.000798	3,887	−0.005230	3,954
Texas.................................	−0.000674	11,571	−0.003386	10,479
Utah..................................	−0.000532	948	−0.001723	667
Vermont...............................	−0.001116	605	−0.008013	697
Virginia...............................	−0.000636	3,870	−0.003336	3,090
Washington............................	−0.000190	956	−0.001070	889
West Virginia..........................	−0.000784	1,344	−0.005315	1,323
Wisconsin.............................	−0.000986	4,628	−0.005562	4,461
Wyoming..............................	−0.001599	718	−0.007708	647

Table D-6. Parameters a and b for Calculating Approximate Standard Errors of Levels for the Detailed Sportspersons Sample

State	Sportspersons and anglers 16+		Hunters 16+	
	a	b	a	b
United States......................	**−0.000020**	**4,289**	**−0.000018**	**3,793**
Alabama.............................	−0.000459	1,570	−0.000489	1,672
Alaska...............................	−0.001213	535	−0.000986	435
Arizona..............................	−0.000405	1,492	−0.000389	1,431
Arkansas............................	−0.001229	2,452	−0.001529	3,050
California...........................	−0.000275	7,111	−0.000265	6,859
Colorado............................	−0.000602	1,924	−0.000649	2,075
Connecticut.........................	−0.000385	976	−0.000429	1,086
Delaware............................	−0.000483	288	−0.000658	392
Florida..............................	−0.000395	4,789	−0.000478	5,788
Georgia..............................	−0.000512	3,106	−0.000472	2,858
Hawaii...............................	−0.000509	454	−0.001043	930
Idaho................................	−0.001216	1,176	−0.001263	1,221
Illinois..............................	−0.000487	4,492	−0.000648	5,979
Indiana..............................	−0.000549	2,501	−0.000654	2,982
Iowa.................................	−0.000888	1,953	−0.000659	1,450
Kansas...............................	−0.000642	1,292	−0.000832	1,673
Kentucky............................	−0.000835	2,592	−0.000679	2,110
Louisiana...........................	−0.000991	3,270	−0.000831	2,743
Maine................................	−0.000954	959	−0.000937	942
Maryland............................	−0.000516	2,087	−0.000397	1,605
Massachusetts.......................	−0.000252	1,221	−0.000278	1,344
Michigan............................	−0.000643	4,874	−0.000592	4,491
Minnesota...........................	−0.001114	4,105	−0.000889	3,278
Mississippi..........................	−0.001033	2,169	−0.001124	2,360
Missouri.............................	−0.000678	2,843	−0.000857	3,597
Montana.............................	−0.001195	832	−0.001299	904
Nebraska............................	−0.000676	851	−0.000707	890
Nevada..............................	−0.000617	893	−0.000576	833
New Hampshire......................	−0.000501	478	−0.000547	522
New Jersey..........................	−0.000252	1,588	−0.000305	1,918
New Mexico.........................	−0.000711	944	−0.001259	1,672
New York............................	−0.000364	5,159	−0.000301	4,277
North Carolina......................	−0.000451	2,646	−0.000616	3,618
North Dakota........................	−0.000814	389	−0.001295	619
Ohio.................................	−0.000421	3,638	−0.000381	3,292
Oklahoma............................	−0.000954	2,454	−0.001042	2,679
Oregon..............................	−0.000652	1,715	−0.000558	1,468
Pennsylvania........................	−0.000635	5,902	−0.000628	5,840
Rhode Island........................	−0.000423	322	−0.000510	389
South Carolina......................	−0.000527	1,616	−0.000696	2,133
South Dakota........................	−0.001088	605	−0.001013	563
Tennessee...........................	−0.000577	2,490	−0.000749	3,232
Texas................................	−0.000603	9,273	−0.000733	11,259
Utah.................................	−0.000616	955	−0.000714	1,106
Vermont.............................	−0.001086	520	−0.001184	567
Virginia.............................	−0.000546	2,930	−0.000658	3,529
Washington..........................	−0.000427	1,913	−0.000305	1,368
West Virginia........................	−0.000781	1,133	−0.000891	1,288
Wisconsin............................	−0.001026	4,165	−0.000832	3,378
Wyoming.............................	−0.001209	452	−0.001693	633

Table D-7. Parameters a, b, and c for Calculating Approximate Standard Errors for Expenditures for the Detailed Sportspersons Sample

State	Sportspersons and anglers 16+			Hunters 16+		
	a	b	c	a	b	c
United States.........................	**0.000209**	**−81,938**	**16,935**	**0.000849**	**−338,404**	**16,347**
Alabama..........................	0.009175	−61,525	5,860	0.024164	−1,049	5,155
Alaska............................	−0.006112	−16,312	2,378	0.021402	39,475	489
Arizona...........................	0.026819	−7,817	2,578	0.092593	−90,851	2,072
Arkansas..........................	0.004633	−23,748	6,426	0.014405	−62,820	5,523
California	0.021384	−70,276	15,458	0.113785	−136,283	6,339
Colorado..........................	0.009864	−19,578	5,293	0.022718	−94,581	3,887
Connecticut.......................	0.001877	−16,928	2,684	0.079125	−34,580	1,895
Delaware..........................	0.040550	−7,042	809	0.105687	−2,637	311
Florida	0.007654	20,508	14,478	0.023874	−155,743	8,973
Georgia...........................	0.014008	−36,268	6,059	0.008831	−95,649	7,863
Hawaii	0.025846	−5,658	1,067	0.097125	−938	788
Idaho.............................	−0.002875	−29,463	3,878	0.016379	−64,453	3,289
Illinois............................	0.019572	10,051	8,854	0.085878	−549,762	11,311
Indiana...........................	0.022696	−22,961	5,102	0.033251	−103,911	8,051
Iowa	0.005064	−20,998	4,528	0.016656	−138,890	5,392
Kansas	0.015860	18,185	1,730	0.021785	−50,528	2,671
Kentucky	0.004591	−41,799	5,443	0.008079	−58,497	4,208
Louisiana	−0.00040	−65,739	6,880	0.019445	−21,541	4,669
Maine	0.017717	−5,998	1,713	0.025284	−13,157	1,841
Maryland	0.008904	−8,843	3,522	0.032998	−11,255	2,731
Massachusetts......................	0.016262	−12,678	3,571	0.024064	−1,953	1,922
Michigan..........................	0.019792	−127,849	11,921	0.040148	−65,705	9,671
Minnesota.........................	0.008800	−47,947	9,688	0.014048	−30,492	6,73
Mississippi	0.016340	−3,615	2,838	0.048203	−12,376	2,679
Missouri	0.010252	−14,938	4,700	0.044792	−43,432	4,274
Montana	0.006249	2,944	2,023	0.012939	−22,671	1,865
Nebraska..........................	0.017333	−3,651	1,663	0.027267	−39,668	2,043
Nevada	0.018933	−14,263	1,569	0.031588	−38,184	1,658
New Hampshire	0.018219	−2,158	896	0.019369	−16,561	1,337
New Jersey........................	0.008872	−21,461	4,161	0.074090	−47,814	2,925
New Mexico........................	0.009851	−15,340	3,013	0.038148	4,904	1,576
New York..........................	0.026625	−55,537	8,963	0.021960	−65,942	13,270
North Carolina	0.002898	−52,854	8,564	0.027058	−70,174	6,255
North Dakota	0.005072	−1,310	842	0.013476	10,740	593
Ohio	0.006294	−16,259	6,658	0.032819	−343,279	12,406
Oklahoma.........................	0.004660	−37,618	7,562	0.020499	−34,984	4,891
Oregon	0.003145	−20,997	4,657	0.039506	−209,288	4,495
Pennsylvania.......................	−0.001615	−16,424	12,085	0.015010	−45,176	9,408
Rhode Island	0.008233	−3,065	823	0.163731	1,552	318
South Carolina	0.006577	−24,715	4,435	0.014150	−45,230	4,751
South Dakota	0.016156	−6,396	1,099	0.041242	13,567	850
Tennessee	0.033971	−12,176	3,739	0.025020	25,879	2,858
Texas.............................	0.002571	−181,509	27,582	0.012511	228,353	16,609
Utah	0.001106	−2,243	3,125	0.011415	−63,829	3,240
Vermont	0.011747	−4,625	1,103	0.008540	−5,531	1,212
Virginia...........................	0.016382	−12,594	5,152	0.014967	−57,318	6,583
Washington........................	0.003760	−21,018	4,033	0.047027	−137,577	2,616
West Virginia	0.006720	−9,550	2,878	0.031204	−15,338	1,413
Wisconsin..........................	0.012407	−19,300	6,202	0.024061	−96,808	6,607
Wyoming	0.012293	−9,179	1,344	0.024311	−20,666	1,350

Table D-8. Parameters a, b, and c for Calculating Approximate Standard Errors for Days or Trips for the Detailed Sportspersons Sample

State	Sportspersons and anglers 16+			Hunters 16+		
	a	b	c	a	b	c
United States........................	**−0.000359**	**−10,379**	**21,216**	**0.000168**	**−11,904**	**12,496**
Alabama.............................	−0.014899	−1,645	10,642	0.010257	−3,745	3,494
Alaska.............................	0.004232	−2,284	1,514	0.017337	−1,630	1,174
Arizona............................	0.009813	−504	1,658	0.025859	−2,427	2,408
Arkansas...........................	−0.000591	−4,532	7,151	0.005331	−5,600	6,560
California..........................	0.005829	−32,577	19,133	0.046419	−14,455	11,763
Colorado...........................	−0.002514	−4,440	6,304	0.005304	−3,344	4,269
Connecticut........................	0.004894	−1,905	2,797	0.032365	−208	1,179
Delaware...........................	0.019930	−260	493	0.042659	−901	837
Florida	0.004327	−8,388	12,123	0.023712	−8,026	8,704
Georgia............................	0.006853	−15,975	7,865	0.000498	−4,557	6,375
Hawaii	0.024692	−3,126	2,236	−0.011390	−629	1,711
Idaho..............................	−0.003745	−3,875	4,263	0.007761	−1,392	1,956
Illinois.............................	−0.001740	−10,299	13,115	0.116103	−25,870	11,750
Indiana............................	0.005471	−5,800	7,756	0.015379	−6,119	5,928
Iowa	−0.002638	−1,789	4,745	0.013073	−5,442	4,003
Kansas	0.016223	−605	1,633	−0.005996	−2,318	4,722
Kentucky	−0.001146	−3,831	5,559	−0.008903	−1,883	5,581
Louisiana	0.005167	−9,551	6,990	0.031739	−9,447	4,809
Maine	−0.001145	−2,421	3,262	0.012469	−2,544	2,121
Maryland	0.015009	−1,757	3,235	−0.000817	−3,341	4,179
Massachusetts......................	0.001279	−5,091	4,088	0.028210	−2,953	2,268
Michigan...........................	0.014345	−13,184	13,688	0.005369	−5,906	7,564
Minnesota..........................	0.003565	−17,781	12,718	−0.002763	−5,610	8,671
Mississippi.........................	0.019493	−15,942	6,461	0.014162	−6,098	5,274
Missouri	−0.002128	−5,253	7,226	0.018480	−8,909	5,746
Montana	0.000449	−2,600	3,680	0.000401	−1,984	2,302
Nebraska...........................	−0.001914	−1,750	2,477	−0.000535	−295	1,450
Nevada............................	0.021810	−2,046	1,649	−0.001816	−1,230	1,883
New Hampshire.....................	0.002071	−1,578	1,470	0.000312	−511	902
New Jersey.........................	0.011720	−5,526	6,959	0.022081	−3,488	3,096
New Mexico........................	0.001275	−6,683	5,081	0.035962	−4,491	2,409
New York..........................	0.006773	−19,672	13,519	−0.006261	−6,261	14,001
North Carolina.....................	−0.003764	−7,850	10,700	0.005307	−10,202	11,887
North Dakota	−0.000254	−1,046	1,099	0.013638	−2,072	1,354
Ohio	−0.002277	−12,642	14,807	0.014951	−10,264	9,111
Oklahoma..........................	0.002908	−8,589	7,908	−0.012896	−7,384	10,343
Oregon	−0.004964	−10,252	11,849	0.014008	−4,387	3,466
Pennsylvania.......................	−0.000351	−9,506	15,294	0.001946	−7,227	10,734
Rhode Island	0.003515	−532	829	0.036010	−680	752
South Carolina......................	0.001822	−4,530	4,244	0.016996	−2,924	3,226
South Dakota	0.006727	−857	1,163	0.014473	−561	1,029
Tennessee	−0.003393	−8,542	10,929	0.014450	−5,875	5,933
Texas..............................	0.008771	−62,115	37,457	0.026724	−40,596	24,438
Utah	−0.000945	−159	2,170	0.009900	−3,490	2,684
Vermont	−0.003874	−1,213	1,671	0.001720	−943	1,254
Virginia............................	−0.003305	−6,179	9,142	0.003533	−4,262	5,955
Washington.........................	0.001423	−4,085	5,250	−0.000778	−1,826	2,912
West Virginia	−0.003294	−831	2,712	0.003483	−2,510	3,463
Wisconsin..........................	−0.000821	−11,365	13,762	0.002687	−8,025	7,969
Wyoming	0.001824	−978	1,466	0.000207	3,198	606

Table D-9. Parameters a and b for Calculating Approximate Standard Errors of Levels of Wildlife-Watching Participants for the Detailed Wildlife-Watching Sample

State	Nonresidential users		Wildlife-watching participants[1]	
	a	b	a	b
United States......................	**-0.000076**	**15,974**	**-0.000040**	**8,555**
Alabama.................................	-0.001806	6,172	-0.000996	3,406
Alaska....................................	-0.003984	1,757	-0.007723	1,368
Arizona..................................	-0.001862	6,858	-0.001138	4,191
Arkansas................................	-0.005383	10,740	-0.003708	7,397
California...............................	-0.001245	32,229	-0.000675	17,485
Colorado................................	-0.002666	8,521	-0.001570	5,017
Connecticut............................	-0.002028	5,136	-0.001170	2,963
Delaware................................	-0.003015	1,797	-0.001488	887
Florida...................................	-0.002113	25,612	-0.001029	12,478
Georgia..................................	-0.002607	15,802	-0.001239	7,512
Hawaii...................................	-0.001747	1,558	-0.001508	1,345
Idaho.....................................	-0.011466	11,088	-0.002755	2,664
Illinois...................................	-0.001118	10,311	-0.001182	10,900
Indiana...................................	-0.002301	10,485	-0.001294	5,899
Iowa......................................	-0.002614	5,750	-0.002397	5,274
Kansas...................................	-0.002324	4,676	-0.001200	2,414
Kentucky................................	-0.001720	5,341	-0.001519	4,717
Louisiana...............................	-0.002007	6,621	-0.001352	4,459
Maine.....................................	-0.003051	3,066	-0.002046	2,056
Maryland................................	-0.001879	7,604	-0.001100	4,449
Massachusetts.........................	-0.001845	8,924	-0.000791	3,824
Michigan................................	-0.002911	22,083	-0.001385	10,506
Minnesota...............................	-0.003859	14,226	-0.002710	9,989
Mississippi.............................	-0.002421	5,085	-0.002331	4,896
Missouri.................................	-0.007940	33,309	-0.002372	9,949
Montana..................................	-0.005126	3,568	-0.003963	2,758
Nebraska................................	-0.002615	3,292	-0.001558	1,961
Nevada...................................	-0.002376	3,438	-0.001641	2,375
New Hampshire.......................	-0.003949	3,767	-0.001860	1,774
New Jersey.............................	-0.001349	8,490	-0.000839	5,282
New Mexico............................	-0.003029	4,023	-0.001796	2,385
New York...............................	-0.001303	18,488	-0.000811	11,505
North Carolina........................	-0.001908	11,203	-0.001382	8,114
North Dakota..........................	-0.003144	1,503	-0.002659	1,271
Ohio......................................	-0.001298	11,210	-0.000884	7,638
Oklahoma...............................	-0.004011	10,317	-0.002253	5,796
Oregon...................................	-0.003939	10,356	-0.001506	3,958
Pennsylvania...........................	-0.002310	21,485	-0.001198	11,142
Rhode Island..........................	-0.001581	1,205	-0.001226	934
South Carolina........................	-0.004009	12,288	-0.001840	5,460
South Dakota..........................	-0.005473	3,043	-0.002845	1,582
Tennessee...............................	-0.002163	9,330	-0.001206	5,202
Texas.....................................	-0.003860	59,315	-0.001142	17,541
Utah......................................	-0.003023	4,685	-0.002427	3,762
Vermont.................................	-0.007125	3,413	-0.003296	1,579
Virginia..................................	-0.002550	13,684	-0.001540	8,266
Washington.............................	-0.002590	11,601	-0.000842	3,773
West Virginia..........................	-0.002233	3,226	-0.001979	2,859
Wisconsin...............................	-0.002881	11,690	-0.002288	9,283
Wyoming................................	-0.004150	1,552	-0.004075	1,524

[1] Use these parameters for total wildlife-watching participants and residential participants.

Table D-10. Parameters a, b, and c for Calculating Approximate Standard Errors for Expenditures and Days or Trips for Detailed Wildlife-Watching Sample

State	Expenditures			Days or trips		
	a	b	c	a	b	c
United States...............	−0.000286	−65,186	37,635	0.000052	543,738	10,948
Alabama.....................	0.030708	−4,434	4,714	−0.022833	−34,485	19,838
Alaska......................	0.041800	−4,269	1,514	−0.029715	−14,349	8,241
Arizona.....................	0.015564	−88,920	7,092	−0.006753	8,600	9,994
Arkansa.....................	0.010470	−232,312	19,942	−0.016982	−55,327	23,242
California	0.018066	−66,438	36,961	0.012283	199,721	11,847
Colorado....................	0.038817	−215,098	11,070	−0.052385	−41,128	50,721
Connecticut.................	0.009671	−39,324	6,004	−0.041089	−115,012	28,194
Delaware....................	0.048255	793	1,135	−0.017715	−10,761	3,753
Florida	0.037237	246,936	15,955	−0.011904	368,712	53,853
Georgia.....................	0.049562	−47,365	13,337	−0.012828	−66,122	35,936
Hawaii	0.073902	−7,392	1,428	−0.107474	−50,423	10,960
Idaho.......................	0.049578	3,816	4,179	−0.012767	26,870	10,809
Illinois.....................	0.023791	−91,738	15,163	0.017880	−26,735	32,660
Indiana.....................	0.031176	−6,949	11,644	−0.031304	−137,397	50,618
Iowa	0.027387	−151,677	10,811	−0.043626	−36,375	39,705
Kansas	0.014086	−26,411	5,617	−0.020112	−42,505	16,304
Kentucky	0.034724	−14,328	9,748	−0.100682	−143,695	76,120
Louisiana	0.077714	−11,409	5,935	−0.079705	−145,421	49,422
Maine	0.023033	−44,469	5,406	−0.017174	−7,365	9,098
Maryland	0.043571	−70,123	6,923	−0.033325	−216,192	46,228
Massachusetts...............	0.006810	−178,680	12,400	−0.031568	−234,200	47,548
Michigan....................	0.040492	−319,042	19,607	−0.018833	−31,270	48,594
Minnesota...................	0.014246	−14,209	13,809	−0.095678	−560,553	139,828
Mississippi	0.124078	18,562	3,885	−0.030843	−100,539	24,176
Missouri	0.034639	−25,636	11,799	−0.010269	219,841	37,795
Montana	0.057903	−22,171	3,776	−0.012332	5,559	10,812
Nebraska....................	0.024994	−4,237	3,539	−0.038650	−12,323	13,951
Nevada......................	0.034440	22,068	4,012	−0.005101	−34,384	8,741
New Hampshire	0.035666	−13,208	2,568	0.022014	−23,662	6,038
New Jersey..................	0.013039	−52,984	9,831	−0.011200	215,547	18,712
New Mexico..................	0.160478	−37,219	3,245	−0.041133	−40,922	17,946
New York....................	0.055761	−88,911	14,702	−0.018354	−352,468	78,358
North Carolina..............	0.016613	−38,392	14,073	−0.014391	−150,974	57,926
North Dakota	0.083798	−1,532	1,564	0.000482	−16,359	3,936
Ohio	0.013567	−190,802	23,398	0.054816	−205,827	28,294
Oklahoma....................	0.016264	−32,772	9,957	0.012938	93,047	14,288
Oregon	0.006779	−12,633	7,354	−0.034862	−36,621	32,540
Pennsylvania................	0.029900	−197,526	29,144	0.024902	969,419	−33,184
Rhode Island	0.030265	−1,717	1,486	−0.069322	−95,835	12,964
South Carolina..............	0.053921	14,141	5,196	−0.019706	−230,401	46,919
South Dakota	0.057120	7,343	999	−0.031149	−123,874	14,456
Tennessee	0.037696	−9,299	8,559	0.000581	38,507	8,480
Texas.......................	0.038651	−443,322	33,784	0.005378	354,179	23,102
Utah	0.056421	9,481	4,059	0.045711	−66,098	23,779
Vermont	0.013746	−43,820	3,010	0.010618	−34,930	7,630
Virginia....................	0.036266	−105,349	16,055	−0.016136	−231,865	58,093
Washington..................	0.018752	−46,218	10,365	−0.015432	−108,529	31,269
West Virginia	0.051192	−2,708	2,632	−0.035244	−80,788	20,819
Wisconsin...................	−0.001127	−25,290	18,720	−0.064163	−592,681	124,050
Wyoming	0.097425	−2,122	1,550	−0.093805	−13,385	14,702